C000045623

beat takeshi vs. takeshi kitano

by casio abe

with a preface by lawrence chua
edited by william o. gardner
and daisuke miyao

translated by william o. gardner
and takeo hori

Originally published in Japanese in 1994 by Chikuma Shobo Publishing Co., Ltd., under the title of *Kitano Takeshi vs. Beat Takeshi* by Casio Abe

English translation rights arranged with Chikuma Shobo Publishing Co., Ltd. through Japan Foreign-Rights Centre

Portions of this book first appeared in the following publications:
"The Long Journey of the Melancholy King" (*Eureka*, February 1998)
"Getting Any?" (*Image Forum*, April 1995)
"Kids Return" (*Film Art Quarterly*, Summer 1996)
"Fireworks" (*Cine-Lesson*, December 1997)
"Kikujiro" (*Tosho Shinbun*, 12 June 1999)
"Brother" (*Eureka*, February 2001)
"Dolls" (Casio Abe fan-site, October 2002)

05   04   03   02   01

Published by Kaya Press, an imprint of Muae Publishing
www.kaya.com

Cover and book design by Sandra Watanabe
Cover art: *Kikujiro* by Takeshi Kitano © Bandai Visual, Tokyo FM, Nippon Herald, and
    Office Kitano
Indexing by Joyce Teague/Paper Pushers

Manufactured in the United States of America

Distributed by D.A.P./Distributed Art Publishers
155 Avenue of the Americas, 2nd Floor
New York, NY 10013
(800) 338–BOOK www.artbook.com

ISBN 1–885030–40–1

Library of Congress Catalog Card Number: 2005920973

This publication is made possible with public funds from the New York State
Council on the Arts, a state agency, as well as Soo Kyung Kim, Wook Hun and
Sun Hee Koo, Eileen Tabios, Ronald and Susan Yanagihara, JP Morgan Chase
SMARTS Regrant Program, the Asian American Arts Alliance, and many others.

table of contents

preface

by lawrence chua

Watching some of Takeshi Kitano's films is like witnessing both a catastrophe and a miracle unfold. They happen with little of the fanfare that we are used to seeing with car crashes, burning buildings, or the arrival of the messiah in Hollywood pictures. There is little of the commentary that accompanies such images on television. That is to say, it is sometimes difficult to know who we are rooting for in these moments. In Kitano's films, those pursuits that anoint masculinity—crime, sex, sports, even violence itself—become arenas of conflict that unravel before our eyes.

The world that Kitano looks at is a man's world, and he looks at it in a dispassionate way. This is accomplished through the use of long static shots that are reminiscent of the work of Yasujiro Ozu and bereft of any sentiment. Kitano has said that his approach to movie violence was influenced by a famous series of photographs of a suspected Viet Cong fighter being executed by a South Vietnamese officer during the 1968 Tet offensive.

But it would be misleading to suggest that Kitano depicts violence with the same voyeurism with which it is reported on American television. There is a difference between dispassion and numbness. In *Beat Takeshi vs. Takeshi Kitano*, Casio Abe's careful meditation on Kitano and his work, the author acknowledges the ways that Hollywood cinema and television are two facets of a spectacular system that dictates the pattern of mass psychology. Abe describes Kitano's artistic strategy as "anti-TV." He acknowledges the ways that one of Japan's most prolific and challenging television personalities, Beat Takeshi, is constituted as an electronic body. Like other such bodies, Beat Takeshi's appears perfect and infinitely reproducible; a body without organs that denies the realities of life and death. Yet the novelist, painter, actor, and director Takeshi Kitano is constantly challenging the conventions of that body. "Criminals are always in close proximity to death," writes Casio Abe. "Takeshi Kitano enjoys exposing his own criminality and death." Beat Takeshi's spectacular body is forged out of a culture in which life has become an eternal non-life. Traditional symbols of death, such as corpses and decay, have given way to aluminum and glass; life is sacrificed to the workings of the machine. In this necrophilous mirror, all life, along with the faculties of reason, sight, hearing, taste, and loving, is transformed into things. Sex becomes a mechanical skill, joy is replaced by fun, tenderness is directed towards machines. The only acceptable desire is the desire to consume endlessly. In order to do this, one is required to live a life uninterrupted by death, which is not life at all. "It seems to me that life and death have very little meaning in themselves, but the way you approach death may give a retrospective meaning to your life," Kitano has said.

Implicit in Kitano's film work is the idea that every act of destruction is also an act of renewal. By looking at death in a truthful way, perhaps life gains more depth.

One of the sentiments Takeshi Kitano spares us is piety. Instead of retreating into a well-rehearsed humanism, his films look at the world in a way that strips it of its innocence. He offers a glimpse of the common ground shared by birth and death, the way things fall apart and come together in the debris of the world. Moments of absolute lucidity and beauty puncture his films like strange dreams. They do not so much depart from the stories he tells as take them somewhere else. They suggest a way of seeing that is liberated by clarity, not tyrannized by passions. Perhaps by witnessing the world in this way, we too can learn to destroy it.

foreword

by daisuke miyao

Takeshi Kitano has been one of the most popular figures in Japan for more than two decades. This popularity comes not from his internationally and critically acclaimed films, but rather from his legendary alter ego: comedian, actor, and social commentator Beat Takeshi. To this day, Kitano is known in Japan more as a popular television celebrity who maintains at least seven regular weekly shows than as a great auteur of cinema—this despite the fact that his seventh film, *Fireworks*, was awarded the Golden Lion (Grand Prix) at the 1997 Venice International Film Festival. In his influential collection of essays on Kitano, *Beat Takeshi vs. Takeshi Kitano*, Casio Abe, one of Japan's preeminent critics of film and culture, explores the meaning of this ambivalent Takeshi Kitano/Beat Takeshi duality, a dichotomy manifested in the critical success of Kitano's films on the one hand, and the enormous popularity of Beat Takeshi as a television personality on the other. As such, Abe's work accomplishes something more significant than just a critical analysis of Kitano's oeuvre: by closely examining Kitano's filmography, Abe comes up with a critique of the nature of television in contemporary Japanese society that has implications for the role of television in contemporary culture around the world.

Abe's strategy in discussing this Takeshi Kitano/Beat Takeshi ambivalence is to view cinema and television as two antagonistic, contrasting entities (though, as he confesses in Chapter 7, this strategy has limited potential in the face of television's enormous power). In Chapter 1, Abe discusses how television in contemporary Japanese society is a space of homogenization from which there can be no deviation, and according to which appropriate answers/responses to all possible questions have already been arranged. In this homogenized space of television, which Abe goes so far as to call a modern disease in Japan, "Beat Takeshi" is a kind of floating sign, though one that lacks both flesh and blood. Even though this charismatic sign called "Beat Takeshi" has succeeded in differentiating itself from other media stars, attracting an enormous audience in the process, it is still exposed as being little more than a visual sign—i.e. just another of the television personalities whose own bodies have been robbed of materiality through the televisionesque narrative of homogenization. Abe argues that for Takeshi Kitano, filmmaking has been a desperate attempt to recover the living flesh and blood of his own body from the repression of television. Obsessed with the theme of suicide, Takeshi Kitano is continually trying to reveal the bodily existence of Beat Takeshi. No surprise, then, that this book is entitled *Beat Takeshi vs. Takeshi Kitano*. Cinema is the space where the director Takeshi Kitano struggles with the televisionesque body of Beat Takeshi.

From Chapter 2 onwards, Abe examines Kitano's first four films in detail. Chapter 2 focuses on *Violent Cop*, Kitano's directorial debut, which, according to Abe, demonstrates the visual motifs of "the continuity of an action" and the "right-angleness of actions," as well as the thematic motif of "double-suicide." As such, the film reveals the physical actuality of the human body. In particular, Abe argues that *Violent Cop*'s preoccupation with the body of the protagonist, which is played by Beat Takeshi, reveals Takeshi Kitano's attempt to regain the reality of his own body, which had been fictionalized in the persona of Beat Takeshi by the space of television.

In Chapter 3, Abe describes Kitano's second film, *Boiling Point*, as exemplifying Kitano's theory of baseball. In this chapter, Abe discusses the concept of "dispersiveness," one of the most remarkable characteristics of modern Japanese society. According to Abe, modern Japanese society is hedged in by strict, boring regulations, just as baseball is a sport filled with strict rules. The theme of suicide in *Boiling Point* exists as a way of emphasizing the actual physicality of the human body.

In Chapter 4, Abe argues that even though the actor Beat Takeshi does not appear in *A Scene at the Sea*, the theme of suicide is acted out by his alter ego, the young deaf-and-mute surfer. According to Abe, these recurrent themes of revealing the physicality of the human body and of suicide (i.e. the killing of the body of Beat Takeshi by the director Takeshi Kitano) are most clearly explored in *Sonatine*, Kitano's fourth film, which is discussed in detail in Chapter 5.

Chapter 6, which is the final chapter of Abe's original book, concludes with a consideration of *The Birth of the Founder*, a Japanese film based on a novel written by Kitano and in which Beat Takeshi appears as an actor, but which is directed by Toshihiro Tenma, Kitano's former assistant director.

The original Japanese version of this book, published in 1994, ends with Abe anticipating Kitano's future career as a filmmaker as well as a television personality. This edition of the book follows Abe's continuing critical examination of Kitano's work by collecting and translating essays written by Abe on all of Kitano's subsequent films to date, from *Getting Any?* to *Dolls*.

In an essay subtitled "The Present of Takeshi Kitano and Beat Takeshi," Abe argues that since his near-fatal motorcycle accident, which took place in August 1994, Kitano has been moving away from the struggle between Takeshi Kitano the filmmaker and Beat Takeshi the television personality. Abe rhetorically claims that Kitano has come to stand "beside television," though still not within it. He argues that given the present condition of Japanese society, cinema has become so trivial and the influence of television so powerful that even the Beat Takeshi/Takeshi Kitano dichotomy on which the film career of Takeshi Kitano has been based has become meaningless. Rather, Abe insists that the filmmaker Takeshi Kitano is now attempting to reconcile or fuse these two aspects. As such, according to Abe, *Fireworks*, originally titled *Hana-Bi*, was Kitano's successful attempt to overcome the dichotomy between "*hana*" (flower), which implies "life," and "*hi*" (fire), which implies "death." In so doing, it works also on the dichotomy that exists between Takeshi Kitano and Beat Takeshi, and between cinema and television. In his review of Kitano's *Brother*, Abe suggests that Kitano's most recent directorial efforts have been an attempt to overcome the dichotomy between "Hollywood cinema" and "Japanese cinema."

To fully appreciate Abe's insightful discussion, it might be helpful to briefly introduce Takeshi Kitano's career here. Takeshi Kitano was born in Tokyo's Adachi ward on January 18, 1947, the youngest of four children. His father, Kikujiro, whose name would become the title of Kitano's eighth film, was a craftsman in lacquer and paint, and his mother, Saki, did piecework at home. After dropping out of Meiji University, where he had been studying engineering, Kitano drifted from job to job, working as a waiter, an airport baggage handler, a taxi driver, and finally, an elevator operator at the France-za burlesque theater in the Asakusa entertainment district of Tokyo. While working in Asakusa, Kitano polished his comedic skills under his "master," Senzaburo Fukami, and in 1972, he debuted on stage at France-za. In 1974, Kitano was asked to step in for the partner of

Jiro Kaneko, another Fukami protégé, and the two formed the stand-up manzai comedy duo that eventually became the Two Beats (Beat Takeshi and Beat Kiyoshi). After their TV debut in 1975 on the program *Rival: Big Laugh!* (Raibaru Daibakusho!)," the Two Beats became national stars of the manzai boom, which started in the late 1970s. Kitano's rapid-fire delivery and deft comments struck a nerve with TV viewers, and his physically expressive power attracted a wide audience, especially among students and young people.

Kitano achieved solo stardom on the TV program *We are wild and crazy guys!* (Oretachi hyokinzoku!) (1981-89), an ensemble show that emphasized ad-libs, running gags, and free-form parodies of popular songs, movies, TV shows, and commercials. Kitano also built a fanatical following with his iconoclastic social commentary on the late-night radio show "All Night Nippon," which aired from 1981 to 1990. In addition to work as an actor in TV dramas, Kitano began acting in films in 1981 in *Migratory Bird on a Dump Car* (Danpu wataridori). In 1983, renowned film director Nagisa Oshima used Beat Takeshi in the role of a a Japanese officer in his *Merry Christmas, Mr. Lawrence*, a film that garnered international attention for Kitano.

Kitano's popularity rose to unprecedented heights in the 1990s, when he appeared in TV shows and commercials, published columns in several magazines and newspapers, and wrote books of poetry and essays, as well as serious novels. He was chosen Japan's most popular TV celebrity six years in a row (between 1990 and 1995), according to an annual poll of NHK, Japan's national TV broadcasting association. (A number of notes regarding Kitano's career, some of which are by Abe himself, have been added in this translated version of Abe's book to introduce specific names, TV program titles, and historical events in Japanese culture and society to non-Japanese readers.)

In 1989, using his real name, Takeshi Kitano made his directorial debut with the film *Violent Cop*. Such a career shift seems reasonable:

Asakusa, where Kitano began his career as a performer, has been a center of urban entertainment since the late-nineteenth century, with cinema (which was first imported from Europe and America) existing there as only one of many *misemono* entertainment shows.[1] Since *Violent Cop*, Kitano has completed a total of nine films, most of which have received significant critical success internationally.

Despite his enduring popularity, Kitano's career weathered critical crises at least twice. In 1986, a weekly tabloid, *FRIDAY*, published photos of a college student with whom Kitano was reportedly having an affair. Kitano and eleven of his entourage, popularly known as Takeshi Army (Takeshi Gundan), invaded the magazine's office, attacked the staffers, and were subsequently arrested. Kitano reached an out-of-court settlement with the magazine, but was required to take a six-month leave from TV to demonstrate his contrition.

The second major crisis took place in the early morning of August 2, 1994, when Kitano crashed his motorcycle into a guardrail in the Shinjuku ward of Tokyo. The crash almost killed him, leaving the right side of his face partially paralyzed. After seven months of rehabilitation, he returned to TV in March 1995. Kitano now confesses that the accident might have been a suicide attempt, although the reason is still not clear even to himself.

When Casio Abe's book *Beat Takeshi vs. Takeshi Kitano* was first published, Kitano had directed only four films, all of which had been largely ignored by Japanese audiences, as well as by most Japanese film critics. Since Beat Takeshi was and continues to be a hugely popular icon in Japanese television, Takeshi Kitano's filmmaking was not considered seriously. As Kitano himself once commented, "Who wants to pay to watch me in a movie theater when you can see me on television for free?" After the financial and critical failure of Kitano's fourth feature, *Sonatine*, Kazuyoshi Okuyama, an influential producer at Shochiku Studio, publicly criticized Kitano's filmmaking in a popular magazine, and announced he would no longer produce Kitano's films.

However, Kitano's films were beginning to attract international praise, and after the financial and critical success of *Fireworks*, his status as a film director became well-recognized in Japan as well. In this sense, Kitano's career resembles that of Akira Kurosawa's, particularly as regards Kurasawa's *Rashomon* (1950). When Kurosawa made *Rashomon*, his producer, Masaichi Nagata, reportedly hated the film, saying "I cannot understand what is going on!" However, after *Rashomon* received the grand prize at the Venice International Film Festival, it was proclaimed a masterpiece upon its return to Japan.

As such, Casio Abe was one of the first film critics in Japan to appreciate Takeshi Kitano's films, and *Beat Takeshi vs. Takeshi Kitano* was one of the first efforts to seriously examine Kitano's films. In addition, Abe's approach to film criticism is rather unique. Even though he analyzes Kitano's films in detail, his description of the scenes is not always strictly precise. According to Abe, when he watches films, even on VCR, he never stops the tape. Of course, in a movie theater, it is impossible to stop and rewind a film. He also never takes notes during a screening. Instead, he goes to see the same film over and over again, taking all his notes right after the film has ended. The rationale for this approach is Abe's belief that film is "living and moving." For Abe, film is "vanishing every moment," and "memory alone enables us to reexperience it." To stop and rewind a VCR screening of a movie is, according to Abe, akin to "treating film as a thing that can be petrified" or as "a corpse that is ready to be examined." Abe insists that he wants to be faithful to the way an actual audience would experience the film in a movie theater.

Abe differentiates "creatively incorrect" memories from "careless" ones, describing the former as constituting "the cutting edge of film criticism in Japan." He insists upon the importance of "opening" a text as opposed to "closing" it through authoritarian discourse. Rather than worshipping a film as a "closed" and "isolated" text, Abe seeks to connect it to the vernacular experience of its audience. Of course, there are also merits in other approaches. For instance, a close shot-by-shot analysis makes it clear how filmmakers try to lead audience members to feel sympathy or empathy for characters through the choice of shot size or editing. Also, such an approach may reveal how "incorrect memories" are re-created in the audience's mind. However, according to Abe, an audience's perception and appreciation of a film comes from its constant flow of movement. Because film is, literally, moving pictures, Abe's attempt to understand cinema in the constant flow of time is both illuminating and valuable.

01

THE DEATH OF MASATAKA ITSUMI

On December 25, 1993, Masataka Itsumi, a popular TV-show host whose bout with cancer had been the focus of intense, day-to-day media attention, finally died. As is well known in Japan, Itsumi's battle with cancer had by then been thoroughly mythologized through the logic of television. In the same way that reports about the minutiae of Emperor Hirohito's *geketsu* ("melena" or "bloody stools") had both exposed and dissolved something that should have remained hidden from outsiders, the development of Masataka Itsumi's disease was also completely dissected in reports about which part of which organ had been surgically removed, or whether he had recovered enough to eat such-and-such food and spend Christmas at home. This dissection process was itself staged as a mythical story by the kind of corrupt reporting that treats everyday trivia as the only reality. In the case of Emperor Hirohito, the character for *ge* ("down" or "lower") that formed part of the rarely heard medical term geketsu seemed symbolic because it seemed to manifest ominously from the "lower" regions of the body. This state—where such words function like tentacles of curiosity that extend into the various "lower" regions of the body—was obscene, as was its goal of crassly exposing that

beat takeshi vs. takeshi kitano

which should remain hidden. Another kind of obscenity could be found in the conscience of the TV narrator, who, right before uttering the word "death," would use instead an inconclusive phrase such as "a serious condition." From this, we can see that obscenity is a multifaceted concept. It is, in short, a mentality that "cleverly keeps a distance from any conclusiveness" while "insolently probing into areas that should be kept hidden"; that is, it disguises the ambiguity of the difference between directness and indirectness.

In 1993, the tabloids feasted in the much same way on another matter regarding obscenity. The English-derived word "hair," not an unusual word in itself, was employed in place of the direct and decisive Japanese words *chimoh* (shameful hair) and *inmoh* (shadow hair). This made it possible to refer to pubic hair without the qualifying characters of *chi* (shame) and *in* (shadow), which in turn made possible the pathology of openly discussing what would normally be talked about in public with some hesitancy. Though seemingly explicit, writings that used this word "hair" were in fact ambiguous and inconclusive. Since the existence of genitals cannot be clearly expressed anyway, the use of the English-derived word "hair" in public has nothing to do with a real attempt to counter censorship, but is rather a manifestation of inconclusiveness.[1] Moreover, the transformation of the word "hair" into this kind of code is obviously unnatural. To use another example, some Japanese actresses and celebrities publish photo collections that show their pubic "hair," yet this "hair" is itself no longer "natural" due to trimming and other artificial processes. As such, it is not something that personalizes that actress or celebrity. Nevertheless, people fuss over pubic hair as if it were somehow determinative. (This same hypocrisy can be found in the attitude displayed by economic critics during the era of the bubble economy. At the time, they were content to maintain the status quo of capitalism, but after the bubble economy collapsed, they were quick to criticize it.) In short, exposing "hair" means sustaining modern society's pathology of making all values indeterminate. To invoke something as "pathological" originally meant "something that is impossible." However, like the "hair" that has been exposed, what is considered pathological in these times is in fact a marker of what is possible, with the result that the amount of pathos to be derived from the use of the term "pathology" is very low. The possibility of showing more "hair" to the public does not mean the end of this pathology of inconclusiveness, but rather its continuation. Modern pathologies (in accordance with what takes place at a "lower" level), reveal themselves not by what is "impossible" but by what is "possible."

The unmistakably obscene reports on the progression of Masataka Itsumi's illness share the same core qualities as this "hair" controversy. Like the term "hair nude," the comments that peppered reports on the progress of Itsumi's illness remained inconclusive while outlining the area they were supposedly hiding. The original source for those first reports on Itsumi's illness had been the emotionally moving press conference where Itsumi, brimming with self-control, had announced that he had cancer. But the truth is that even before he came to personify openness about cancer and cancer notification,[2] almost single-handedly disseminating these topics within the circuitry of the media, Itsumi was already a mythical figure. An emblem of success for salarymen who had gone into second careers, Itsumi's squareness, eagerness, and down-to-earthness—qualities not generally considered compatible with the entertainment industry—had paradoxically come to be seen as the newest thing in this contemporary age of television. However, the short period of glory he enjoyed from the time he became a freelance TV host to when he lost his battle with cancer was cruelly, if unintentionally, undercut by remarks made by the very people expressing concern for him. What they in essence said was: "The television industry is filled with monsters.

Within that industry, Masataka Itsumi's kindness to others was rare and unique, but his salaryman sensibility never left him, even when he was at the peak of his popularity. Because show business is a world in which monsters rule, Itsumi accumulated stress and as a result succumbed to cancer. His death is thus doubly sad because it was that of a heroic warrior." In reality, the mentality that can only discuss Itsumi's cancer and death within these parameters is exactly that of the "salaryman," and not of a human being. Ichiro Furutachi, a personality who, like Itsumi, had once been a newscaster, memorably expressed something to the effect that "Mr. Itsumi was, on the surface, a newscaster through and through, but inside he was a very emotionally volatile 'human being.' I cannot find any love for him in those who claim his was a heroic warrior's death caused by stress."

On a different note, one wonders whether the people who knew Itsumi really spoke their true thoughts about him. Isn't the idea that "he died a tragic, heroic warrior's death due to stress resulting from his gentleness of heart" just an idiotic, prefabricated "story" peddled by the media? Let's say for the sake of argument that most of Itsumi's so-called "friends"—those who reminisced about his life and talked about his death at his funeral—had willingly placed themselves into the media's automatically prepared "story." Whatever they said would thus have been drained of all substantive meaning except to the extent that the relative differences among them could be emphasized in statements such as "I was closer to him than anyone else when he was alive" or "When he was alive, I was much closer to him than most people realize." However, such an assumption may in fact be cruel. It is true that when celebrity soundbites about Itsumi were edited and broadcast in sequence, the result was necessarily competitive, pitting everyone against everyone else for the glory of "who was closest to Itsumi when he was alive." But in reality, these celebrities may have had no other motive than to pour out their sorrow as human beings.

If the people who talked of Itsumi's death were guilty of any sin, it was only of allowing images of themselves to be used in the orchestration of such relativity through the discourse of television.

Not only did television obscenely expose the weak foundations on which the celebrities close to Itsumi stood, it enhanced this pathological situation by reducing everything to a state of comparison. Take the tabloid reporters, who often approached those attending Masataka Itsumi's funeral with questions like "Aren't you sad now that Mr. Itsumi has passed away?" (This is obviously not a literal quote, but quite honestly, such fatuities require neither precision nor accuracy.) Anyone who cannot detect pathological elements in such a "question" has had their sensibilities completely eroded by television. After all, this "question" is not a "question." It is an "answer." The tabloid reporters were throwing out a predetermined "answer"—"Mr. Itsumi has died and I am sad"— in the form of a "question." The first thing that whoever had a microphone thrust into their face in this way said was "Yes," or something to that effect. The second question that tabloid reporters would ask went something like: "What kind of person was Mr. Itsumi?" In truth, such a leading "question" expects no true "answer" in the real sense of the word. By asking it, the tabloid reporters were only giving those being questioned the chance to respond with, "Mr. Itsumi was a good man . . ." Prejudiced in this way, the people being questioned were unable to say anything else, thus prematurely forestalling spontaneous conversation or any possibility of veering in an unforeseen direction with their response. Such reporters thrive on imprinting a prefabricated "story" that their subjects are forced to regurgitate. Tabloid reporters are, in this way, television itself. Even people who supposedly existed in their own private spaces until television showed up are instantly pulled into television by the microphone placed before them. Manipulated so as to outline the "story" that television has prepared, they too are forced to become television itself.

beat takeshi vs. takeshi kitano

Due perhaps to some prearranged agreement, the only person not subjected to the unceremonious thrusting of tabloid microphones was Beat Takeshi, probably the most newsworthy person connected with Itsumi's death. All we saw of Beat Takeshi was a shot of him sitting in the front row at the funeral, an image that was broadcast without interpretation. His face, devoid of televisionesque expressions, displayed no emotions and existed only as itself. His figure, clad in simple black clothes, was repeatedly broadcast in two different clips. One was relatively short, but revealed that Beat Takeshi's naked face, when not covered with make-up, is covered with small, light-colored blotches.

In the second, slightly longer clip, Beat Takeshi is in the grips of a continuous, sorrow-filled movement: sitting in a chair with his legs slightly spread apart, he looks down, gripping his knees, shoulders tensed. His shoulders shake periodically. He is crying. This comes as a shock: we are seeing a side of the television signal called "Beat Takeshi" that has never before been shown. Any attempt to treat the "Beat Takeshi" of this moment as a television signal would be impossible because the naked essence of that signal is too explicit; Beat Takeshi's presence is too rooted in reality to be treated as an object of flattery or hackneyed expression. Because his sorrow could not be interpreted through the ready-made "story" prepared by the television reporters, the tabloid hosts were forced to repeat the clip over and over until it was reduced through reproduction. But, as anyone could see—and unlike the other celebrities caught by the camera—the Beat Takeshi who was speechless in the face of Itsumi's death was not television.

QUESTIONER = ANSWERER

The disease where reporters throw out "answers" in the form of "questions" is none other than the reality of television, whose only expectation is for an already prepared "story" to function.

television is only the modern age

But common sense tells us that for the questioner to simultaneously be the answerer is illogical and discomfiting. As the television object and subject casually merge into one another, the distance that should exist between questioner and answerer disappears. It is natural to expect that this "answer-question" polarity would develop into either an attack on one by the other or some synthesis of the two. But such a possibility is completely precluded by the merging of the subject and object. The actions of the subject or the object are greedily absorbed into the other's counteractions, and each swallows the other whole.

On a different note, does the questioner, who is simultaneously also the answerer, perceive a lack of purpose in his or her own words? If the action of asking something becomes, in that moment, the answer, then its *raison d'être* is negated the moment one opens one's mouth. Wouldn't it also be possible to imagine a situation in which an answer is degraded into nothing more than a question? In such a case, the questioner would never be saying anything, neither question nor answer, and would not even be conscious of the impossibility inherent in his or her own words, since the very attempt to question would itself morph into an answer.

We can call a person who has combined his or her own questions and answers out of some sense of obligation to reinscribe a "story" prepared by someone else the "questioner=answerer." Would such a person be able to separate his or her own "questions" and "answers?" For this to be possible, one must first possess a self-reflexive gaze. One must then be able to analyze the circuitry—of which one is a part—that has produced the story—of which one is also a part. But such self-reflexive thinking would itself only be able to go as far as re-recognizing that, in the end, one is a priori just a cog in the wheel of the story. Moreover, those who mix "questions" into their own "answers" merely because of externally imposed time restraints do not possess the discipline of thought necessary to even entertain such a hypothesis. Such self-questioning would lead directly back to the eternal purgatory of compulsively mixing one's "answers" with one's "questions."

This issue isn't limited to the problem of the TV reporter, nor is it exclusive to those who attended Masataka Itsumi's funeral. Having one's thoughts co-opted by a preexisting "story," having someone else's answers blended into one's questions, and having one's answers thoroughly permeated with someone else's questions are all everyday occurrences. The "questioner=answerer" avoids drawing his or her own conclusions, ultimately preserving only a vague sense of self. Even if this person tried to have a dialogue with him or herself, it would be impossible to determine if the phrases being generated were questions or answers. Such a mental state is nothing more than "self-love."

The reality is that the spectacle of questions and answers being merely two sides of the same coin is rampant on the medium called television. For example, nobody expects an unanswerable question on a television quiz show. On the one hand, those who create the questions wouldn't present one without a specific answer in mind. And, on the other hand, the answerer unequivocally agrees to be questioned. But isn't unequivocally agreeing to being questioned in and of itself an answer? Instead of choosing to answer, the answerer is required to do so. As a result, one should not imagine that the number of questions on TV quiz shows corresponds to the number of answers, since all that exists there is an aggregate of "question=answer" "question=answer" etc. equations that add up to nothing. Television shows on which the questioners and the answerers merge always promote the worship of the illusion that there is no distance between the audience and the show that is constantly being touted.

Since television shows are always developing, they now have multiple answerers who create the appearance of undeniable difference.

Each response is stamped with the name of an individual, but such discrepancies are ultimately reined back within the functional parameters of generating laughter. Within such a context, the personalized differences in the answers organize the uniformity of the answerers even more. The host, who takes on the role of the questioner, is also incorporated into this enormous uniformity. In other words, television becomes one enormous area of uniformity. The television quiz show *Heisei Board of Education*[3] can be considered entertaining only in a comparison where that show's uniformity is judged as having a finer texture than others. In this magnetic field of uniformity, there are, naturally, television questions and television answers, as well as ready-made "stories" that become apparent through those questions and answers. In sum, the "story" prepared by television is one that takes as its thesis the idea that all things are equivalent, and therefore that all things exist merely to be rearranged. It also assumes that, without exception, uniformity connects all questions and answers with the Sign of Equality ($=$).

SELF-REFERENCE AND THAT WHICH IS NOT SPOKEN

When one views this "uniformity" from another angle, one realizes that television self-references television. It is clear that this is the locus of television's problem. Television always says that it is television. Television questions and simultaneously answers that its question is a question. Or it raises a question that already includes its answer. In this way, television says nothing. A unique set of values comes into play as a result. According to those who appear on television, going with the flow is the only worthwhile way to behave. In order to avoid being treated as a foreign object, one must never hint even casually at one's presence, much less strenuously argue for it. Instead, one should give oneself over to and participate in that circuitry through which television self-references itself. All that is required is that one become a speaker for television itself. This is the television viewer's ultimate criteria, and television performers who do not obey this rule are considered "inferior" to those who do. Television is, after all, a thoroughly relativistic space where viewers are constantly comparing people and waiting faithfully for the moment when they will form a judgment as to "who is inferior to whom in the realm of television uniformity." I use the word "faithfully" to indicate the incredible patience with which television viewers never fail to tame their boredom.

In this context, Beat Takeshi is a superior television entity. He thoroughly understands television uniformity, and manages to avoid contradicting it by never asserting himself on it. This is what makes him so intriguing. When Beat Takeshi first appeared on the entertainment scene during the *manzai*[4] craze, he had a peculiar mannerism: while performing with his partner, his arms would almost always hang lifelessly by his side. By disassociating himself from "speaking with his hands," he ended up emphasizing his words. His arms moved away from his body only when performing those functions typically performed purely as hands—for example, jabbing at or hitting his partner on the head—and he never failed to add a hint of childish playfulness to those moments when he pointed at his partner, thoroughly disempowering the inherently political nature such a gesture usually possesses. This suppression of hand gestures, coupled with his irresponsible way of talking, always enabled him to avoid seeming pushy, even when blurting out opinions. Consequently, he never stood out. (Later, when Beat Takeshi became a film director under his real name, Takeshi Kitano, he again used this technique, directing his actors to speak with their arms dangling at their sides so as to prevent awkwardness with their hands. This also resulted in the self-imposed directorial rule of trying to show only the upper arms of an actor, coolly cutting off the rest with the bottom of the frame.)

It is also worth noting that in the variety shows he appeared on after leaving manzai—visits that increasingly took place in television-ordained settings—his hands would often be touching his face. Touching one's face with one's hand is a symptom of self-love, but as long as television viewers are themselves soaked in self-love, it's not one that will invite disgust. That is, anything that does not disrupt the television viewer's self-love is fine. In fact, in our age of television, the absence of self-love is a much hated, unacceptable vulgarity.

Beat Takeshi also thoroughly understands that television is a relativistic space where he can only exist in relation to something else: for example, as "the one who is more honest about his real feelings," or "the one who is more adorable," or "the one who is more dangerous," or "the one who is more bashful." And he felt that being praised by television viewers merely for being "better than" his manzai partner Beat Kiyoshi was both monotonous and unwise. Perhaps it was in order to broaden the variety of people he could reflect off of that he placed himself next to Akashiya Samma, Koji Ishizaka, Hiroki Matsukata, or Masataka Itsumi, or that he took part in the "Takeshi Gundan"[5]—choices that probably brought a degree of freedom to the relativistic space he was required to inhabit.

Beat Takeshi is always just "wise" enough. This is because he knows all too well that in television, being considered "too wise" means being called not wise at all. As a result, he has a wonderfully sensitive quality of restraint. By being "wise" enough but not "too wise," his "wiseness" on TV is enhanced. This method of accumulation perfectly matches the tactics of television, a medium that is appreciated cumulatively and unconsciously. At the same time, Beat Takeshi often acts in unexpected, outrageous ways. When looked at more closely, his outrageous actions are always linked with embarassment, and so do not in fact seem outrageous. Takeshi, who always seems to exude a sense of risk has, on closer examination, always stayed within a safety zone on television. While exclaiming the fake, censored-on-television word "*omanta!*"[6] to touch upon the evil areas of the television viewer's psyche, he would simultaneously signal "embarrassment" to let viewers perceive the risk he himself had just flirted with moments earlier. In other words, his risks are equipped with a self-consciousness that renders them safe. In that sense, he is a highly self-referential presence—"highly" because his self-referencing isn't restricted only to "speaking one's own emotions or biography." Actually, the "self" that can be found in Takeshi Kitano the film director is totally annihilated on television. All that we see on television is a television self. Because television expresses nothing more than television, when inside it, anyone who does not express his or her own real sense of self ends up being paradoxically referred to as a "television self." In television-speak, that is the sophisticated way in which to refer to oneself.

The essays written under the name Beat Takeshi use language that anyone could easily use. His words are not what makes Beat Takeshi unique: they express only that he had nothing to say as himself. Thus, whether Beat Takeshi or Fumio Takada transcribed the manuscript from taped statements is unimportant.[7] Even if one knows that in his book, *Film Theory Without Honor* (Jingi naki eigaron, 1996) Beat Takeshi shockingly praises *Ghost* (Zucker 1991), a movie one should be viscerally repulsed by—or shows a surprisingly tolerant opinion of Kurosawa's latest film, or puts down Martin Scorsese's *GoodFellas* (1990), a film he needs to come to terms with given his own leanings, or praises Verhoeven's *Total Recall* (1990) for misguided reasons that have nothing to do with film—when one finds out that he is speaking under the name "Beat Takeshi," one must resign oneself to the fact that Takeshi is not expressing his own opinions as himself, and is instead only hoping to have his opinions quoted by know-it-all film buffs. Note that in these cases, the first

television is only the modern age

person singular that he uses is *"ore"* or *"oira,"* not the seemingly self-loving *"boku."* [8] In this way, he gives those who accept Kitano as Kitano an opportunity to hesitate.

Since Beat Takeshi's manzai days, it has been apparent that he is actually not saying anything, even when he seems to be. One look at his manzai style confirms this. For example, he would affectionately ridicule a list of various stereotypes, but never himself. This listing of stereotypes would frequently be followed by the qualifying phrase "or something like that," a cautionary measure that made certain that his expression of intent always reversed itself, becoming meaningless. (Another noteworthy expression of his was the frequently inserted "Hey, you idiot!"—a maneuver probably intended to show that his words were on the side of an inoffensive "evil.") In any case, he never speaks from his real self while in the realm of television. Why? Because not speaking from one's real self means being insubstantial, and Beat Takeshi wants to be insubstantial. Even when he speaks about his own personal experiences—about the *"FRIDAY* Assault Incident" for example [9]—he laughs them off and plays them down, making them palatable to his viewers. Again, this is because he himself wants to be insubstantial. As someone who resides in the inverted space called television, he knows that being adequately insubstantial will entitle him to that special aura reserved only for television performers. All television lovers immediately recognize the ridiculousness of those performers who, hesitating, fail to wrap themselves in insubstantiality.

We need to note here that Beat Takeshi's "embarrassment" is identical to the circuitry that television uses to refer to itself as television. In other words, the "boyish" and "mischievous" smile that occasionally breaks through Beat Takeshi's deadpan Asian face is television. On a physical level, television is also Beat Takeshi's tic-like mannerism of periodically twisting his neck as if to relieve shoulder tension. This spasmodic gesture occurs when, for example, he is in the process of revealing his counterpart's weaknesses. By inscribing his own physical presence on television, he also evokes chuckles. This enables him to simultaneously be both question and answer. If such simultaneity is the essence of television, then Beat Takeshi is simultaneously a "visceral physical presence" and "someone who evokes chuckles." This is, once again, a microcosm of television's function. In reality, the only way Beat Takeshi asserts himself on television is through his embarrassed smile and his repetitive, neck-twisting twitch. But even those smiles and gestures are, on television, transformed into extremely television-like signals.

The process of creating these signals is, of course, a subtle one. Because only Beat Takeshi can emit them, he alone shoulders the function of instantly reversing poles from television, that enormous magnetic field of uniformity, to its antithesis, individuality. On another note, this aggregate of the different individual aspects called "Beat Takeshi" is an extremely musical signal. If one could express how these changes in body and expression are made manifest while ignoring their meanings and attributes, one might use such temporal descriptions as "flickering" or "vibrating"—or, more precisely, purely musical terms that signal changes in key such as "modulation" and "restoring to the dominant." Through his use of restraint, he is able to harmonize with his surroundings under any circumstance, as if playing a chord. In other words, his body vibrates within uniformity, and that vibration is also musical. This is a gift granted only to the signal called "Beat Takeshi."

Nevertheless, "Beat Takeshi" is obviously a flesh-and-blood entity. And in contrast to the slight, wavering details of his physical presence as a TV personality, which manifest as musical flickerings amidst the uniformity of television, Beat Takeshi the actor leaps beyond the confines of that uniformity in a single bound. Surely this is due to his instinctual understanding that difference, not uniformity, is what prevails in the space of drama. In short, Beat Takeshi the actor acts boldly within the screen, while Takeshi Kitano, the director who will later direct that actor, painstakingly molds this quality of boldness into an even more naked boldness. With this in mind, and before discussing the specific films Takeshi Kitano directed, I'd like to roughly sketch out the painstaking quality of Takeshi Kitano's directing, and also to review the process by which he constructed Beat Takeshi the actor.

NAGISA OSHIMA/TAKESHI KITANO

In the late June 1993 edition of *Cinema News Quarterly* (Kinema Junpo), Hiro-o Otaka wrote of Kitano's films that: "Much as there is a clear connection between the Okinawa baseball scene in *Boiling Point* and Nagisa Oshima's *Ceremony*, I have always felt the hovering influence of Oshima's cinema on Kitano's films." He goes on to describe a fairy-tale-like story about the period in the late 1960s when Takeshi Kitano was making a living as a bartender. At that time, Kazuo Komizu[10] was one of his customers. During the course of their conversations, they playfully made a promise that came to fruition close to twenty years later in *Those Who Inherit the Stars* (Hoshi wo tsugu mono, 1990), a film that Kitano produced and Komizu directed. From this story, we can see that Takeshi Kitano was a young cinephile at the time. Hence, we can easily imagine how Japanese cinema of the period "in which Nagisa Oshima existed" helped to create Takeshi Kitano's cinematic sensibility. (French cinema "in which Godard existed" may also have contributed to his directoral sensibility. Proof of this can be found in the frequent inclusion of nonsensical fight scenes that take place next to vehicles in *Boiling Point* and *A Scene at the Sea* . These scenes appear at first to be a development of the "two-picture cartoon" technique[11] that resembles manzai. However, they also connect with the sensibility of the scene in Godard's *Masculine-Feminine* [1966] in which a couple exchanges vows of love in the foreground, oblivious to the carnage taking place in the background. It also conjures up the absurd chaos of the highway traffic jam in *Weekend* [Godard 1968].)

One finds even more similarities between Oshima and Kitano in the ways that both use actors. After being ordered by his film company to use the dull and inexperienced actress Yuki Tominaga for his debut feature, Nagisa Oshima began to use actresses such as Kayoko Honoo, Saeda Kawaguchi, Rie Yokoyama, Emiko Iwasaki, and Hiromi Kurita—all of whom only had one film under their belts—as the stars of his subsequent films. A similar tendency can be detected in Kitano's use of the already popular Maiko Kawakami and Yuriko Ishida in his first and second films respectively, though he never used them again, and of the then-unknown Hiroko Oshima and Aya Kokumai as the leads for his third and fourth films.

Oshima has an inherent talent for finding the distance between the cinematic and the non-cinematic. His ability to handle ideas that in lesser hands would probably not even constitute a film requires not only technical prowess but unique good fortune as well. On the other hand, Kitano's films are almost compulsively permeated with the beautiful, accumulated essence of cinematic expression: abbreviated storytelling and characterizations, and the precise depiction of the state and texture of things (including characters) within the sparest of storylines (though *Boiling Point* is pregnant with a mesmerizing schizophrenia that contradicts this last quality). Together, these create a rich, cinematic spell that emphasizes the characters who are talking rather than the content of their dialogue. (This is taken a step further in dialogue scenes where Kitano deletes the talking subject from the frame, filming instead the character who is listening. In these moments, he manipulates silence twice: first, by showing a person who is not talking, and on top of that, by presenting an expressionless person so that the shot is "silenced." The editing of these spare shots together creates a shock.) As a result, his films are not about camerawork, but about editing until absolutely no excess fat remains. They overflow with the depth of silent films (and this is without even mentioning *A Scene at the Sea*, where the two leading characters are deaf). Precisely because of their soundless state, Kitano's films invite viewers to look closer at what is actually happening in the frame. It is also worth mentioning that Kitano's work seems to have inherited the cinematic mantle of Sadao Yamanaka's ellipses and Robert Bresson's editing (though Takeshi Kitano has never written a self-conscious treatise on film directing to rival Bresson's *Notes on the Cinematographer;* I have already referred to Kitano's book *Film Theory Without Honor* in a negative light). Furthermore, the viewer inevitably feels that Kitano's ellipses have a "student film" quality to them in that "he only photographs what is photogenic."[12] Thus it is also possible to understand the view that Kitano's directing methods clash with the ten "formulas" that make movie entertainment what it is.[13]

On the other hand, Kitano's directing methods can also be interpreted as the discarding of images that is made necessary by Kitano's love of speed. (Speed here refers not only to practical issues of production, but also to the way that the artist in Kitano cannot help but eliminate the pedantic moments a storyline requires from the images he creates.) Such a claim can only be made because Kitano's films are pregnant with unique and organic structural properties. He eliminates narrational effects characteristic to movies in ways that would normally distort them to the point where they were no longer entertaining. However, his films would be in danger of degenerating into mere "Art" if that were all that was going on.

I can nevertheless defend Kitano—even after having accepted all of the above—because he understands the essential elements required to make a film a "movie." Kitano has an especially firm grasp on the power of light. Many of his films are shot on relatively short schedules and, due to his preference for not following established movie conventions, on actual locations. This frequently results in scenes that are overcast. The cloudiness of the weather never dulls the images, however. Kitano understands what needs to be inserted amongst the greys: people in motion. For example, there is a scene in *A Scene at the Sea* (Ano natsu, ichiban shizukana umi, 1991) where Takako (Hiroko Oshima) comes to the beach to watch her boyfriend Shigeru (Claude Maki) practice surfing. The screen is almost completely grey, filled unceremoniously by a concrete breakwater. Into this mostly grey frame, unadorned except for a bit of texture, Kitano throws the stark movement of Takako descending stairs in the background and eventually sitting down on the beach. Similarly spare images are repeatedly presented throughout *A Scene at the Sea,* extending a sense of the everyday. This is the essence of Kitano.

Kitano inserts a scene that is particularly impressive for its unusual light into this sense of the commonplace. In it, Shigeru's surfboard is shown on the beach, foreshadowing his death. The weak sunlight that angles through the thin clouds seem haunted by otherworldliness. This light, which signals a change in the tone of the imagery, is charged with a miraculous but functional beauty. Because of this one moment of light, all the greyness that had been the film's key tone until this point shines metaphorically back into the past, creating an entirely new and specific meaning from that moment on. In other words, this change in light saturation from one scene to the next helps us to reframe all the scenes preceding Shigeru's death from the perspective of after his death.

television is only the modern age

In the same way that the strangeness of the light marking Shigeru's death is a response to the grey that had been the film's key tone until then, certain scenes or shots from one part of *A Scene at the Sea* reflect different scenes and shots from other parts of the film. What is being reflected varies according to the scene. For example, the silent shot of the ocean that opens the film represents the point of view of Shigeru, who is deaf. Though this shot seems objective at first, it is actually subjective. Only when looking back can one see how it matches the deadly serious attitude with which Shigeru stares at the ocean. After this opening, Shigeru's point-of-view shots are consistently eliminated. When one realizes this, it becomes apparent that Kitano intends to contrast the opening shot with all the film's subsequent shots. In other words, he shows us Shigeru's subjective "view" in the opening of the film, but throughout the rest of the film, Shigeru is depicted objectively. Kitano integrates these two views at the end of the film with the words "The Quietest Ocean That Summer."[14] This organizing principle is responsible for the film's symphonic sensibility. (The most obvious example of how certain parts of the film reflect back on others is the series of outtakes that runs at the end of the film, referred to by Kitano as "extra goodies." These show more of the relationship between Shigeru and Takako, thus reflecting back upon the content of the film "proper.") This, in turn, changes into sorrow about the "Shigeru that used to be here" and the "Shigeru that no longer exists." (Although these components are always characterized by a thorough exactness, Joe Hisaishi's synthesized musical score at the end of the film facilely connects the film's symphonic sense with a musical symphony, thus revolting against Kitano's one cinematic commandment: that "the viewer should quietly become aware of things.")

A sudden change in light connects with beauty in one of the scenes in *Sonatine* (Sonachine, 1993) as well. When Murakawa (Beat

Takeshi) learns that his underworld boss has framed him, he raids the Okinawa hotel room where his boss has headed. Though we see shots of Murakawa using a semi-automatic rifle to blow away the gathered gangsters, we are never shown how he enters the room, how he begins the attack, or how he defends himself against counterattacks. This has all been abbreviated. The only exception occurs when one of Murakawa's underlings, Ryoji (Masanobu Katsumura), is shown sneaking into an electrical closet to create a hotel-wide blackout just before the assault. Otherwise, the circumstances just prior to Murakawa's raid are shown only through a night exterior of the completely darkened hotel taken from the hotel's parking lot. One of the hotel rooms suddenly fills with an intense, rapidly flickering light accompanied by loud gunfire. Even from a distance, the audience is able to understand that this periodic, intense light in a dark room is in fact gunfire erupting from the barrel of Murakawa's semi-automatic. The audience does not see the slaughter itself; they are merely watching the light. Still, they know that the abstraction of flickering light is more brutal than an explicit display of slaughter. This is pure cinema. Yet to place one's faith in light alone rather than on drama or dialogue requires talent.

This cinematic efficiency of expression through light does not exist in Nagisa Oshima's films. Oshima is a filmmaker who expresses things skillfully, but he prefers to pour his energy into giving overwhelming impact and continuity (or continuity of intervals in some cases) to his images. As a result, his color schemes and his films as a whole are powerful and have "bulk." Though Kitano's films stand out because of their violence, Kitano, unlike Oshima, actually prefers subtlety over power. The amount of attention that Kitano pays to linearly connecting the uniformity of each scene is particularly subtle.

In what way did Nagisa Oshima influence Takeshi Kitano, then? The truth is that Oshima's biggest influence has been on "how to direct Beat Takeshi." The first film in which Beat Takeshi made his mark as a film actor was none other than Oshima's *Merry Christmas, Mr. Lawrence* (Senjou no merii kurisumasu, 1983). In it, Oshima highlighted the unnerving quality of Beat Takeshi's deadpan expression by placing Tom Conti, a Westerner, next to him. A Westerner's deadpan expression indicates a highly developed mental and psychological state. But a deadpan expression on an Asian face turns the Asian into an object like a stone or a tree. The content of the Asian's thoughts are completely erased by this deadpan expression—not just pushed aside and hidden, but eradicated. Oshima's talent for bringing out the beauty of an actor's deadpan expression is apparent in his use of Yusuke Kawazu in *The Cruel Story of Youth* (Seishun zankoku monogatari, 1960) and in the title role of *Boy* (Shonen, 1969)—a fact that Oshima has himself acknowledged in books such as *Oshima Nagisa 1960* (1993) and others. But in *Merry Christmas, Mr. Lawrence*, Takeshi's deadpan expression is even further objectified in contrast to those of the Westerners. At the same time, Oshima strips away Takeshi's superficiality as a televisionesque virtue that floats in television. Oshima often appears on Takeshi's TV shows, but unlike Takeshi, he negates all the "tenuous feelings of modern society" that Takeshi exhibits. As a result, Takeshi's audience appreciates Takeshi even more.

Oshima also eliminated Takeshi's familiar gesture of slightly raising his left shoulder while spasmodically twisting his neck and laughing with embarrassment. These would have become signals of television. (Note that the actor Beat Takeshi was still developing at this point and hadn't let go of the habit of shaking his body while talking. Still, he manifests physically in this film in a way that is completely different from the television personality Beat Takeshi.) In this way—and in particular through the use of close-ups—Oshima fixed only the naked essence of Takeshi in the frame.

© JEREMY THOMAS

There is also Takeshi's unforgettable smile in the last scene of *Merry Christmas, Mr. Lawrence* to consider. *"Merii Kurisumasu, Merii Kurisumasu, Misutaa Rohrensu,"* he says. While moving in the context of the drama, the pathos of these English words, which are spoken with a heavy Japanese accent, is aided by a perspective that views Japanese people as foreign objects. Takeshi's smile at the end of the film was widely commented upon as having a "rightness to it that was hard to express in words." This "hard to express in words" quality was the furthest one could get from the embarrassed smile that Takeshi showed on television. Oshima's insight that Takeshi and all Japanese people are viewed as foreign objects by Westerners is even more strongly reinforced by the fact that Takeshi shaved his head for the role. By objectifying Takeshi, Oshima made it possible for viewers to see in Takeshi's smile their own split—their own nakedness. This is what made it "hard to express in words."

CRIMINAL FLESH IS A FOREIGN OBJECT

After *Merry Christmas, Mr. Lawrence*, Takeshi would, (albeit intermittently) express a part of himself that was more object than mood or sign, even when appearing on TV. The three criminals that he portrayed in made-for-TV movies—Kiyoshi Okubo, Jesus Sengoku, and Hui Ro Kim—are examples of this (though, to be exact, one of these men was a criminal only according to the media). His portrayal of the serial rapist Kiyoshi Okubo was the most menacing of these roles, encompassing an abnormally wide range for a character.[15]

Okubo jumps from being called "my sweet boy" ("*bokuchan*") by his mother, an experience that exposes his Oedipal complex as an extreme form of wimpiness, to the obnoxious self-consciousness of a New Leftist or poet, then bloats into monstrosity when cursing at and begging for mercy from an interrogating police officer. Finally, his violence is thrust upon us in the rape scene. Since the drama is structured through the repeated use of flashbacks during Okubo's interrogation, the viewers feel particularly uneasy about the zigzagging swings of character evidenced by Okubo=Takeshi. In the rape scene, the skillfulness with which he slaps the victim, forces her legs open, and threatens her conveys a visceralness that seems to violate TV production codes. This would become the archetype for the fight scenes in Takeshi's own films. Takeshi's specialty in his fight scenes is the headbutt, a fact that appears to be based on his own physical sensibility. A person who favors headbutts is someone who knows that his own head can create an impact on an enemy. Such a person thinks of his own body not as a container for thoughts or a soul, but as a thing in and of itself. This sensibility—i.e. one that realizes that the body is an accumulation of functions, an object—is the dominant quality of Takeshi's portrayal of Kiyoshi Okubo in the rape scene, and it brutalized the television screen in unexpected ways.

In this sense, Takeshi's serial rapist can be paired with the creepiness and excessive self-consciousness that Kazuya Nakayama[16] brought to his portayal of Kiyoshi Tatsuta, the protagonist in Mamoru Watanabe's *Serial Killer: Cold-Blooded* (Renzoku satsujinki: reiketsu, 1984) based on the life of Kiyotaka Katsuta.[17] If we limit our gaze to the realm of television, the versimilitude displayed by Okubo=Takeshi ranks among the following iconic potrayals of villains: first, the overpoweringly fleshy sorrowfulness of Yasuo Daichi in *The Fukagawa Psycho-Killer Case* (Fukagawa toorima satsujin jiken, 1983), a portrayal that shows the "fallen hero" to be a man who is unconsciously driven to self-destruction out of relentless failures and fear of his father; second, Shigeru Izumiya in *The Yoshinobu-chan Kidnapping Case* (Yoshinobu-chan yukai jiken, 1979), an extremely physical embodiment of Tamotsu Obara that inscribed onto Izumiya's own body the often forgotten fact that Obara, rumored to be the postwar period's most heinous criminal, was mentally retarded. The quality of criminality depicted in all these characters, including Okubo=Takeshi, is so powerful on a physical level that it makes one forget the obvious fact that these are merely illusions created through acting.

Such a degree of criminality cannot be brought to life by just any means. For example, it is rare for a high degree of criminality to be depicted in popular novels featuring criminals. Only the novels of Bou Nishimura[18] have been able to achieve this. If one attempts to analyze a criminal with one's intellect, the criminal's "criminality" all but disappears. Only by completely descending to the side of the criminal, as Bou Nishimura does—i.e. only by physically feeling what the criminal does (an act that, while different in content, resembles a demonic possession)—does it become possible to portray him.

Two other roles played by Takeshi on television were less successful. In one, his portrayal of Jesus Sengoku as a good-natured old man referred to as "ol' man" by his followers regrettably failed to capture Sengoku's physical presence.[19] In the other, his portrayal of Hui Ro Kim was weakened by media manipulations of the actual Hui Ro Kim.[20] This in turn exposed the real Takeshi as a television personality who also manipulates the media.

The next noteworthy portrayal of a criminal by Takeshi was that of the professional killer hired to kill Chairman Nagano of the Toyota Trading Company in Yojiro Takita's *Comic Magazine* (Komikku zasshi nanka iranai!, 1986). This film, which stitches together artifice and fact while giving a quirky tour of contemporary social mores, is violently invaded by Takeshi's performance as the Hired Killer near the end of the film. The actual scene of Chairman Nagano's murder had been accidentally broadcast live on television, so those images were still fresh in the minds of viewers when this film was released. Keeping this in mind, Takeshi attempts to trace not just the killer's behavior, but his very viscerality. The media's violence, the violence of realism, fictional violence, Takeshi's own violence, and the film's (the filmmaker's) violence all come together within Takeshi, creating the illusion that Takeshi himself is being turned inside out, and that his portrayal has actually taken on its own body. (Of course, another reason why his portrayal is so believable is due to the "*FRIDAY* Assault Incident," which happened in much the same fashion.) The violence in this short scene obviously has less impact than the live footage of the event that had been captured by television cameras, but it is equipped with the evil of something inverted and wrong. As such, the reenactment goes further than the actual footage in describing the multiple meanings of violence. In the movie version, Takeshi conveys that he is a "goner" the moment he appears among the hordes of news reporters gathered around the apartment room where Chairman Nagano is hiding. His very body becomes the actual proof of violence stripped to its core. Takeshi knocks on a door. He removes the bars on the kitchen window next to the door. He breaks the glass, then enters the room through the broken window. Like the actual incident, these movements are carried out in full view of the media, and performed with the original perpetrator's unhesitating forcefulness and infantile persistence.

This quality of violence in Takeshi is repeated in his films. Such infantile persistence is particularly apparent in *Boiling Point* (3–4 x jugatsu, 1990)—for example, in the scene where Takeshi, playing an Okinawan gangster, comes out of a building after having been humiliated by the yakuza (gangster) boss. Oblivious to the fact that his underlings are hanging around, he repeatedly kicks the boss's car. Such persistent violence is also on view in the scene when Takeshi, absorbed in an informal game of baseball on the beach, persistently throws a rubber ball at his lover, who is standing in the batter's box.

The Takeshi Kitano who became a film director was made aware of his inherent physicality through the many criminal portrayals performed by his other half, Takeshi the actor. He has enlarged upon this in his overall attitude towards acting and in all the films he's directed. The manifestation of a televisionized physicality that is the mistake of so many Japanese films today does not exist in Kitano's films—neither for him nor for his entire cast.

This can be seen in the way that Kitano deliberately and completely confines the televisionesque body of Eiji Minakata (playing an assassin) in *Sonatine*. As Takeshi Kitano himself explains:

What cracked me up was the leader of the Chambara Trio.[21] I used that old guy as a contract killer. . . . What you see is a lot better than what I started with, actually. When I said that he was a killer, he said, "A killer?" and willingly agreed. So then I said, "You're carrying fishing gear," and he began to panic. 'Cause he was thinking, all black clothes, a raincoat and a white necktie or something like that. So I said, "No, that's not what I mean. You're a killer with fishing gear." So he came back looking like he was about to go fishing. "Is this what you mean?" I said, "That's great." Then I said, "When you come to the front of the house of the person you're about to kill, check your surroundings," and so he starts to look around intently, with this look in his eyes like he's obviously about to kill

television is only the modern age

somebody! [Laughs] Everybody fell over with laughter. And I thought, Damn! I said the wrong thing. So I said, "I'm sorry, I really hate to do this, but I've gotten rid of the contract killer. It's just a regular fisherman." "Oh, a fisherman?" Then I said, "A fisherman who has no place to stay for the night comes along, and he's wondering whether the house is empty. How's that?" This confused him even more! [Laughter] And I almost threw up my hands.[22]

Despite its apparent cruelty, this handling of Eiji Minakata is based on a film aesthetic that is not bound by televisionesque evasions of the flesh. Minakata's wandering around the peripheries of the frame with his fishing gear brings to mind the rhetoric of Kitano's films since *Violent Cop* (Sono otoko, kyobo ni tsuki, 1989), where tension is created from the unexpected direction of the killing bullet. Unlike *Violent Cop*, however, this use of the unexpected direction in *Sonatine* is brought about invisibly through the use of editing (as in the scene where the Okinawan gang boss is assassinated). In this, one can observe the maturity of Kitano as a film director for whom editing is critically important.

In any case, it should be stated that Kitano's portrayal of a series of criminals has made it possible for him to completely avoid the phenomenon of televisionesque flesh in his own films. The alienness of the criminal's flesh and its ambivalence about not being assimilated into the establishment always thrusts itself at the television viewers. To those who are not criminals, the bodies of criminals seem abnormally elongated and unbalanced, either lacking in something or excessive in some way. This is obviously not true on a physical level; rather, criminals are semantically deformed. Instead of blending in with their surroundings, their existence is thrown into relief. In this sense, they become "hard." While non-criminals spontaneously embody spirituality and gentleness, criminals often embody materiality through their physical presence. Criminals are always in close proximity to death, a subject we will explore further when we look at Takeshi's individual films. By revolting against the accepted order—i.e. one slanted towards valuing life—some criminals may develop a mindset that does not loathe death, and as a result will gamble with their own lives. In other words, they connect up with a value—be it hedonism, evil, vainglory, or extreme opportunism—that is different from life, using their own lives as collateral. Such criminals are permeated by the stench of death.

For example—and this is something everyone intuits—tattoos, which are a trademark of criminals in Japan, point not toward *élan vital,* the expansion of life, but *flan vital,* the contraction of life.[23] But instead of seeing tattoos as stylized patterns that tie criminals to themselves, binding them to who they are, couldn't they also be seen as, for example, the poison that their bodies are filled with by their unhealthy lives and that rises to stain their skin? In other words, as a symptom of the violation of the surface? Seen this way, death itself stains the criminals with a patterning that even further reinforces the physical alienation that is their aesthetic value. Takeshi has been fond of portraying criminals in his films; even his detective in *Violent Cop,* whose warped obssessiveness and recklessness violates all professional codes of conduct, exudes the pungent smell of criminality. In his subsequent two films, he again portrays gangsters. Takeshi Kitano enjoys exposing his own criminality and death. In a scene in *Sonatine,* Murakawa, portrayed by Takeshi, is enjoying a bucolic rendezvous with Miyuki (Aya Kokumai) that is interrupted by a sudden, short squall. The rain-drenched Kokumai, whose healthy nipples show through a white t-shirt worn over her naked flesh, is contrasted with Takeshi, whose tattoo-covered body is visible through his white shirt—an obvious juxtaposition of Life and Death.

television is only the modern age

To further expand on this book's opening topic of television, a Beat Takeshi-type criminal is obviously not going to be reinserted into the "uniformity" that is the primary characteristic of television. In television, which is by nature an enormous arena of uniformity, the other does not exist. (The only exceptions to this are criminals featured on the news or maliciously observed celebrities, who also manage to capture a kind of otherness.) However, in his best moments, the actor Beat Takeshi becomes the Other=Foreign Object—a feat that he himself, not viewer animosity, brings about. The moment that this happens, we lose sight of how the magnetic force field of televisionesque uniformity—an arena so ubiquitous that within it all questions and answers are connected with an equal sign—operates. Thus, at best, Beat Takeshi is either absolutely a question or absolutely an answer, but definitely not an "answer=question." He is not a deferred object behind which a "story" hides.

DIRECTOR = STAR

It's obvious from the first that Beat Takeshi is conscious of the space of televisionesque uniformity called "question=answer." Moreover, the signal he emits has a yin-yang simultaneity that allows it to switch between different meanings. As such, his very television signal-like movements could be described as a kind of "blinking." Although he is a part of the "uniformity" of television, the equal sign only connects him to the parameters of his own "excessiveness" and "embarrassment." Because he never connects things with an equal sign when they should not be, he never assists in television's concoction of a "story." This means that he never supports the neverending evil of "uniformity." Upon closer examination, Takeshi's morality can be detected in this. He may continue to manifest brilliantly as a tiny descrepancy within the powerful space of uniformity called television, but that uniformity remains unshakeable.

Contrary to our expectations, the actor Beat Takeshi appears on television or in movies as a singularly foreign object (other). Usually—in TV for example—that otherness is collected within sameness. TV is constantly struggling to put the other within sameness. However, as mentioned before, Beat Takeshi is able to preserve that otherness by positioning himself on the screen as only an independent "question" or an independent "answer." In other words, the battle over uniformity shifts away from a formula that connects with an equal sign—for example, "question=answer"—to one that connects with an arrow—"question → answer." In order to achieve this, Takeshi might have forced himself into a "director=star" framework similar to that of the "questioner=answerer."

Everyone knows that the moniker "Beat Takeshi" conceals the real name, "Takeshi Kitano." The name "Takeshi Kitano" was probably already in circulation before it was parenthetically presented in reports on the "*FRIDAY* Assault Incident." According to common journalistic practice, criminals are referred to by their real names. We know this because at the time of the "*FRIDAY* Assault Incident," a particular Minister of Justice disgraced himself by using the strange sounding "*Beat-kun*"[24] when he said with a knowing wink, "I can understand Beat-kun's feelings well." Everyone must have been aware that "Takeshi Kitano-san" would have been the most appropriate form of address for a Cabinet member, someone who should always strive to generalize problems.[25] This means that by the mid 1980s (when the incident took place), everyone already knew that the musical waverings of "Beat Takeshi" were supported by the calm consciousness of "Takeshi Kitano." Soon after this incident, it was reported that Kinji Fukasaku had stepped down from directing the film *Violent Cop* because Kitano could not be on location for the number of days Fukasaku required, and that Takeshi Kitano = Beat Takeshi would henceforth serve as both director and star of the movie. Takeshi's birth as a "director=star" might have been the product of chance, but it gave the first hints of a premonition that "Takeshi Kitano" would use the weapon of otherness called "Beat Takeshi the Actor" in his struggle to drive a stake through the uniformity of television.

On a different note, what does it mean for a film director to do double duty as a starring actor? How is that director's self-consciousness smashed and then reconstructed? Here is some interesting testimony about Clint Eastwood, now recognized as one of the most successful director/stars, from Sondra Locke, his co-star and wife:

> While shooting scenes for *The Gauntlet*, Clint would talk to me without raising his voice, just mouthing his words. Even when he was also in the shot, if he wanted the other actors to speed up, he would wave to them from outside the frame. He would even talk to me while I was doing a take.[26]

What takes place on the set of an Eastwood film is something peculiar to the early days of cinema, when the great silent films were being churned out. It is clear from the films of Charlie Chaplin that delegating all decisions to Chaplin alone (the actor also functioned as the director) must have resulted in an exceptionally efficient production. (When Chaplin's back was to the camera, or when he was only partially in the frame, he could keep the framed part of his body in the shot as the actor while directing with the part outside of the frame. By splitting himself up by function in this way, Charlie Chaplin became a multifaceted character. Such a working style must have been even more feasible in the silent-movie era, before synchronous sound recording.) The astounding style of moviemaking that came out of the early days of cinema is something we can only marvel at now. Take Jackie Chan, for instance. Because he performs even the most dangerous daredevil stunts himself, and because his films are an endless barrage of spur-of-the-moment movie ideas and action scenes, the brisk pace on his sets must be accelerated even further when he both edits and stars in the same movie. Even more activity is made possible in the process of making a film when "the director=the star"—in other words, when the subjective and the objective are one and the same. For example, when capturing a shot of the protagonist's feet, the director=star is able to operate the camera from a position that the cameraman would not be able to reach. In this way, the camera is itself out of necessity sucked into the movements of the director=star.

Another type of director=star is represented by Orson Welles. Such a type transcends the Chaplin-type technique of using one's own image as an actor in an unadulterated shot. The Orson Welles-type director=star realizes that films are predicated on the editing process, and puts enormous effort into dispersing his or her own voice and physical presence within that linear time-frame called a film through editing. This brings into being a kind of objectivity, albeit one with a more complex circuitry. However, the director=star must possess a degree of self-adulation that reaches perverse heights in order to do this. Even without an Orson Welles level of ego, objectivity always finds its way into a "director=star" film since the director=star needs to be able to objectify him or herself from the camera's perspective. Moreover, the director=star cannot watch his or her own eyes the way that someone who stands before a mirror can. Also, a film cannot exclusively show only one individual. Obviously, then, an editing process intervenes here on behalf of the "director=star." This is something that Orson Welles was able to accomplish to a high degree in the sensual medium of cinema, where time and space are intermittent, and where new time-spaces occur every moment. In such a realm, it is necessary to thrust one's figure forward. Unlike the Chaplin-type director=star who desires self-promotion, Orson Welles had the mentality of a "trickster." Therefore—although others might have difficulty taking this seriously—Orson Welles might even have wanted to expand his body until it was almost spherical in order to make his image appear larger and more dominant on the screen. Welles' true filmic nature lies in the fact that such a sphere is ultimately an aberration within film's rectangular frame. Drifting between a familiar, unchanging voice and unfamiliar, renewing flesh, his films maintain an uncanny equilibrium between cinematic assimilation and the accentuation of cinematic minutiae. That this simply feels right is a testament to the masterfulness of his films.

In contrast, it may be of interest to consider Shoji Kaneko, the "screenplay writer=star" of *Ryuji* (Ryuji, Kawashima 1983). Kaneko exists on the other end of this spectrum. *Ryuji*, with its numerous and sometimes suffocatingly self-adulatory shots of Kaneko looking at himself in a mirror, is a twisted masterpiece haunted by the dim light given off by those who do not possess the talent of an Orson Welles. Though permeated by a kind of self-adulation, *Ryuji* expresses a surprising modesty on screen. The image of Kaneko's face floating on the surface of this extremely grainy film announces the all-too-real fact that Kaneko is dying in real life, and thus never comes into focus in the audience's mind. Moreover, despite the obvious beauty of Kaneko's voice, it is somehow possessed by a vagueness that echoes the weakness of something ephemeral and distant. *Ryuji* is probably a masterpiece precisely because it manages a fragile equilibrium between self-love and ambiguity. Regardless of its intention, *Ryuji* has the effect of enveloping its audience in something other than the proximity of self-adulation, something far away. Furthermore, the mirror-image relationships formed in *Ryuji* between the characters jointly played by Shoji Kaneko, Kinzoh Sakura, and Koji Kita are very weak, as relationships tend to be in this "contemporary age." *Ryuji*'s narrative depicts this. Though it might only have happened by chance, the audience probably senses that this film's form, which fuses the danger (darkness) of the characters' linkages with the light of the film and the darkness of their faces, is close to miraculous.

Both the primitive appeal of Clint Eastwood's films, in which director and star coincide, and those of Orson Welles, which are accompanied by the thrill of discovering that the star's image and voice can be dispersed through editing, are readily recognizable in Takeshi Kitano's films. Moreover, Kitano's sets have been stamped with a name comparable to that of a Welles or an Eastwood, and the awareness that such a person is actually on set appeals to the crew, who want to remain anonymous. (This helps to explain the on-set meglomania described by producer Kazuyoshi Okuyama in his essay "Parting Ways with Beat Takeshi."[27] It's worth noting that, aside from actual interviews with Kitano, this wonderful essay by Okuyama has the strongest analysis and is the most affectionate of all the materials written in connection with *Sonatine*'s publicity. Ironically, by writing so wonderfully about their parting of ways, Okuyama also inadvertantly revealed that he was the producer most worthy of being in Takeshi Kitano's orbit. Naturally, his essay suggests a possible future reunion between Takeshi Kitano and Kazuyoshi Okuyama.)

But once one accepts the commonalities that exist between the sets of Takeshi Kitano=Beat Takeshi and those of Clint Eastwood or Orson Welles, it becomes obvious that Takeshi's "director=star" films rest upon a completely different foundation: the films of directors like Beat Takeshi=Takeshi Kitano are fundamentally different from older films because they always need to be conscious of film's neighboring medium—television. Kitano's films are organized only according to reasons personal to Kitano. In other words, Kitano starts off by acknowledging the established fact of the Beat Takeshi that floats around in television. To counteract this, he makes films. Thus, what he initially accomplishes in his films is a pure critique aimed at the contemporary age "in which television exists." (This is evident from the previously quoted statement by Takeshi Kitano about the leader of the Chambara Trio. What is impressive about it is the distance—a "critic's distance"—that Takeshi Kitano creates between himself and television.) Kitano's films use the "director=star" equation, a circuitry that resembles the dangerous, televisionesque uniformity of "questioner=answerer." However, he uses it in opposition to television, which relentlessly "says nothing" in a fervently superficial way by making its performers act as both questioner and answerer. Kitano's films express anti-television. He is able to fix a shocking physicality in the movie frame that doesn't exist in television. His assertion that "I am an object" further deepens this gap between film and television. Although he might be attracted to the hard-boiled style solely from an artistic point of view, he ends up using it, however incidentally, to critique the "Contemporary Age."

Because this critique is based on the singularity of Beat Takeshi's body, it can never be quoted by others in the way that his words are on quoted on television. The greatest virtue that Takeshi Kitano has discovered in film is "solitude." Any rationale for him to call his films his "toys" can only be discovered in the "scent of solitude" they exude. In his own personal way, Beat Takeshi=Takeshi Kitano organizes the film shoot location called the "festival place" (which it probably is in many senses) for the sole purpose of satisfying himself. When seeing Kitano rush to the movie set, squeezing scarce time out of a busy schedule, one invariably senses the solitude of a king.

The films of Beat Takeshi＝Takeshi Kitano reveal a latent personal split within himself. The person gazing at himself is Takeshi Kitano, and the self that is the object of the gaze is Beat Takeshi. The importance of this to Takeshi Kitano＝Beat Takeshi can be understood from the fact that Takeshi Kitano the actor is faithfully credited as Beat Takeshi. This is in sharp contrast to actors in the Takeshi Army such as Yanagi Yurei (Masahiko Ono), Guadalcanal Taka (Takahito Iguchi), and Dankan (Minoru Iizuka), each of whom are credited under their real names. Excuses such as "I want to wipe away any hints of television from my films," or "with a silly stage name, the cinematic nature of the credits would be lost," are all overturned when Takeshi Kitano is credited as "Beat Takeshi." What Kitano is doing here is fixing his gaze on the essence of matters. By crediting Yanagi Yurei and the others under their real names, Kitano keeps them as objects. In order to objectify himself, however, he had to make "Beat Takeshi" an object. This is what gives specificity and substance to the arrow in the structure of the uniformity-challenging "question → answer."

In his films, Kitano constructs a Beat Takeshi that is diametrically opposed to the television version—one that is, in other words, an object. By doing this, he simultaneously murders and "suicides" Beat Takeshi. Obviously, the phrasing "suicides Beat Takeshi" may sound odd, but for Takeshi Kitano, "suicide" functions as a transitive verb. The Japanese word for "suicide," *jisatsu*, includes an object.[28] The self referred to in this character encompasses not only Takeshi Kitano himself, but also his other expression of self, "Beat Takeshi." When seen from a broader perspective, this character "ji" is somewhat problematic since it contains that infinitely evil uniformity called television. Moreover, this "ji" that is the self also reflects the narcissistic tendency that lingers around the television viewer. This is the "ji" that Kitano murders.

television is only the modern age

The contemporary age's self-revolving "questioner=answerer" diagram, where only a shallow story exists, takes on a solidity that makes removing the equal sign difficult. In essence, the "question=answer" theory contains a postponing function that prevents the clear, naked expression of both question and answer. This being so, let's think of a method that will allow us to burn away the equal sign that exists in "question=answer" while decisively impressing upon the viewer that an equal sign does exist. In his films, Kitano always (and the reason for this "always" will be explained in a later chapter) shows himself "suiciding" Beat Takeshi. In so doing, he is gambling, half-smeared with futility, on the possibility that the equal sign in "question=answer" can be replaced by an arrow indicating change. This is the essence of Takeshi Kitano's critique. It goes without saying that one can see in it his revolt against television. At the same time, by filling his films with objects (i.e. with himself), he saves Japanese movies, which have hit an all-time low due to their lack of objects. This is also part of his critique. Even within this contemporary age, where all forms of expression turn into critiques, Takeshi Kitano=Beat Takeshi lives self-consciously by rejecting televisionesque chatter and introducing instead a critical silence. Such a silence is, truly, the otherness that can potentially counter the din of television. But given the way things are now, inserting such an objectivity into the syntax of film is not the best approach—nor is it even possible. Still, even an awareness of such an impossibility constitutes a critique.

At this point, let's figure out the direction in which the self-consciousness in Takeshi Kitano's films is heading. I mentioned before that Kitano's films are films about editing. In a film with a Takeshi Kitano style of editing, the space between shots is especially sensational. Naturally, a large part of the rationale behind such a technique is a dramatist's eye toward creating shocking effects. But the desire to slice up the flesh of Beat Takeshi through editing must also be at work. This Kitano-type desire to slice oneself up, as opposed to the Wellesian desire to make oneself omnipresent, is a rare commodity for a film director. Regardless of how many pieces Beat Takeshi is sliced up into, however, he is not provided to the viewers because his films are about objects as pure objects, and thus are about nakedness.

THE ELIMINATION QUEST AND URGENCY

What moves the audience first in the films of Takeshi Kitano=Beat Takeshi? From a moral standpoint, what is most moving is Takeshi Kitano=Beat Takeshi's sure grasp of himself. In fact, when asked by Takeshi Yamaguchi, "Do you rely on someone else to judge your acting?" Kitano answered "No, I don't. After appearing on thousands of TV shows, I have a good sense of what my own acting is like and how my expressions look." [29] This is a particularly memorable comment on the sure sense of self that initially became apparent in Kitano's television work and that was further refined in those films he acted in but did not direct.

Is it possible to be moved merely by a sure grasp of self? The "director=star" Takeshi Kitano → Beat Takeshi generally appears first as the subject, then as an object. When considering this, one can't help but notice that the materiality of Takeshi Kitano as a subject exists before Beat Takeshi is realized as an object. In other words, this is not a case where Takeshi Kitano attempts to transform Beat Takeshi into an object through trial and error. The heart's tendency to insert emotional judgments when excavating the essence of matters makes it difficult to classify objects as merely objects. In that sense, the heart always simply replaces an object with a heart. In contrast to this, the only thing that can conceive of an object as an object is, obviously, thought. Moreover, one must possess a detached mindset that tries to apply thought only to objects. In other words, eliminating emotion from the thoughts one entertains about oneself only becomes possible by being steadfast in one's will to completely construct an object. Being able to recognize that one is merely an object requires this level of mental discipline. Kitano's mental discipline should thus be commended here, since being emotionally impressed by such things as Takeshi Kitano's "sure grasp of his self" or the fact that "he is a rare instance of someone who has not lost his sense of self" would be insufficient.

However, excavating Takeshi's material presence based on the order in which Takeshi Kitano = Beat Takeshi appears may already be taking us in the wrong direction. Couldn't a reversal take place in which Beat Takeshi the object exists before thought itself, thus making it possible for him to "think" as an object? Wouldn't his thinking then be free from rhetorical embellishments, and instead of being thoughts about objects, be the thoughts of an object itself? Normally, the idea of "objects having thoughts" would be considered impossible—but aren't audiences moved by a Takeshi Kitano = Beat Takeshi film precisely because of the specific methods he uses to break open what is normally thought of as impossible?

In any case, when thinking about objects, it is essential to eliminate everything that's extraneous, not just emotions. Hollywood's Golden Age is so named because it was an era in which this kind of elimination successfully took place. It is a well-known fact that the screwball comedy was the twisted result of the Hollywood Production Code, which, among other things, demanded that beds in which lovers or married couples slept together be eliminated. The elimination of unnecessary sentiment is also synonymous with the elimination of extraneous expository dialogue. This both illustrates and reveals the historical importance of Kitano's attempt to resuscitate the inherent power of films to say a lot using only a few words.

This resuscitation has more urgency than people may realize for Takeshi Kitano, who feels a sense of crisis regarding film. It's probably fair to say that the crisis regarding screenwriters started with the French New Wave, but Kitano's sense of urgency, which exists at a level beyond cinematic history, rises far above a lazy insistence on obeying the "Ten Golden Rules of Moviemaking." This sense of urgency has the potential to overturn the existing values of cinema itself.

Why is rushing ahead with such urgency so important? Anyone who can't answer this question must be thoroughly anesthetized to television's proliferation. We require immediate emergency treatment for television's gradual wearing away at our sensitivity. And in this day and age, when everyone unintentionally mimics television's embarrassed laughter, what can shoot television down if not truthful silence and violence? Let's freeze that embarrassed laughter with truthful silence and violence. The people who are in the best position to do this—the people in a position to "betray" television—are themselves television people. Takeshi Kitano is probably not unaware of this.

Naoto Takenaka[30] approaches this issue from a slightly different position. Everyday reality is mundanely overturned in open-ended films such as *The Sky Can't Be This Blue* (Sora ga konnani aoi wakeganai, 1993) and *The Grave and Divorce* (Ohaka to rikon, 1993) which appeared around the same time as the once-popular "skillfully crude" cartoons.[31] Though this might at first seem to be a technique that allows for ambiguity, it actually comes from an entirely different place. Takenaka's work always possesses a quality of unrushed latency. His films, like Kitano's, utilize an economy of expression. However, unlike Kitano's films, which overwhelm, they are modest and thus in danger of being lumped together with other, inferior films. Given that Takenaka was acclaimed for his ability to instantly subvert himself to the accompaniment of violent laughter, such modesty is surprising. Still, this modesty is itself probably responsible for the individuality he found for himself in the arena of film. In any case, it is telling that Takenaka first became entranced by film's generosity after appearing in softcore porn at the beginning of his career.

If Takenaka captivates audiences with his "miniature garden"-like tepidness, thrusting the morality of his films at the audience slowly and in a half-embarrassed way, then what does Kitano's urgency—an urgency that could easily be confused with a hard-boiled style—indicate about his dispositions and views beyond commands that can easily be turned into slogans such as "protect cinema from television"? Maybe because Kitano understands that everything is plunging relentlessly toward death, urgency becomes his willful way of willfully not being left behind. On a different note, this urgency could also be understood on the level of Takeshi Kitano=Beat Takeshi's physicality. Didn't "Beat Takeshi," the stand-up comedian who first appeared on television, always have a sense of urgency about him? Think of the way he would go through a litany of complaints against stereotypical characters, and of his anger toward the thick-headed responses of his manzai partner, Beat Kiyoshi. We can call this urgency at the level of the heartbeat. This is why, when he began editing his own films (which can be described as "unfolding with detachment"), he showed a tendency to eliminate scenes that dragged, urgently piling scenes on top of each other and urgently killing off characters. In so doing, he was able to situate his films as foreign objects=others at the opposite end of the spectrum from televisionesque uniformity. It should be noted here that television's constant equation of questions with answers in order to create a space of uniformity looks urgent precisely because of its relentless renewal of uniformity. In reality, television is an infinite malignancy that drags on and on—i.e. an eternal postponement. This can be compared to the movement of a clock's second hand, which, though initially seeming to possess a kind of urgency, has nothing to do with urgency at all when viewed from the perspective of the totality of time. What we need to figure out is if Takeshi understands the televisionesque contemporary age as being urgent, when in fact television is only the contemporary age. Television marches forward like the second hand on a clock, but we cannot call that movement urgent.

Takeshi Kitano=Beat Takeshi creates—probably intentionally—an extremely seductive misunderstanding about the urgency of our times. Even though no such thing exists, he mistakenly thinks it does. This is something we can't afford to overlook when discussing Takeshi Kitano's auteurial secrets and intricacies.

02

violent cop
double suicide

In an article entitled "The Current State of Japanese Cinema," the critic Sadao Yamane wrote:

> When I saw Takeshi Kitano's *Sonatine*, it made me think of the "*ketsu*" aspect of *kishotenketsu*.[1] Kitano has now directed four films, and they actually seem to fit nicely into the kishotenketsu structure.
>
> In *Violent Cop*, the film's star, Beat Takeshi=Takeshi Kitano, also happened by chance to become its director, resulting in a powerful, violent first film (*ki*). In addition to directing and starring in his second film, *Boiling Point,* he also wrote its original screenplay, in which the everydayness of backlot baseball explodes into violence against the backdrop of Okinawa (*sho*). In *A Scene at the Sea*, Kitano's third film, he changed tactics and moved away from the violence of the second film, "quietly" crafting a seaside love story that had no dialogue or dramatic effects. Although he was not the film's star, he was its editor and also performed scriptwriting and directing duties (*ten*). In *Sonatine*, his fourth film, he simultaneously functioned as writer, director, and editor, in addition to returning as its star. While this fourth film summed up the

main elements of his three previous ones—showing both the brutal violence of the Okinawan gangsters' internecine war and the parallel everyday quietness of the beach—he concludes the drama in a startling manner. One can't help feeling that now another period has been demarcated (ketsu).[2]

The above gives a very accurate, if rough overview of Kitano's filmography. At this point, I would like to interpret Takeshi Kitano's films using Sadao Yamane's technique of outlining Takeshi=Takeshi's function in each of his films. This makes it possible for us to examine the films from the perspective of "how do they exist" instead of summarizing "what we see."

Our guide in this endeavour will be Makoto Shinozaki's article "Those Who Sullenly Fight On," the only systematic and accurate theory about Kitano to be published thus far in a film journal (it was written after the release of Kitano's second film).[3] Shinozaki opens his essay abstractly with this statement:

"I was convinced of the emergence of a new breed of film director within minutes of *Violent Cop*'s opening, with its images and sounds that pulse with 'cinematic blood.'" Everyone in the audience must have felt this same shiver of recognition. Let's now examine how *Violent Cop* was born from this opening scene that pulses with "cinematic blood."[4]

THE OPENING OF "VIOLENT COP"

We are first presented with a close-up of the almost too nakedly exposed, bespectacled face of a homeless man. His unreadable expression and his twisted, toothless mouth, which appears to be laughing, displays an alcoholic numbness that is unmistakeably the

violent cop double suicide

zero degree of facial expressions. The camera then pulls back slightly to show a brutal assault that seems to have been inspired by an early '80s incident in which schoolboys assaulted homeless people in Yokohama. (Needless to say, it also conjures up the scene in which street kids assault a crippled beggar in the opening of Buñuel's *Los Olvidados*). All that is shown on screen as the youths jab at the back of the homeless man's head are the boys' hands. The homeless man, unable to bear the attack, attempts to escape on his hands and knees (though here, as in the opening shot, his expression does not change). The camera follows him, mostly through a dolly shot, revealing the number of boys participating in the assault and that it is taking place in a city park at night. What is initially striking about the boys' violence is its persistence, which the dolly shot conveys very well. Finally, after being dragged along by one of the boys' bicycles, the homeless man faints. (We learn only later that he has fainted. Based on what we are initially shown, the homeless man appears to have died.) Up to this point, the scene has been filmed in a continuous dolly shot that moves along a horizontal axis. After this scene, however, we briefly see vertically composed shots of the boys who, having let off steam, are heading home on their bikes through an inner-city tunnel lit with orange lights. Let's call the effect of this transition from a horizontal movement to a vertical composition the impact of the "right angle."

The next sequence, which takes place some time later, shows one of the boys involved in the attack entering a white, modern-looking house in what seems to be a residential area. The camera, which is pulled back as far as possible, remains in place even after the boy disappears into the house. Following a brief pause during which nobody is on-screen, we see Beat Takeshi (playing Detective Azuma) enter the frame from the right and walk towards the house. He rings the doorbell. After a moment, the boy's mother opens the door.

Takeshi says that he is with the police, and succinctly announces that he is there to talk to the boy, an exchange that is shown in a precise shot-reverse shot. (Because of Takeshi's deadpan expression, we do not interpret or expect anything beyond what he actually says.) Having confirmed that the boy's room is on the second floor, he starts for the stairs, though he has not been ushered in. He stands in front of the door to the boy's room. The composition of the frame at this point is crowded. A shamanic mask that looks like a Japanese demon hangs on the door, probably put there by the boy. Its protruding nose lunges oppressively toward Takeshi, again at a "right angle." He knocks on the door. Though he only knocks twice, it is with a forcefulness that feels monomaniacally persistent. The boy, who probably thinks it's his mother, does not immediately open the door. Instead, he answers, "Stop bugging me. What do you want?"

The moment the door finally does open, Takeshi coolly punches the boy somewhere in the chest. The boy falls to the floor in pain as Takeshi continues to persistently slap him. Actually, the hand Takeshi uses to beat the boy is offscreen below the shot, but the violence of the slapping sounds echoes in the imagination of the viewer. Takeshi then kicks the boy a couple of times. Here again, the point where Takeshi's foot comes in contact with the boy is offscreen. The camera finally moves to one side, showing us the boy, who raises his upper body off the floor slightly, shrinking away from the looming figure of Takeshi. We notice blood flowing from his nose.

TAKESHI: Tomorrow, come to the precinct with your cronies.

BOY: What did I do? I haven't done anything.

The boy does not conceal his terror as he says this, and his body actually twitches with fear. In profile, we see Takeshi, savoring the moment. He pauses for effect while staring at the boy with a deadpan expression, then starts into him again, saying "Oh, you didn't do anything?" After another pause, during which this question has time to sink in, he suddenly exclaims, "Then I haven't done anything either. Brat!" and gives the boy a powerful headbutt. Because this head breaks the silence of a "pause," its impact stands out even more than the other depictions of violence we have seen until this point (a directorial feat). The boy cries. The scene soon changes back to the previous long shot of the boy's house, although this time Takeshi is exiting. He turns to the right and exits the frame.

The next morning, a small boat and its captain are shown moving down a river while the sound of the boat's engine reverberates in the background. Just ahead, a bridge is visible, forming yet another "right angle" to the direction of the boat. The clatter of an empty can being thrown echoes across the image. As we wonder what this could mean, we make out a group of boys (if the boys we had seen previously were high-school or junior-high-school boys, then these are clearly elementary-school students) who are leaning over the handrail of the bridge, throwing empty cans at the boat. Confused, the captain looks up. The moment that the boat passes directly under the bridge is captured in a bird's-eye shot with the boys in the foreground with their backs to us (it goes without saying that this "right angle" between the boat and the bridge the boys are standing on is emphasized by the angle of the camera, which is perpendicular to the water). On the far side of the frame, we see a full shot of the boat captain yelling "Hey!" as the boys yell back, "Idiot!" Then, using a match-on action technique, the camera frames the boys from behind as they run across the bridge. Here again, taking the river as its axis, the camera's orientation changes from parallel to the river to coming at it from a "right angle."

To top all this off, the film's main musical theme—an updated version of Erik Satie's "Trois Gnossiennes, Lent"—kicks in. Using an extremely long lens, the camera shows the boys in a static shot as they walk away, eventually picking up from beyond the arc of the bridge first the head, then the upper body, and then the entire figure of Takeshi as he walks toward the camera. Through this dolly shot, which captures him from the side at a "right angle," we come to realize that the length of time Takeshi is shown walking contradicts narrative efficiency, continuing for over a minute until he enters the police precinct. At this point, the shot changes, and he walks down a hallway and enters his office.

At this point, I will stop this trivial chronological description of scenes. The truth is, what I've described is already more than enough. Everything that needs to be said about this film is contained in the scenes described above. All that needs to be recognized is that the condition of this film's existence is woven together from the concept of time that has repeatedly been emphasized by such words as "persistence," "continuity," and "length," together with the spatial concept of the "impact of the right angle." Other critical issues are also contained in these scenes, however. For example, the transmission of violence (the phrase "the transmission of violence" is actually Makoto Shinozaki's) from the boys who assault the homeless man, to Takeshi, who abuses one of those boys with a zealousness that goes beyond his duties as a detective, to the elementary-school boys who throw empty cans at the passing boat captain from a bridge. Another issue is the way that what is happening in the film or where it is happening sometimes only becomes clear "after the fact." Then there is the way that Erik Satie's "Trois Gnossiennes, Lent" is used on the sound-track. And, obviously, we must also consider "violence" itself. In this chapter, I will illustrate how these concepts and facts organically blend together to form *Violent Cop*'s unique rhetoric.

VARIOUS ASPECTS OF "CONTINUITY"

Let's now consider the quality of "continuity." The fact that this film's running time qualifies it as a feature-length "entertainment film" despite the drastic paring down of Hisashi Nozawa's original screen-play seems almost entirely due to the way that individual actions are "continued" in it. Depicting the persistence of violence through its "continuity" requires stripping violence down to its essence. And nat-urally, the first in line to create this kind of effect is Detective Azuma, portrayed by Takeshi, whose persistent violence reaches its first apotheosis when he repeatedly and persistently slaps a drug dealer during a raid on a deal going down in a nightclub bathroom. This sense of "continuity" is not only conveyed through violence, however; it can also be seen in the way that Azuma is constantly shown

walking throughout the film. (Yukihiro Udagawa sheds light on this point in an excellent arti-cle entitled "Brilliantly Sculpting the Modern Moment."[5] In it, he points out that these inter-spersed walking scenes, a com-mon denominator of Kitano's films, gives them a physical rhythm that even links up with slapstick comedy.) Once, when

beat takeshi vs. takeshi kitano

Takeshi was asked in an interview, "Why do you shoot scenes in your movies where all we see is you walking?" he jokingly responded, "Because that's part of the TV-cop-show formula." This comment does not need to be taken seriously, however, since nothing is ever exposed through the walking scenes that take place on television cop shows. In *Violent Cop*, however, the degree to which Azuma is laid bare when he walks testifies to the truly phenomenal physicality of Takeshi's performance.

Let's describe Takeshi's "walk" as precisely as possible. In the opening scene, where it is captured from the side, his thigh and calf muscles appear to be well developed, and he walks as if being propelled vigorously forward. His hips do not move up and down. His powerful walk seems to conform to the stereotypical Japanese habit of keeping the hips in a perpetually low position. However, quite a different impression is given by the frontal-view shots of Takeshi walking, where he appears quite bowlegged (a fact that becomes even clearer in full frontal-view shots of him running). The fact that Takeshi's feet do not even manage to perform the basic repetitive action of making contact with the ground starting from the heels, shifting forward, and then pushing away with the toes contradicts the sense we had gotten of Takeshi's powerful stride from the side-view shots. Furthermore, the right side of Takeshi's upper body moves rhythmically up and down with each step, giving the false impression of a limp. However, as we confirmed earlier, his hips actually remain even as he walks, which means that the swaying in his upper body is generated by something in his upper body. As such, it fulfills the same function as the repetitive shoulder and neck spasms that are symptomatic of a whole body twitch. Is the shakiness of Takeshi's right side, which seems to increase with each step as the scenes of him walking change from full to medium shots, merely an optical illusion? In any case, this powerfully propelled walk, which

violent cop double suicide

makes it seem as if he's carrying a bomb in his upper body, must put considerable strain on his hips and knees. What is it about Takeshi's gait that requires so much explanation? We can decisively dissect the complicated structure of Takeshi's walk because the scenes of him walking are repeated so many times. In this way, Takeshi shows the subtle, bare nature of his own flesh.

Actually, a number of bodies in this film are stripped naked in this manner. This extends even to the smaller roles. Take, for instance, Nito, played by Ittoku Kishibe, who appears on the surface to be a restaurateur, but who is actually a drug lord. Nito is always reprimanding his subordinate Kiyohiro, played by Hakuryu (whom we will discuss in detail later), for his lack of self-restraint. Nito knows that Kiyohiro commits murders that haven't been ordered out of a mistaken sense of duty, and that, moreover, he does this because he enjoys it. However, when Nito discovers that Kiyohiro assaulted Detective Azuma's younger sister, Akari (Maiko Kawakami) and ordered his gay cronies to gang-rape her, he gives Kiyohiro an ultimatum: "Don't ever show your face here again." A scene prior to this shows Nito punching Kiyohiro several times in his otherwise empty president's office. The spectacle of these punches could be perceived by the audience as persistence, but what does this persistence expose about Nito? It does not come out of a need to merely execute a task, nor is it an expression of resentment. Nito's violence is persistent simply because he gets carried away by the fervor of the moment. As conveyed through Ittoku Kishibe's acting, physical strength, and athletic abilities, Nito's repeated punching of Kiyohiro reveals only his own fragility. Because Nito is incapable of becoming a subject in actions involving his physicality, he will eventually be mercilessly shot and killed by the battered and wounded dog, Azuma.

Unlike Nito, Azuma (Takeshi) and Kiyohiro (Hakuryu) share a common quality of violent persistence that is reinforced by their repressed cruelty and violent passions. The fact that the two are caught in a tug-of-war that causes them to plunge together toward their doom—the end of the movie even hints at a homoerotic love—results from these similarities. The terrifying quality of Azuma's persistent violence erupts again after he breaks into a condo where Kiyohiro has a love nest with his homosexual lover. Under the pretext of conducting a search, Azuma plants evidence that makes it possible for him to take Kiyohiro into custody, then forces Kiyohiro to confess in a locker room. Most of this violence is never actually shown on-screen. We are instead shown the figure of Azuma's subordinate, Kikuchi (Makoto Ashikawa), shaking with fear as he keeps watch so that nobody will notice this act of brutality that is taking place in, of all places, a police precinct. However, the persistent, muffled echoes of Kiyohiro's body being smashed against lockers alerts the audience to the appalling transgressions taking place behind the door in front of which Kikuchi stands. This same technique of indirection is used at the end of *Sonatine*, where the slaughter taking place in a hotel is conveyed only through changes in light. After all, isn't the use of sound and light to enact violence itself cinematic? Since audiences tend to be more sensitive to sound than to light, the "muffledness" of the noises in this sequence must add a chilling sense of realism. The violence Azuma commits in the locker room is immediately transferred to Kiyohiro, who is soon thereafter released from custody (thus resulting in the previously mentioned transmission of violence).

"RIGHT-ANGLENESS" OF ACTIONS

What kind of a character is Kiyohiro? It is immediately apparent that he is a man who brings the "right-angleness" of violence upon himself. The scene in the night harbor where Kiyohiro makes his first appearance and where we quickly understand his role as a drug dealer is a high-angle crane shot that foreshadows what can be called Kiyohiro's "right-angular" attention-grabbing powers. In this scene, Kiyohiro is trying to sell another dealer drugs he has procured from someone in the police department. When the drug dealer complains about the price of the goods, he incurs Kiyohiro's wrath and is killed with persistently repetitive knife stabs to the stomach that take place at a "right angle." This fixation with the abdomen resurfaces again later when Kiyohiro manages to corner Azuma after having failed to shoot him in front of a movie theater. Kiyohiro persistently digs into Azuma's already wounded abdomen with the tip of his shoe, then tries to finish Azuma off by sticking a gun barrel to his forehead at a "right angle." This assault is met by a counterattack: Azuma, using the knife he had grabbed from Kiyohiro, slashes at Kiyohiro's legs at a "right angle." In other words, the venom of Kiyohiro's homicidal "right-angleness" is ultimately sucked out by Azuma's right-angular actions. In any case, it becomes clear that Kiyohiro's natural reflex is always a "right-angle" action to the abdomen, as can be seen in his two-step approach to killing: as a rule, he first uses a knife, and only when that fails, reaches for a gun.

The scene in which Kiyohiro confronts one of the several dealers he had been methodically tracking down for having squealed on him to the police is framed in a brilliantly controlled way through the "perpendicularity" of the camera and the movements of the figures. Kiyohiro drags one of the dealers to the roof of an old building and backs him up against the edge. He is planning on pushing the dealer off the building's roof and making it look like a suicide. The camera angles, which alternate between shots looking down at the ground from the roof and looking up towards the top of the building, attempt to emphasize the building's height. But the decisive moment of "right-angleness" appears right before the dealer falls from the building to his

death, when he just barely manages to grab onto the edge of the roof. The tip of Kiyohiro's knife is shown inching along the five fingers of the dealer's right hand, prying them off at a "right angle." In this scene, Kiyohiro's act of drawing lines of blood across the dealer's fingers at a right angle leaves a stronger impression of violence than the dealer's fall, which is a physical movement perpendicular to the ground.

The first time that Kiyohiro and Azuma meet (although they are merely shown synchronously and in passing in the same shot) is at night on top of an overpass that is itself at a "right angle" to the ground. Captured in one "continuum," we first see Azuma, who is climbing the stairs of the overpass, and then, after a short lag, Kiyohiro as he turns onto the overpass at a "right angle" and begins descending the same stairs. This leads to the climax of the scene, which occurs when the two pass each other mid-stairway. By following the two characters in this manner, the movement of "continuity" is related to that of "right-angleness." This first encounter is foreshadowed just prior to this when Azuma, having determined the whereabouts of a dealer connected to Kiyohiro, confirms that that dealer has not yet been killed. The dealer tells Azuma, "You're going to be next," to which Azuma responds with the parting shot, "Nah, *you're* the one who should be worried." We then see Azuma's figure at night heading toward the previously mentioned overpass. The camera that follows him emphasizes only those moments when he turns street corners at a "right angle."

We have now reached the point where we can discuss *Violent Cop*'s point of maximum (although of short duration) violence, which

violent cop double suicide

is brought about by "right-angle" actions—i.e. actions whose "right-angleness" guarantees sudden, unpredictable eruptions. It comes in the previously mentioned scene where Kiyohiro ambushes Azuma in front of a movie theater (the Shochiku Central 2 in Higashi Ginza, incidentally). The action proceeds as follows: Azuma, trailed by Kiyohiro, walks down the street at night and reaches the entrance to the Shochiku Central 2 movie theater. The moment Azuma, sensing danger, turns around, Kiyohiro stabs him in the side with a knife. Azuma grabs the blade with his bare hands, however, and won't let go. A struggle ensues between Kiyohiro, who tries to stab Azuma again, and Azuma, who keeps his grip on the knife while trying to push it away. Azuma headbutts Kiyohiro, who falls on his back. As Kiyohiro sits up, he pulls out a gun, and, smiling easily, slowly extends his arm toward Azuma. He is about to shoot when Azuma hits the gun with a sideways kick. The bullet flies off in an unexpected direction, striking one of two girls who (we assume) have just come out of the movie theater. The second girl screams. The girl who has been shot had been standing exactly to the side of the gun that had been pointed at Azuma. This means that by kicking the gun, Azuma had changed the its "right-angle" direction. This killing—which could almost be mistaken for the accidental death of a passerby on a movie set—thus remains consistent with the film's theme, whereby "right angles" function as the angle of death. The fact that in this case the victim is a moviegoer—that is, a "friend to movies"—impresses the cruelty of the killing's unpredictability upon the viewer even more strongly.

But let us examine once more the fact that Kiyohiro tried at first to stab Azuma in the abdomen. Kiyohiro's fixation on the abdomen contrasts nicely with Azuma's fixation with the head. As was mentioned in the passage about *Violent Cop*'s opening scene, Azuma's forte is "slapping" and "headbutts," both of which are normally attacks to the head. Thus, when Kiyohiro tries to stab Azuma in the abdomen, he opens himself up to a countering headbutt from Azuma, who holds onto the blade of Kiyohiro's knife with his bare palms. There is probably a suggestion here that a fixation on the abdomen is feminine while a fixation on the head is masculine. Thus, it seems appropriate that Kiyohiro wears a white turtleneck and is homosexual. So is the masculine portrait of Azuma as someone who cares for his younger sister, which brings to mind the character Shintaro Katsu, who cares for his younger sister, Naoko Otani, in Yasuzo Masumura's *The Great Ode to Yakuza*.[6] As Shinozaki writes:

> The most fascinating character in the two films that Takeshi Kitano has directed so far is probably *Violent Cop*'s psychopathic killer Kiyohiro, played by Hakuryu. This is not because his profession as established by the story is that of a killer, nor is it because the specific methods he uses are incomprehensibly cruel. Incidentally, he does wear a faint smile while killing an informant who is clinging to a roof, but that has nothing to do with his "liking to kill," as another of the film's characters claims. Rather, it seems that Kiyohiro's urge to kill increases uncontrollably with each killing. Nito, the drug-dealing kingpin who controls Kiyohiro from the shadows, recognizes this. This is why, after warning Kiyohiro "Don't do any killings that I didn't order," he asks Shinkai, his right-hand man, "Do we have someone to take care of *that*, if we need to?" as soon as Kiyohiro leaves the room.[7]

A COMPOSITE OF "CONTINUITY" AND "RIGHT ANGLES"

"Continuity" and "right-angleness" are also intricately woven together in the scene that comes right after the opening of the film, resulting in miraculously rich actions. Azuma and four of his colleagues are conducting a search for a certain drug addict, and, after various complications, finally manage to track the man down. The sense of continuity in this scene is first evoked in the breathtaking chase between the fleeing drug addict and Azuma that takes them all over town. "Right-angleness" is actively injected into the scene when Kikuchi, Azuma's subordinate who had been temporarily eliminated from the chase when the drug addict punched him, drives up alongside Azuma, who has temporarily lost sight of his quarry. They are on a street alongside a river crossed by many bridges. Relying on his instincts, Azuma tells Kikuchi where to drive in order to cut the drug addict off. Humorous give-and-takes lines are mixed into the scene—for example, when Azuma tells Kikuchi to "make a right" where it is prohibited and is, as a result, blindsided by Kikuchi, who makes a left turn instead. (Angered by this, Azuma switches with Kikuchi so that he can drive himself.) As the two spot the figure of the drug addict running across a bridge on the other side of the river, the continuous flow of images that had captured the "right-angleness" of the cop car's "right" and "left" turns results in a more complicated, and therefore more fertile, movement. Combining "continuity" and "right-angleness," the scene proceeds to transcend even this basic movement when, through the windshield of the car and along a straight line, the camera frames the back of the drug addict as he flees. (This is in itself truly wonderful, with images of the city—not to mention the movement of the fleeing drug addict and the car—organically inserted into each stage of the action, all of which is captured by Yasushi Sasakibara's camerawork and editing).

Azuma, who appears to be a bad driver, tailgates the fleeing drug addict, taunting "I'm gonna run you over, I'm gonna run you over," then actually does hit him by mistake. Azuma slams on the brakes, and he and Kikuchi are horror-stricken when the drug addict, who they assume is lying on the ground, does not respond. Azuma glares at Kikuchi as he says with trepidation, "If we're out of luck, he may be dead." He then notices the drug addict, who is standing next to them holding an aluminum bat, once again at a "right angle" to the driver's seat and in an "unexpected direction." He realizes this too late, however, and the drug addict smashes in the driver's-seat window, climbs onto the hood of the car, and begins maniacally attacking the windshield, which is itself at a "right angle" to the window that had just been destroyed. (The idea that windshields can yield beautiful cracks is repeated in *Boiling Point*.) Infuriated, Azuma backs the car up, causing the the drug addict to fall to the ground in front of the car. Letting his rage get the better of him, Azuma steers the car forward and runs down the drug addict, who had just managed to get to his feet. Having at last gotten his prey, Azuma gets out of the car and "persistently" continues to kick the prone man. In this scene, the "persistency," "continuity," "unexpectedness," and "right-angleness" that are the film's trump cards are intricately intermingled and shuffled like playing cards, making it the pinnacle of *Violent Cop*'s action sequences.

Looked at in this way, it becomes clear that the action sequences in *Violent Cop* are realized by precise calculations. With the possible exception of some of Shintaro Katsu's work, these action sequences are without peer, not only among the films of other contemporary directors, but among Kitano's other films as well. In this sense, *Violent Cop* could be called Kitano's best work. The film's "right-angleness" also affects the characters' positioning in claustrophobic spaces. I won't point out each and every example of this, but there are a number of scenes where two figures are positioned at a slight distance from each other, resulting in a 90-degree angle. And when the corpse of the drug-dealing detective who was Azuma's only close friend within the precinct is found hanging underneath a bridge as a suicide (he was probably killed by Kiyohiro), we shouldn't forget that the relationship formed by the corpse and the bridge is also that of a "right angle." (Actually, the angle formed by the corpse and the bridge is never fully revealed, since the corpse is shown only from the point of view of the boat captain, who happens to be passing by in his boat.)

TO DEPICT AND DECEIVE

Using *Violent Cop* as an example, Makoto Shinozaki also explains how "What is essential in film is not 'explaining' but 'depicting.'" The mental disorder of Azuma's younger sister, Akari (Maiko Kawakami), is conveyed through layered "depictions" rather than through "explanations." As Shinozaki astutely and correctly points out, Akari's mental disorder can be surmised from "the stuffed animal peeking out from a paper bag that Azuma holds in the hospital scene (a gift that obviously doesn't correspond with the apparent age of his sister), as well as from the look in his sister's eyes in the taxi." Since both these examples are brief on-screen "depictions," how would someone who missed them be able to confirm the mental illness of Azuma's sister?

First, as Shinozaki points out, there is the hospital scene. In it, we see Azuma greeting a girl who appears to be his younger sister as she is being released from a hospital. But the reason why the sister was in the hospital is not, for the moment, clear. (Her attending doctor, by the way, is portrayed by Bang-ho Cho of *Empire of Brats*[8] and *March Comes in Like a Lion*.[9] Because we are not shown a frontal shot of the doctor, the audience only recognizes a figure that looks like Cho from a partial profile, and learns "after the fact" from the credits at the end that he was indeed Bang-ho Cho.) In the next scene, Azuma and his sister come across an outdoor festival as they are driving home. They get out of the car to check it out. At this point, the audience senses something strange in Akari's unusual attachment to a pinwheel bought at the festival. In the scene where

the two stare at the sea after having visited the festival and before heading home, we realize that it is so late that the sun has already begun to set in the west. This implies that instead of going home, which should have been their first priority, the two have spent an inordinate length of time at the festival.

Several scenes later, Azuma comes home to the apartment he shares with his sister only to find that, while he was gone, his sister has taken in a lover off the street. The audience must wonder at this point about his sister's lack of sexual morals or weak sense of chastity. Prior to this, however, there has been no explicit mention of her mental illness, or that she is in a critical stage of recovery.

Even when this information is first mentioned, the words have a veneer of fakeness to them. While staking out the activities of a drug dealer in a discotheque, Azuma casually comments to Kikuchi, his subordinate, that "My sister was in the hospital." When Kikuchi immediately asks, "What was wrong with her?" Azuma responds, "Her head," making a joke out of it. In a later scene, Azuma, on his way home from work, sits down next to his sister, who has been spending time alone on the bank of a river. He looks at her tenderly. Here again, the conversation seems fake to the point of abnormality:

AKARI: You can catch fish here.

AZUMA: Did you go play at least a little?

AKARI: 'Cause this isn't the ocean.

violent cop double suicide

When the fact that Azuma's sister has a mental disorder is at last clearly stated, the announcement does not come in the simple form of an "explanation," but is instead reflexively accompanied by the added embroidery of action. Bleeding profusely from his forehead, Kiyohiro (Hakuryu), who has been incarcerated on trumped-up charges inside the police precinct's locker room, attempts to assert himself in the face of Azuma's crazed attack by pushing Azuma's buttons. (One could even say that by making comments that further enrage Azuma, and by matching Azuma's fury with his own, Kiyohiro exacerbates the situation until both are at an explosive level of tension.) Kiyohiro's taunt—"Brother and sister alike, you're all psychos, aren't you?"—reignites Azuma's persistent assault. In *Violent Cop*, "explanations" never function merely as explanations.

The concepts of "younger sister," "incarceration," "action," and "insanity" are all tied together in the dialogue and the dramatics of this locker-room scene. It is helpful at this point to remember that Kiyohiro is someone who transcribes actions while further complicating them. Thus, the "younger sister" is "incarcerated" in a warehouse, gang-raped by Kiyohiro's gay cronies, and injected with heroin. Her "insanity" is fully revealed at this point, and as

a result, Azuma finally shoots and kills her out of pity. In this way, her flesh is forcibly and organically intertwined with "action." In other words, "depiction," "anti-explanation" (i.e. the retroactive construction of meaning), "fakeness," and "complicated transcriptions" are the film's structural components, lending it a narrative style

beat takeshi vs. takeshi kitano

appropriate for a "hard-boiled" movie. Though the storyline here clearly does not have the maze-like quality of Howard Hawks' *The Big Sleep* (1948), Kitano nonetheless deserves praise for his ability to pare down a script until it is disciplined enough to work as a "hard-boiled" film. Thus the resentment of *Violent Cop*'s original screenwriter towards Kitano due to extensive dialogue cuts must have been unrelated to the quality of the filmmaking itself.

BROTHERHOOD BETWEEN ENEMIES

Violent Cop is unmistakably a film about "suicide," although this fact is not as plainly stated as in *Sonatine*. This explains why its main musical theme is Erik Satie's "Trois Gnossiennes, Lent," the depressing piece played during Maurice Ronet's suicide scene in Louis Malle's *A Time to Live, A Time to Die* (1963).

What exactly are the elements that make *Violent Cop* a "suicide" film? Criminal natures can be divided into two types, depending on whether the crime committed was motivated by simple and optimistic pragmatic calculation or not. The "degree of suicide" in those who commit criminal acts is increased when a crime can be said to require a high degree of gambling with one's fate. In other words, anyone who knows that they will be discovered and punished for a crime and is still driven to commit it must, to some degree, be operating so as to "terminate oneself, the one who commits crimes." This is another way of describing "suicide." *Violent Cop* contains the single-minded drive to perform such an act, though we can't see this if we look only at the character of Azuma (Takeshi).

What I want to point out here is the senselessness of the acts committed by Azuma and Kiyohiro, both of whom have many criminal traits. As is appropriate for a renegade cop, Azuma takes his sometimes illegal investigations further than necessary, thus defying the will of the young, elitist Head of Police (Shiro Sano). Although Azuma does have some awareness of his weakness—i.e. his inability to desist from extra-legal activities—he can't help but take the excessive steps that he does. Why? Because Azuma's homicidal impulses and resentments (and perhaps also his sense of being joined in struggle with Kiyohiro) "swell up beyond his control," to use Makoto Shinozaki's description of Kiyohiro's experiences. Furthermore, Azuma himself has probably never before experienced the eruption of such violent emotions, which had always lain dormant. And letting oneself experience something for the first time, sheerly for the pleasure of it, is innocence itself.

When Takeshi meets Hakuryu—a man who, like himself, senselessly intensifies violent abuse—he is confronted with his diametrically opposed double. The two exist as intricately reflecting mirror images, entering into regions of "commonality" and even "collaboration" that lead Shinkai, another of Nito's underlings, to exclaim at the end of the film, "Each and every one of you is mad!" "Collaboration" is, after all, another word for "brotherhood." The film's modern sensibility ultimately lies in the realization that brotherhood can exist only in extremes and between enemies. Many people define themselves by their enemies, but the senseless ways that enemies who are identical taunt each other in pursuit of mutual destruction can only be defined as "suicide."

Various kinds of "suicide" exist, but the ugliest is the "theatrical" suicide that depends upon some form of judgment from another person. The next lowest in estimation would be the "passive suicide," which is carried out through a self-neglect that can always be interrupted and therefore deferred. It is also noteworthy that "suicide" (self-killing) secretly contains a circuitry that subtly corresponds to concepts such as "self-depiction," "self-consolation" (masturbation), and "self-abandonment." Thus, in its broadest sense, "suicide"—and even more so "a suicide that senselessly pursues the destruction of an enemy similar to oneself"—makes a powerful ethical statement about our contemporary age. In such a suicide, what we have is a consistent pattern of behavior instead of a singular incident that results from a spur-of-the-moment decision. Such consistency also contains a senseless and furious objectivity.

In order to highlight this senselessness, it is thus dramatically appropriate for Takeshi's Azuma to become more conspicuous about his animosity toward Hakuryu's Kiyohiro after he is dismissed from the police force. If we consider Azuma's state of mind at this point, we can see that since he is no longer a cop, becoming a gangster is all that is left him (and in fact, Beat Takeshi actually does start portraying gangsters from his next film on). With his sister abducted and with no hope of her mental condition improving, there is nothing left to keep him from pouring all of his passion into erasing all traces of himself. (In this respect, *Violent Cop* also recalls *The Great Ode to Yakuza*, in which Shintaro Katsu acknowledges Masakazu Tamura as the lover of his sister [Naoko Otani], then, in the last scene of the film, sets off to kill the contract killer of a the rival mob organization. In its degree of despair, Katsu's act is completely "suicidal," since his back is up against a wall and he has no escape routes.) Those who from the first have never had anything must go back to a pure "state of having nothing." Thus Azuma dies, not in an unrestricted space, but in the very specific space called the "flesh of Hakuryu=Kiyohiro." And how else can one describe this state of mind if not by using the word "love?"

Thus, one immediately senses that the scene in *Violent Cop* where a gun barrel is pushed against Takeshi's forehead at a right angle has the same force as the scene in *Sonatine* where Takeshi points a gun barrel at the side of his own head at a right angle. Such a standoff can be represented by a diagram in which each half of the two-headed eagle brought into existence by both Takeshi and Hakuryu (Takeshi's

violent cop double suicide

alter ego) tries to bite off the other's head. Another possibility is the cliché of a snake that, hungering for its own extinction, swallows its own tail. Perhaps the kind of "suicide" depicted in *Violent Cop*, which connotes a brotherhood with one's enemy, should be placed in higher esteem than the direct expression of "suicide" in *Sonatine*. After all, it manages to create a moral resonance on par with its emotional impact, and, in this way, succeeds in capturing a modern sensibility.

That this film's modernism is the modernism of rage can be understood from its last scene. When Takeshi and Hakuryu die at the end of a harrowing battle, their only survivor and heir is Takeshi's subordinate, the weak and conventional Kikuchi (Makoto Ashikawa). One might assume at first that Kikuchi, having survived such scenes of carnage, and having matured into a stalwart, would inherit the mental state of his ex-superior, Azuma, who was even willing to use brutality to catch a criminal. When Kikuchi walks toward the camera in exactly the same way Azuma had walked across the overpass in the film's opening, we instantly recognize this as a retracing of Azuma's mental state. Any expectations that *Violent Cop* will descend into a Kurosawaesque modernistic moralism whereby technique is passed on from mentor to disciple (as in films like *Red Beard* [Akahige, 1965] and *Stray Dog* [Nora inu, 1949]) are completely betrayed, however. In the final scene, it becomes clear that the mantle Kikuchi assumes is not Azuma's, but, surprisingly, that of the corrupt detective whose body was found as a suicide. In this way, the film's modern sensibility is preserved.

beat takeshi vs. takeshi kitano

In reality, a speck of opacity remains in this attempt to morally praise *Violent Cop* as a film about "brotherhood." That is, such praise is made impossible by the opacity of "Beat Takeshi's" expressions, which have been stripped naked through the continuity of actions. Isn't it possible to say that for Azuma (Takeshi), it is "despair" and not "brotherhood" that has run rampant, escalating out of his control? The film's violence displays a kind of primal nakedness that cannot be reclaimed by any reputable "brotherhood." Thus, "Beat Takeshi" as directed by "Takeshi Kitano" may have performed more "nakedly" than even he had intended. These impressions, which are supported by a vigorous sense of "continuity," will be reinforced in yet another form as "discontinuous accidental discharge" in Kitano's next film, *Boiling Point*.

03

a theory of baseball
(with anti-suicide contraption attached)

Makoto Shinozaki writes about Kitano's next film, *Boiling Point*, as follows:

> Though *Boiling Point* is brimming with an exclusively cine-matic vigor and allure, it simultaneously exudes a feeling of incongruity that can't be wiped away regardless of how many times one sees it. What is the reason for this?
>
> As mentioned earlier, *Boiling Point* was based on the director's own script, making it possible for the director to revise it—creating and adding new scenes as needed. In addi-tion, it was mostly shot in order from the first scene on. Despite this, several scenes, or rather specific images that comprise those scenes, seem as if they did not diverge from the original conception at all. In other words, an oddly overdetermined principle of composition appears here and there throughout the film.
>
> Starting with the shot of the baseball field that opens the film, our attention is excessively drawn to the way the charac-ters are placed on the screen. Because every scene, including those with medium shots, is shot in such a way that the char-acters' heads are positioned exactly in the middle of the frame,

the somewhat vague blue sky ends up being included in the top half of the composition.[1]

Shinozaki's claim is, in fact, correct. Here are some key characteristics of the film's compositon and camerawork: the insertion of unstable frontal compositions; shorter takes than in *Violent Cop*; a non-aesthetic laxity resulting from the unnecessary inclusion of sky in the frame; long shots characterized by a fatal inability to integrate numerous scattered characters; and the frequent use of wide-angle lenses in locations where there's not enough room to accomodate the camera, resulting in images that could only be called awkward.

Thus, the virtues of Kitano's previous film have disappeared in *Boiling Point*—for example, the rich essence of "continual movement" that organically braids together various components of movement (e.g. the camera, the characters) based on the the principle of "right-angleness." In this second film, all attempts to read the norms of camerawork and the intentions of the director seem to end in vain. The fact is, "diffusion" envelops every aspect of *Boiling Point* in the same way that "continuity" envelops every aspect of *Violent Cop*. Thus, the previous film's catharsis—in which Takeshi and Hakuryu, expanding on the violence that was their common code, bring about their mutual destruction—does not exist here at all.

Is this because Hisashi Nozawa's original screenplay for *Violent Cop*, as unsatisfactory as it may have been, prevented the kinds improvisations that took place on the film set from completely doing away with his story's consistency? That is, while the limitations of story effectively disciplined production in *Violent Cop*, in *Boiling Point*, the screenplay lacked restraint because it was written by Takeshi Kitano? Or was the film's scatteredness influenced by the change of cinematographers from the accomplished Yasushi Sasakibara, who (for example in Ryuichi Hiroki's *City of the Devil*

a theory of baseball

[Maohgai, 1993]) masterfully organizes "right-angleness" as cinematic necessity and not just virtuoso techinique, to Katsumi Yanagishima? Or is it simply that this film is worse than the previous one? My answer to all these questions is no.

BASEBALL IS "REALITY"

Since the original Japanese title of this film, *3-4 x October*, is a baseball score, (according to Toshiro Ogata, this score "refers to a reversal of fortune along the lines of the saying 'beware of a cornered animal'") I would like to offer the following "theory on baseball."

Baseball must be very difficult for fans of a sport like rugby to decipher aesthetically. Baseball is a sport about "diffusion." This diffusion originates in the "allocation of roles" created by some kind of contract or arrangement. All nine players, including the pitcher, catcher, and outfielders, are positioned decoratively according to an arrangement made by some unknown person, who forces solitude upon them. For example, although it's not logically impossible for the rightfielder to be positioned next to the pitcher as he is going into his windup, it is impossible for the pitcher or catcher to be positioned next to an outfielder. Baseball is thus almost completely unrelated to the hand-to-hand anarchy of athletes swarming in pursuit of a ball, where the limited numbers of possible changes in organizational structure are brought about by the critical juncture called the ball. As a result, baseball has nothing in common

beat takeshi vs. takeshi kitano

with the fertile beauty of an organizing structure that metamorphosizes from moment to moment. Instead, it could be said to possess
the static beauty of nine player positions. However, such a view
might lead to a simplistic "cynical value system" where everything
ends up being about overcoming "boredom" and "standing at attention." After all, how could one permit the "boredom" of having the
attention of some of the players focused wholly on the critical juncture called the ball, while other members of the team do not react to
it at all? (For example, consider whether the centerfielder would
move in a situation with no outs and the bases empty if the batter hit
a foul fly in the catcher's direction.)

Enlarging upon this theme, baseball is a sport that forbids the
crossing of boundaries. It is thoroughly immersed in the impassable
"dualism" of defense and offense. Let's say for example that the third
batter hits a fly that the opposing team's rightfielder catches. How
can one explain the weak link between that opposing team's rightfielder and the first batter, who'd grounded out to third base two bat-
ters back? This weakness is another reason for the relative
coagulation that is inevitably brought about by this "dualism." Thus,
in *Boiling Point*, when Masaki (Masahiko Ono) continues to stand in
the third-base coach's box after Kazuo (Minoru Iizuka) is tagged out
and the teams switch sides, he is berated. This berating is clearly
based on a reaction called "the denial of crossing lines."

After being called out at third base, Kazuo also rebukes
Masaki for not signalling to him by, for example, waving his arms.
But does Kazuo want to be discriminated against by having his own
decisions controlled by the third-base coach, someone who is tech-
nically not even a player? If so, he is like a dog who "enjoys being
dominated by others." Furthermore, the coach's exaggerated gestures are not aesthetic. Could there be an uglier gesture? In sports
such as soccer, signals from those who stand outside of the playing

field are forbidden. The static structure required to read such signals does not even exist in soccer, where judgements intricately metamorphosize in various ways. Such sports do use signals, but because they consist of glances (eye contact) between teammates, and so are for the most part concealed from spectators, they appear modest or beautiful.

Baseball's "rules" are not subject to aesthetic considerations. They are fundamentally different from soccer's, according to which everyone except the goalkeeper is forbidden from using their hands, or rugby's, where players are forbidden from passing the ball forward. The rules of both soccer and rugby result in a kind of *flan vital*: they add aesthetic unity to the fundamentally anarchic conditions the sports are striving to achieve. In contrast, baseball's rules enact an arbitrary contract that serves to further manage the game—making it more boring in the process. It would probably be a mistake to presume that baseball's rules were organically formed, as they were in rugby and soccer. They must have been created in the abstract as an empty theory by a weak mind.

In another of *Boiling Point*'s scenes, Masaki, who has hit a home run, runs past Kazuo, the previous runner on base, and is consequently called out on an error. This moment captures the essence of baseball's "bureaucratic absurdity." What other sport contains moments when the faster runner is considered less worthy of acclaim than the slower one—or in other words, that go against the glorification of the flesh? Having written this much, however, I would like to direct the reader's attention to the following matter. The words that have just been used to describe baseball—"rules," "boredom," "cynical value system," "bureaucratic absurdity," and "standing at attention"— can all be said to function as metaphors for reality. Thus, baseball expresses that very reality that is full of "boredom" and immeasurably bound by "rules."

THE FORMATION OF "DIFFUSION" BY PROTAGONISTS

I have already mentioned that baseball is a sport about standing by alertly. All the players on both teams, except for those directly involved in a play, are held in a state of alert waiting. As a result, baseball's most thrilling triples or breathtaking defensive plays always occur as "accidental discharges." To sum up, baseball is the very "reality" in which those who are trapped in the "impossibility" of a managed awareness yearn for an "accidental discharge" that will break the "boredom" of "diffusion." This theory would still make sense if one were to replace the word "baseball" with *Boiling Point's* Japanese title, *3–4 x October* (3–4 x jugatsu). In fact, the film *3–4 x October* is itself a theory about baseball, which automatically makes it a theory about reality.

The film thus directs us toward "diffusion." The camerawork refuses to delineate organic linkages along temporal lines, and even locations are "halved" in a diffusive way between Tokyo and Okinawa. Meanwhile, all the film's featured characters—Masaki; Kazuo; Iguchi (Takahito Iguchi), a reformed ex-gangster now uncomfortable as a snack-bar manager; Uehara (Beat Takeshi), an Okinawan gangster in the midst of a whirlwind downfall brought about by his self-destructive lifestyle; and Uehara's henchman, Tamaki (Katsuo Tokashiki)—are "assigned their separate positions" and scattered. Although they make contact with each other in their respective sections of the film, no one character is allowed to occupy a central position throughout the entire film.

Though his existential deadpan expression is striking, how could Masaki (Masahiko Ono)—whose sickly, long face sits awkwardly in close-ups, and whose smiling face leaves an indelible impression of bucktoothedness—be the protagonist of a film unless it were one that was meant to convey "diffusion?" One might argue

that Masaki must be the primary subject of the film because, in the end, the entire film is revealed to have been his dream. In reality, the idea of Masaki as the film's primary protagonist merely allows for the role of the protagonist to be passed along to others who occupy the same space. Masaki operates as a kind of catalyst who, paradoxically, metamorphosizes into the final protagonist. A different real protagonist exists for each part of the film: at various points it is Takeshi, Tokashiki, Iguchi, Iizuka, and Bengal, playing a Tokyo gangster whose frailty, cunning, and vindictiveness is momentarily transformed into a terrifying reality. (One of the high points in Bengal's acting comes when, threatened by Iguchi, he repeats "Iguchi-san" over and over, gradually shifting to a Korean-Japanese pronunciation that exposes the mystery of where he comes from.) At another point, the protagonist could also be said to be the black woman in a white one-piece dress whose unforgettable, dazzling elegance while catching a rubber ball on a white beach in Okinawa is captured in slow motion. (Also wonderful is the long shot that shows her solitary figure abandoned on a white road in Okinawa after Uehara, irritated because she is making the car hot, kicks her out.) Or it could even be the Oedipal punk who yearns for a motorcycle even though he has no license, dyes his hair red, and keeps getting mixed up in painful ordeals, thus functioning as comic relief. In this way, the film's central axis "diffuses" into many layers. Among these various layers, there is one actor who leaves an undeniable impression of physicality on par with the marvelous,

beat takeshi vs. takeshi kitano

self-evident physical presence of Takeshi and Tokashiki. That person is Minoru Iizuka=Dankan.

The transcendental qualities of baseball can be found in the film as well. This is why the coffee shop waitress Sayaka (Yuriko Ishida) and Masaki propitiously start behaving like lovers in the scene where they meet by chance for the first time.

DISPERSION OF VIOLENCE = ACCIDENTAL DISCHARGE

In this film, "violence" is dispersed as well—that is, if dispersion is taken as the the antonym of continuity. (None of the walking scenes so wonderful in *Violent Cop* are in evidence in this film. In their place are cars, bicycles, motorcycles, and even offscreen airplanes, all of which evoke a sense of travel that creates a curious correspondence with the "dispersive" quality of the film.) As a result, *Boiling Point* does not possess the excitement of *Violent Cop*, where violence is transmitted from one character to another and weaves toward a conclusion. For example, about halfway through *Boiling Point*, a gun is required for Iguchi to enact his revenge, thus creating the pretext that takes the protagonists to Okinawa. After some further twists and turns of plot, a gun is appropriated. However, it is never actually fired except by Uehara and his cronies, who are part of a subplot (though it accidentally discharges once). By the end of the film, the use of the gun as a weapon of vengeance has completely vanished. What appears instead is a trailer truck that Masaki will use to crash into the rival gang's headquarters as the instrument=weapon of a

a theory of baseball

spectacular suicide (or, if one includes Sayaka, a double-suicide). The narrative strand of the movie that the gun was supposed to carry forward thus becomes a victim of discontinuity. This discontinuity is so thorough that even this suicide by explosion and burning is ultimately revealed to be an impossibility through the film's it-was-all-a-dream punch line. (Kitano's nihilistic perception of reality is strongly in evidence here.)

Under such conditions, violence can only be assigned the role of subject on a moment-to-moment basis. In *Boiling Point*, the subjects of violence are, on the one hand, those sickly-faced people who look as if they have lead poisoning (let's call their color "yakuza color"), or, on the other hand, those who carry grudges. The latter are capable of perpetrating violence in the middle of the day. (Such acts of violence clearly convey a "persistence" that is related to the "continuity" of action, but they don't take up much screen time.) Both Takeshi and Tokashiki can be found in this second category, as can Bengal, who slaps the manager of the gas station where Masaki works. The pale faces, on the other hand, become active at night. (Hakuryu from *Violent Cop* is almost completely so.) Iguchi can be counted in this category: he attacks Bengal, his former underling, at night after Bengal taunts, "The next time I see you, I'm just gonna call you 'Iguchi.'" Another pale face, Minoru Iizuka, proves that any character in a Kitano film who is able to defeat an opponent with a single blow can never be the subject of violence. Iizuka puts away a young biker punk with whom he has had a misunderstanding with a single head-butt. Earlier, I mentioned that a headbutt is the manifestation of a pure physicality. Iizuka's headbutt foregrounds the physical while leaning toward "positivity" and away from "negativity." That is, his power is being exercised through a singular action, not a repeated one.

In contrast to Iizuka, Uehara, as portrayed by Takeshi, represents repetition and persistence. Why is it that Takeshi's violence always takes the form of a persistent continuity? Uehara ignores the protests of the junior crony guarding a fellow gangster's car at the yakuza headquarters and, filled with pent-up anger, repeatedly kicks the vehicle. He attacks a fellow gangster who had been teasing him about the money he embezzled at a karaoke bar. Using a beer bottle, he repeatedly hits the other gangster over the head with a curious stop-and-go persistence. (The wonderful quality of the odd tag team of Uehara and Tamaki [Tokashiki] clearly signals the inner workings of slapstick comedy. For example, when another gangster who sees Uehara's attack on his buddy stands up, Tamaki momentarily interrupts his dance with a black woman, uses his boxing expertise to knock the gangster out with one punch, and resumes dancing.[2] But Uehara's repetitive attacking motions become a strange form of repetition without any sense of enforcement.) Or, in another case, Uehara=Takeshi takes advantage of his pitcher's privilege by persistently throwing a rubber ball at his lover, who is standing in the batter's box during an informal game of baseball on the beach. Later, in a car and elsewhere, he repeatedly pushes at the back of her head with his hand. What is being proven here is the "negativity" of the flesh called Takeshi. This becomes even more explicit when he is contrasted with Minoru Iizuka. Any action that is not singular is shown to be spiteful and warped, and moreover a kind of frailty. But this frailty, when presented as repetition, can become a "violence" that simulates strength. Perhaps Tokashiki's boxing abilities can thus be considered a kind of dance that effortlessly stitches together graceful singular actions with the frailty of persistence. If this is true, then *Boiling Point* can be said to have a "dispersive" tendency with regards to its display of violence. This contrasts with *Violent Cop,* which centers around Takeshi and Hakuryu, two characters who embody the same "right-angled" quality of violence despite fixating on different objects ("head" and "abdomen"). *Boiling Point*'s rape or

a theory of baseball

sodomy scene, which will be discussed later, is one example of this tendency toward dispersive violence.

Yet there are also instances in which violence that has been "dispersed" manifests as actual violence—for example, when there is an "accidental discharge." An accidental discharge takes place when an outbreak of violence happens unexpectedly, in a "dispersive" manner, and from an unanticipated direction. In *Boiling Point*, guns "accidentally discharge" twice. The first occurs when Uehara and Tamaki enter the offices of the yakuza bosses, who have demanded that Uehara cut off of one digit of a finger as repayment for embezzling money from the gang.[3] Uehara carries under his arm a bouquet of bird-of-paradise flowers that hides a machine gun. The gun accidentally discharges and rattles away in an unforeseen direction. This gives pause to the gathered Okinawan gangsters (portrayed by Etsushi Toyokawa, Johnny Okura, and others), giving Uehara a chance to mow them down with his bouquet. The second accidental discharge takes place when Masaki, having failed to avenge Iguchi's lynching at the yakuza headquarters, leaves Kazuo (Minoru Iizuka) and his best friend (Makoto Ashikawa), who have been taken hostage. He returns to his car, intent on launching a second attack on the headquarters with Sayaka, his lover, in the passenger seat. As he is making adjustments to a gun, it accidentally discharges, shattering the car's windshield. (As if reminding us of the equally wonderful shattered-windshield scene from *Violent Cop*, the frame is filled with beautiful, delicate white light from the cracks that have spread

beat takeshi vs. takeshi kitano

across the glass.) This accidental discharge is made even more thorough by the "dispersed" manner in which it is revealed, with the image of "Iizuka and Ashikawa being held hostage" sandwiched between the "moment of accidental discharge" (in a shot from the side exterior of the car) and "the shattered windshield."

An especially memorable instance of an abstract "accidental discharge" that is realized without guns takes place in one of the Okinawa sequences. Uehara and Tamaki, having obtained a gun, bid farewell to Masaki and Kazuo, who have also accomplished their goal of finding a gun. Uehara and Tamaki then head by car to the gang headquarters, which they've decided to attack. The figure of Takeshi as Uehara is captured here in a close-up through the windshield as he sits in the passenger seat of the moving car. At this point, four flashes of what seem to be premonitory visions by Uehara are inserted into the scene in an "accidental-discharge-like manner." These flashes are so short and sudden that at first it isn't clear what is happening, but they are dutifully repeated later in the film as incidents that actually take place. As such, they are only understood "after the fact." Here is a list of the flashes, in the order in which they appear:

1. Etsushi Toyokawa, who portrays the Okinawa yakuza boss, being shot and killed (leaving an instantaneous impression of violence).

a theory of baseball

2. Uehara crowning himself with a wreath of bird-of-para-dise flowers (iconic imagery that also, in a flash, gives an abrupt impression of strangeness).

3. Uehara, extremely aroused at the approaching "do-or-die" moment, engaging in rough sex that almost seems like rape with his mistress in a car. (This image is presented only for a moment, and is almost impossible decipher. I was able to write the above only after watching the entire film, where these shots are repeated. What, then, is an audience to perceive from this image, which flashes by in an instant? Only things such as "mystery," "a vague scent of crime," and "a premonition of some kind of disturbance.")

4. A medium shot of Uehara in a car with the door ajar and his legs hanging out. The absolute blankness of his expression is violently disturbed in the next moment by the blood gushing from his chest. (At this point, the audience feels certain that they have been watching quick inserts of premonitory visions akin to those in Nicholas Roeg's *Don't Look Back* [1973]. But the sense of order that attends this certainty suffers from a simultaneous sense of artificiality. In other words, the scenes hinted at in the first three flashes actually take place in the film as predicted in relatively quick succession, but the fourth premonitory flash is realized only after quite some time has passed. Here also, "accidental discharge" is connected with "diffusion.")

In another instance, "diffusion" also appears as an imbalance in the laws of cause and effect. As Masaki and Kazuo are about to leave Okinawa, Tamaki, who has come to see them off, gives Masaki a gift along with some bills. This incongruous gift, a good-luck charm for uncomplicated births, should not be shrugged off as a joke. It should, rather, be accepted as a disordering of the linear narrative—in other words, as a narrative "diffusion." (As if enmeshed in this "diffusion," Tamaki goes to the airport to see Masaki and Kazuo off, even though he has already said good-bye to them.) In another example, Masaki, who has been absent from work, nods yes when a coworker asks, "Are you coming to work tomorrow?" However, he dies in an explosion soon afterwards, negating his nod of assent.

As the above makes clear, various intentions related to "diffusion" and "accidental discharge" are spread like a web throughout this film, making up its cinematic grammar. Obviously, violence occurs repetitively in this film, as in *Violent Cop*, but since there is no transfer of passion, it gives the impression of "diffusion," not of "transmission." Masahiko Ono's unreadable face contributes greatly to this impression. His expressions are "non-conductive"; they break off all "transmission" of organic movements. As long as the film's "diffusion" is centered around this attribute, Ono is the film's protagonist. Thus, passing judgment on *Boiling Point* based on the physical quality of its camerawork would be an utterly meaningless task.

Whether or not this film delivers the same catharsis of *Violent Cop* is actually a delicate question. The very end of the film, when the credits begin to roll, is especially "diffusional," coming as it does after the "punch line of the dream," which dutifully announces that this film follows the grammar of "diffusion." Here, a wide-angle lens shows another baseball game, this time from an indeterminate vantage point that no longer seeks to create drama. Instead, it fosters "a vague mood" that is unusual in films. The sound at this point is also extremely vague and diffused, lacking the centralization required to distribute sound between foreground and background according to relative importance. This is, however, how reality displays itself.

a theory of baseball

Could it then be said that a catharsis takes place in the scene just prior to this one when Masaki and Sayaka crash their trailer truck into the gang headquarters and die in an explosion? In his previously cited article, Makoto Shinozaki writes about the uncomfortable atmosphere caused by the film's composition before going on to describe the film's hard-to-ignore attractions. He discusses the wonderful trailer-truck explosion scene within the framework of a "theory on violence":

> Probably the most violent moment in Boiling Point happens when the trailer truck, carrying Masaki and his lover, Sayaka, crashes into the Otomo family's gang headquarters, explodes into flames as Masaki's friend Kazuo watches. Obviously, the scene's violence is not derived from the showiness of the exploding trailer truck. On the contrary, Kitano distances himself from making a meaningless spectacle out of this scene, as is clear if one looks at the specific images . . . On what basis then do I call this the film's most violent scene? On the fact that there is no apparent rationale justifying Masaki's and Sayaka's decision to take such a life-or-death action . . . Sayaka, who rides with Masaki in the trailer truck, is not even given the solid pretext that her actions are motivated by her love for Masaki. There are, in the end, no whispered words of love passed between the two when they park the truck on the street and stand forlornly in the dark. After a few wordless moments, they slowly walk toward the trailer truck with steps that are far from determined, and in fact rather devoid of confidence. The two lonely souls sit shoulder to shoulder in the darkness of the truck's cab, quietly looking in front of them . . . After pushing away Kazuo's attempts to stop them, they crash into the gang headquarters, exploding and going up in flames before his very

eyes. Kazuo, who is powerless, can only watch as the flames blaze away. His astonishment is also the audience's . . . This chain of standoffish and brusque images that reject story or character psychology is what cinema should be.[4]

Rather than being cathartic, this scene's impact, as outlined by Shinozaki is that of an "accidental discharge" in the truest sense. Thus, it would not be an overstatement to call such a moment, in which an image has no alternative but to transcend itself without recourse to organic explanation, "cinema itself."

AN ORGANIZATIONAL THEORY CONCERNING "DIFFUSION"

While in Okinawa, Takeshi's Uehara brings together a curious collection of characters whose number is momentarily increased by Masaki and Kazuo. The rules of this collective can be said to have evolved from the Azuma–Kiyohiro brotherhood presented by Kitano in his previous film, *Violent Cop*. Within it, the laws of cause and effect have collapsed.

Let's examine how Uehara, under pressure to return embezzled money and to cut off his finger, uses this collapse in the laws of cause and effect to escape the crisis of having to maim himself. First, Uehara forces Tamaki, who at this point is closer to being his best friend than an underling, to have sex with his mistress. For a while, Uehara fondles Kazuo's masculine body while watching his mistress reluctantly (he had threatened her as well) have sex with Tamaki. Approaching their bed, he tells Tamaki to "switch." Tamaki, who naturally thinks Uehara wants to take his place, starts to offer him his spot. However, Tamaki is mistaken: Uehara wants to switch positions with his mistress. Uehara then pins down the protesting and

unwilling Tamaki and rapes him. Afterwards, Uehara's attitude towards Tamaki abruptly changes. He insists that Tamaki must be prepared cut off a digit of his finger as punishment for having had sex with Uehara's mistress. Uehara then wrestles Tamaki to the floor with the help of his mistress and Kazuo (a further collapse of the laws of cause and effect), and eventually succeeds in cutting Tamaki's finger off. In terms of drama, this bogus logic could be called a confusion in the laws of cause and effect (or, more simply, a "comedic sensibility").

In reality, however, doesn't this sort of entanglement happen because Uehara has an almost pathological inability to distinguish between self and other? Uehara seems to seriously believe that cutting off Tamaki's finger is the same as cutting off his own, and he truly believes that sodomizing Tamaki, who has had sex with his mistress, is the same as having sex with his mistress. Obviously, Tamaki also plays a role in concocting Uehara's illusion. It is precisely at this juncture that the wonderful consensuality described earlier between Uehara and Tamaki—Uehara hits someone over the head with a beer bottle while Tamaki foils the counterattack—comes to mind. Uehara is Tamaki and Tamaki is Uehara. This explains why, in the karaoke bar, they repeat each other's movements as if they were mirror images.

That Uehara exists simultaneously as "two people" is actually important within the following context: it shakes up the concept of ji (self) in jisatsu (suicide). The gravity pulling the Azuma–Kiyohiro linkage together in *Violent Cop* eventually brings them to the same place; the tension between them is partially resolved through mutual annihilation. In *Violent Cop*, both characters have the same intensity of suicidal ambitions. However, the relationship between Uehara and Tamaki is less rigid than the fateful relationship between Azuma–Kiyohiro. For example, Uehara's cutting off of Tamaki's finger could, from the outside, be considered self-inflicted damage. Within the context of Uehara's physicality, however, this is obviously not the case. Uehara specifically intended to cut off Tamaki's finger instead of his own, and to do so, he hatched a complicated and self-contradictory plan. By acting on this plan, however, Uehara's inability to distinguish between himself and others is subjected to a reality check. Within this group he has collected, Uehara's warped subjectivity and sense of reality are intertwined with a high degree of freedom. Tamaki is not merely an instrument in Uehara's hands, because Uehara respects Tamaki's individuality, including his sexuality. Then, betraying this trust, Uehara treats Tamaki as his plaything.

Why does one get the impression that *Boiling Point* suddenly seems more tense when its setting shifts to Okinawa? Is it because Takeshi and Tokashiki, portraying Uehara and Tamaki, both have charismatic physical presences? This may be the case, but the most one can say is that it results from Uehara being an extremely "tentacular" presence who unites the figures that populate the film. Of course, the impression of Uehara's tentacles stems in part from his bisexual preferences. Uehara is a "spider" whose capacity to have sex indiscriminately and whose inability to be quantified sexually ties different men and women together in a variety of webs. (A specific manifestation of this web are popsicles, that strange food that, while obviously a part of this world, seem somehow to lose their substance and become part of another world. Spanning both the material and the spiritual, popsicles can stimulate an artist's alchemical imagination.)

Until now, our discussion has unfolded around the axis of Uehara and Tamaki, but a similarly pathological lack of discrimination

between self and other may also exist between Uehara and his mistress. In any case, because Uehara's web is loosely woven, it does not create the kind of catastrophic bond that exists between Azuma-Kiyohiro. In other words, this spider's web acts as a preventative barrier against "suicide." Uehara is a gangster who is directed towards self-annihilation, but the death being enacted here cannot be considered suicide, even in its broader sense. What Kitano shows us in this film is not his own suicide, but the suicide of the other—namely, of Masaki and Sayaka (though, once again, even this double-suicide is ultimately deferred through the film's dream punch line). The preventative barrier against suicide that Uehara weaves between the members of his entourage is complicated. Oddly enough, a hint of love exists in the web connecting Uehara, Tamaki, Uehara's mistress, and the black woman (as well as Masaki and Kazuo). At the same time, there is also a tinge of hatred. One is even led to suspect that Uehara's "sullenness" is what connects everyone together. In other words, the group created by Uehara is so flexible that even "sullenness" can be considered a basis for its bonds. Uehara, who transforms himself by extending the tentacles of his sexuality like an amoeba, resembles both himself and others. This tentacular form is the basis of the contraption he uses to "disperse" the possibility of suicide that obsessively haunts him.

The group that collects around Uehara may also reflect Beat Takeshi's theory of organization regarding brotherhoods. If this is so, the Takeshi Army would be its real-life expression. Takeshi's organizational theory is founded on "dispersion" rather than solidarity. We can therefore claim that in *Boiling Point*, Kitano judges "dispersion" to be an ideal, not a modern pathology. As long as disbursement stays connected with reality—i.e. as long as reality is seen as a form of "disbursement"—then valuing "dispersion," which is connected with reality, becomes a deterrent against despair. This explains why the Okinawa scenes are able to exude a somewhat idyllic mood, even though they all lunge toward a tragic and bloody end. "Dispersion" is doubtless the word that comes to Takeshi Kitano when he attempts to structurally define his own nakedness. *Boiling Point* is thus the next stage of development for both Takeshi's unadorned "theory on suicide," and its antithesis, the "theory on brotherhood" that he first develops in *Violent Cop*.

Paradise seems to hold an irresistible attraction for Kitano. His fourth film, *Sonatine,* is also set in Okinawa, where Kitano again organizes a loosely knit group that spends its time "alertly waiting." However, *Sonatine*'s ending is totally different from those of his previous films, since almost everyone in the group dies. At the end of *Boiling Point*, Uehara, the group's central figure, releases the black woman, his mistress, Masaki, and Kazuo in the direction of life. With *Sonatine,* however, a pessimism leading to death again enters the consciousness of Takeshi Kitano.

04

the quietest ocean, after death

A WOUND DRAWN ACROSS THE WORLD

In *Film Art Quarterly*'s "This Month's Contributors" section from late November 1991, Saburo Kawamoto writes: "I was moved by [Takeshi Kitano's] *A Scene at the Sea*. It reminded me of Polanski's *Two Men and a Wardrobe*." *Two Men and a Wardrobe* (1958) features a series of simple scenes in which two workers who have been ordered to dispose of a wardrobe repeatedly meet with failure. Eventually, they carry the wardrobe into the ocean. The film's dialogue is kept to an absolute minimum, and the scenes of the two men carrying the wardrobe resemble the scenes from *A Scene at the Sea* where its main protagonists, Shigeru and Takako, walk with their surfboard. The presence of the ocean makes this an understandable association, of course. As might be expected given the political climate at the time of its release, *Two Men and a Wardrobe* won emotional praise as a work describing the wanderings of youth who have lost their way in a world controlled by adults.

Yet aren't Shigeru and Takako in *A Scene at the Sea* judged even more harshly than the "two men" who carry the wardrobe? Especially since neither of them can be integrated into the world's materialistic circuitry—Shigeru is deaf and works as a garbage collector, a generally unpopular profession—and thus are basically superfluous? The real problem, however, is that those who attempt to use their hands and bodies to communicate with Shigeru at a level beyond mere silent understanding completely expose the extent of their communicative abilities. (Fujiwara, who plays the manager of a surfing store in this film, is repeatedly exposed in this way.) Another problem is that Shigeru, who should be sheltered by various societal considerations, throws himself vigorously into the joy of surfing without considering his social position. When he is surfing, the axis of coordinates that would make it possible to relegate Shigeru to the ranks of the weak is lost.

Who exactly is this Shigeru if not one of the weak? His presence has the strength of an "outsider" who cannot be incorporated into any part of the world. This is not an acquired strength, however. Rather, Shigeru is, at root level, a deep wound (="a trace") that has been drawn across the world. The depth of this wound is a powerful surplus in a world that basically does not accept any wounds, particularly those that contain the attributes of "surplus" and not of "lack." This goes against nature. In other words, "the trace" called Shigeru is also a fallacy.

For example, in one scene, Takako comes to the beach to watch Shigeru surf. She sits on the sand and girlishly starts to fold his clothes, which have been left beside her. The moment she looks up to try to locate him on the waves, he throws a pebble at her, and she realizes that he is beside her. Takako then moves closer to him, leaving behind his clothes. At this point, the novice surfer who is dating the "Orange Woman" comes out of the sea and sits down next to Shigeru's pile of clothes. In this way, Shigeru's clothes are cut off from the organic circuitry of the world, becoming an alien "trace" that has lost any sense of belonging.

Or consider this scene: the garbage-truck driver, portrayed by Sabu Kawahara, forcibly pulls Shigeru away from the beach where he

the quietest ocean, after death.

has been hanging out with friends, and drags him back to the work of collecting garbage, which he'd been too absorbed with surfing to pay attention to. (Obviously this use of force is motivated by the selfless intention to rescue Shigeru in the social sense.) As a result, Shigeru ends up collecting garbage in the totally incongruous getup of a wet suit. At that moment, Shigeru becomes "a trace" that creates disharmony within the world.

Or the following scene: Shigeru sits in his room in front of the surfing-contest application he has gotten from the owner of the surfing shop. He starts to fill out the application with false information such as "Weight=2 kilograms" "Blood Type=E" "Name=Gorbachev" etc. as if to defiantly show that "This kind of thing isn't the reason I surf!" Once again it is Takako who, in much the same way that she folded Shigeru's abandoned clothes on the beach, starts to correct these warped "traces" that "those who are cursed" characteristically leave behind.

The film's methodology proceeds as follows: Shigeru leaves a "trace." This "trace" gains a kind of strength because it is protected by a fallacy, but its cursedness is eventually corrected by Takako's love. However, because Takako is not a perfect person, Shigeru's "traces" are occasionally left uncorrected. After his death, Shigeru's "traces" will reach a point where they can be recaptured in the past tense as images from when he was alive. (These "traces" achieve a higher level of emotional accumulation at the end of the film, which exhibits various "extra-goodie" shots composed mostly of snapshots.)

beat takeshi vs. takeshi kitano

THE ABSENCE OF SHIGERU'S POINT OF VIEW

The sorrow of separation evoked in this film is not to be found solely by focussing our gaze on Shigeru, who brings upon himself the tragedy of a "premature death." It springs forth only when one considers Shigeru's existence in the context of Takako or the garbage-truck driver, neither of whom Shigeru treats well. This "infraction" by Shigeru registers cinematically: after the film's opening, no shots are taken from Shigeru's point of view. (As mentioned earlier, this opening shot shows us the "soundless blue sea." Because there is no sound, we realize "after the fact" that it is taken from Shigeru's point of view. This opening sequence, which consists of a soundless image, is the exact opposite of the credit sequence at the end of the film, where we hear the sound of waves against a black screen.) It would probably be a mistake to assume that Shigeru's point-of-view shots were eliminated from all but the opening of the film in order to show Shigeru, who is deaf, as he is, thus giving the film a completely objective viewpoint. We are also frequently shown shots—for example, images of Shigeru riding and falling into waves—from the point of view of Takako, who is also handicapped in this way. In other words, the elimination of Shigeru's point of view correlates intimately with the fact that he does not look at Takako. (Shigeru obviously cares for Takako. There is certainly something moving about the persistence he displays in the scene where their feelings for each other reach a crisis, and he tries to attract her attention by throwing his shoes to where she'll see them from her second-floor window. Their relationship requires no words, and one could say that such serene love containing only silent communication is charged with an unworldly, angelic beauty. However, the point of this discussion is to understand what exactly Shigeru means in this particular film.) Shigeru watches the sea. Or his attention is directed at surfing. Takako, on the other hand,

the quietest ocean, after death.

watches Shigeru. Couldn't the unidirectionality of Takako's love for Shigeru also be seen as a kind a vindictive "infraction" on Shigeru's part? In the end, this vindictiveness is itself transformed into sorrow.

Takeshi Kitano, the director, is completely conscious of this. First of all, he eliminates Shigeru's point-of-view shots, a decision that sometimes results in compositional abnormalities. In one scene, Shigeru is taking a lunch break with his boss, the garbage-truck driver, between shifts of hauling garbage. While the driver is eating his lunch, Shigeru stares at magazine photographs of a surfer performing beautiful stunts. Framing just the photographs (in a normal way) would make the shot appear to be from Shigeru's point of view, so Kitano is forced to use a too-tight composition in which the back of Shigeru's head appears out of focus in the foreground. In another scene, Shigeru is prevented from riding a bus with the new surfboard he has just purchased. He is as a result separated from Takako, who is already on the bus, and he heads home alone. Takako, who is still on the bus, feels torn about having left Shigeru behind. (As proof of this, she never sits down, though the bus is nearly empty.) Eventually, she gets off and runs back along the path the bus has just traveled, toward Shigeru. The use of parallel editing in this scene implies that from here on the gap between Shigeru and Takako will narrow again, and that their relationship will gradually recover. But when the two eventually meet up, their figures are shown in shot-reverse shots that are notable for their contrast. Unlike Shigeru, who is shown alone (hence, from Takako's point of view), Takako is shown in an over-the-shoulder shot (hence in an objective view) from Shigeru's side. The forced inclusion of the back of Shigeru's out-of-focus head in the foreground gives the shot's composition a strange look. (Yukihiro Udagawa is correct when he writes that this sequence is "boring" since its sole purpose is to show the recovery of Shigeru and Takako's love. However, if Shigeru's missing point-of-view shots are taken into consideration, this scene has a considerable importance that can only be understood at the end of the film. Up until this point, Shigeru and Takako were always and without exception shown walking in the same direction. As a result, the absence or presence of their point-of-view shots could not be contrasted. It can thus be presumed that Kitano, the director, clearly intended to thrill the audience at this point by having two people who had always been walking in the same direction approach each other for the first time.)

A scene shot from the point of view of "The Mini-Truck Man" (Susumu Terajima) takes place at the end of the movie. In it, Takako pastes snapshots of Shigeru and herself—their shared memories—onto Shigeru's keepsake, the surfboard. Takako, who can finally be found in someone else's point-of-view shot, achieves a mutual directionality she was unable to realize with Shigeru, and is thus redeemed. (Since Takako sets the surfboard covered with photographs adrift on the ocean, the end of her love for Shigeru and the beginning her love for the "Mini-Truck Man," a person who actually looks at her, may be inferred.)

The sea never watches Shigeru. That is, we never see Shigeru on the beach or riding his surfboard from the point of view of the ocean. On the contrary, from the opening shot, it is Shigeru who watches the sea. In this relationship, Shigeru is also a human being who has been alienated by unidirectionality. Eventually, the sea gives Shigeru death. Mutual directionality between Shigeru and the sea is finally realized, though in an extremely warped way.

THE SORROW OF BESTIALITY

Shigeru, whose point of view is presented only once, is treated like a kind of object. The positioning of Shigeru's head in the foreground of the scene where he's gazing at a surfing magazine could be

the quietest ocean, after death.

described as a "secondary reflection within the frame"; he is being viewed as an object from the perspective of the photographs in the magazine. At this moment, the audience is forced to acknowledge an existential sorrow that hovers around Shigeru. This existential sorrow is a kind of bestiality. Takeshi Kitano did not choose a deaf and mute protagonist in order to insert a note of social reality about the hearing impaired. Words were eliminated from the film in order to realize Shigeru's pure bestiality. In reality, only bestiality is pure. This is what differentiates Shigeru from the protagonists in *Two Men and a Wardrobe*. Although those characters are wrapped up in slapstick-like repetitive actions, Polanski's own critical conscience ensures that they still occupy the position of the "anti-social" within society. Shigeru's characterization is stereotypical—for example, he has a girlfriend that he probably met at a school for the deaf and is only able to find work in a 3K job[1]—but because he is never reduced to any kind of socialization, he remains a completely "bestial" young man. This bestiality is what allows him to become obsessed with surfing. (Claude Maki's role as Shigeru must have determined his real-life character—he ended up playing the "role" of a truly "bestial" young man when he was part of a scandal that took place after he starred in the film. This means that Kitano cast Claude Maki as a Type, in the purely Eisenstenian sense.) In complete contrast to Shigeru's "bestiality," human impurity is depicted as a form of "diffusion," much as it is in *Boiling Point*. Thus, the conversation between the wetsuited youths who watch Shigeru surf and who later become his surfing buddies was probably improvised. Filled with unnecessary, unedited repetitions, the dialogue is generally diffuse and has no central organizing through-line; in fact, the conversation is unintelligent and accidental almost to the point of being detestable. The naked, unmediated condition of the meaninglessly proliferating "world" shown here by Takeshi Kitano transcends the caricatures and worn-out clichés of critical conscience in a way that is consistent with our previous discussions about *Boiling Point*.

Obviously, it is not unreasonable to look for a filmic rationale for why Shigeru can't talk. Script supervisor, Hideko Nakada, (who later co-wrote the screenplay for *Many Happy Returns*) explains:

> Of course, we could have had the protagonists be two regular people and just had them not talk. You know how love stories get sappy the instant the characters speak dialogue? For instance, in this film, in the bus scene, if the protagonist had said something like "You go ahead. I'll run after you" to the girl, it would've automatically become corny, you know? And if you explain things with dialogue, the audience always knows what's going to happen next. So, by getting rid of the dialogue, we wanted the audience to wonder, "What's coming next?" Also, with a book, the reader imagines all sorts of things from the words, but in a movie, you show most of the information through images. If you add words on top of the images, you end up limiting the richness of the images. Of course there are films that do require dialogue. It'd probably be a problem not to have dialogue in "gag" movies. But, you know, movies show things through images after all. It's like in judo: I don't like seeing people win by accumulating points. If an opponent clumsily stumbles or trips and that happens three times, it's a game, but it's better if there's a dynamic flip-over-the-shoulder, right? In the same way, if we're dealing with moving images, I think you should go with just the strength of the images.[2]

WALKING TOWARD THE SOURCE

It is impossible to conduct a resonant textual analysis of *A Scene at the Sea* (a film in which Beat Takeshi did not appear) in a book such as this that locates "how did Takeshi Kitano direct Beat Takeshi?" at the center of its argument. If we choose to look at Kitano's films through the prism of Takeshi Kitano=Beat Takeshi, it would be unacceptable to write only about how Kitano finally realized this film as its director, writer, and editor. We would also need to describe how the presence called Takeshi Kitano=Beat Takeshi can exist transcendentally and without intermediaries within the film's images, and simultaneously how he was able to direct himself. First, however, a discussion of the kind of camerawork employed in this film would not be irrelevant. Koshi Ueno writes about this as follows:

> For his third film, *A Scene at the Sea*, Kitano on the one hand pares the story down to its minimum, to its bone, while simultaneously reconsidering film grammar itself. In other words, the most basic building blocks of film such as "watching someone" and "being watched by someone" are innocently used. While manifesting the nature of the gaze in an utterly fresh way, *A Scene at the Sea* simultaneously taps out its own peculiar rhythm.[3]

I mentioned before that *A Scene at the Sea* achieves a sense of vindictiveness and hopelessness by eliminating shots from Shigeru's point of view. This elicits from the audience a sense of sorrow at having to separate from this bestial youth. From the beginning, it's obvious that the film's rhythm is initiated by its frequent walking scenes. The essence of this rhythm is one of "repetition," which is evoked not only in the walking scenes, but also in the plot itself. A typical example of repetition in the plot can be found in the two young boys (Katsuya Koiso and Toshio Matsui) who switch allegiance from soccer to surfing after watching the two protagonists. The "tracing" subsequently performed by these two boys is accompanied by the clumsiness and frailty inevitable to those who do not

possess bestiality. The boys' fragile speech patterns, as well as their unsophisticated taste—which allows them to buy a chintzy, outdated red surfboard from a pawn shop—are what make it possible for us to describe them as "reduced." Such characteristics can be inversely justified by the boys' roles as "transmitters." In contrast to *Violent Cop*, in which brutality rages toward an apotheosis through the transmission of violence, "love" is unmistakably being transmitted throughout this film, along with a passion for surfing and colorful clothes. The two soccer-playing youths are at the center of this transmission.

Given that the film's walking scenes form the basis of its rhythm, it might seem as if *A Scene at the Sea* resembles *Violent Cop*, but precisely the opposite is true. It could be said that *Violent Cop* is clearly propelled forward by Takeshi's Detective Azuma and his powerful walk—especially since his destination throughout most of the film is unclear. But the side shots of Shigeru and Takako carrying their surfboard that rhythmically decorate *A Scene at the Sea* do not possess the power to propel the film's drama forward. Instead, they are for various reasons used like insert shots. It could be argued that all the scenes in this film are used as so-called "inserts," and so do not provide dramatic propulsion for the film. In that sense, they are "innocent." Furthermore, the walking scenes fail to delineate the indeterminate space of the film. The paths traced by the two protagonists as they walk to and from the beach near Yokosuka or the surfing-competition grounds of the Bousou Peninsula are diligently depicted. One could obviously say that these shots make it possible to accumulate a greater

the quietest ocean, after death.

awareness of the minute discrepancies that occur through repetition. However, if they were eliminated on the grounds of narrative economy, the film's basic strategy of "paring the story down to its very marrow" would collapse.

The crux of the problem lies elsewhere. Simply put, what emerges from the diligently captured side shots of the to-and-fro walking is a movement from the right of the screen to the left, or from the left to the right. Let's restrict ourselves for now to a consideration of the movement from left to right—i.e. a movement from the "present" to "the moment following the present." (This temporal association is clear from the direction of wipe effects or from the directionality in Eisenstein's "vertical montage" analysis of the alignment between a music score and the screen image.) Looked at in this way, an opposite directionality—in other words, a movement from right to left—would imply "moving upstream toward the present," creating a temporal vector "toward the origin." The film's nostalgia can be largely attributed to this. If this seems too farfetched, one could say instead that the sense of nostalgia we get from the film is brought about by the "childishness" of the somewhat obsessive depiction of the path to and the path back. Even in this case, we can see how this film is fully supported by the sense of going back "toward the origin." From this, we gradually become aware that Shigeru might represent Takeshi Kitano's past. Actually, introducing the idea of "origins" makes it possible to juxtapose ideas described in phrases such as "the soundless state," "wordless, primitive communication methods," "obsession with placing a

beat takeshi vs. takeshi kitano

board on waves and riding it," "impressions of asexuality," and "the protagonist's social maladaptivity."

Does this then imply that *A Scene at the Sea* is a kind of paradise through which Takeshi Kitano=Beat Takeshi achieves a pure nostalgia? As Tarkovsky demonstrated cinematically, nostalgia itself connotes a negative state in which a human unable to maintain an organic relationship with the world dies a meaningless, alienated death. Nostalgia is a poison implicit to modernity; it's the quality that most reliably ensures death. The human figure who co-exists with such a nostalgia can only be captured as a floating fragment, an indeterminacy suspended in midair. Perhaps this film's protagonist, Shigeru, could thus be said to have been granted death by that fountainhead of nostalgia, the ocean.

Such matters cannot be so simply defined, however. In reality, even if Claude Maki, in the role of Shigeru, is a reflection of Takeshi Kitano=Beat Takeshi as a youth, Takeshi Kitano=Beat Takeshi outlives him because Shigeru dies in the film. "The February camellia bleeds in my palm/Without hesitation I say that the death of others is my shield" (from Kunio Tsukamoto's *Seisanzu*, a poem said to have been written in response to Yukio Mishima's death).[4] In reality, this film laughs off the "death of others." In the scene after Takako makes up with Shigeru—she had become jealous after misinterpreting his relationship with the "Orange Woman"—the two are shown sitting side by side on a beach. We are shown from their point of view the figure of a man riding his bike on the opposite bank's pier. Suddenly, the man plunges into the sea with his bike. This could be compared to the physical gag that runs throughout the film in which a man with a surfboard (mostly the novice surfer who is dating the "Orange Woman") repeatedly falls down just before entering the sea. These instances are all revealed at this point to be metaphors for the "death of others."

the quietest ocean, after death.

Being able to laugh off the "death of others" is in fact a "shield" against one's own death; it becomes a commandment that wards off one's own mortality. Epicurus' well-known philosophical proposition that "death does not exist" argues that that since someone else's death is not one's own, and since no subject called the self will exist to feel their own death, death ultimately does not exist. But for a person obsessed with death, the ethics of deriving lessons from the "death of others" is related to one's own survival, and, as such, is an ultimate issue.

For these reasons, Shigeru's death in this film holds a dual meaning. On the one hand, it represents a funeral for Takeshi Kitano=Beat Takeshi's past. On the other, it is a deterrent against the seductions of suicide. This is where Takeshi=Takeshi's essence is revealed.

TAKESHI KITANO'S TOMB

But this film also simultaneously possesses a wholeness that distances it from such a reading. From the beginning, Takeshi=Takeshi could be suspected of performing funeral rites not only for his past self but also for his present self. His absence from the screen as an actor is a scheme that allows him to present a landscape that does not contain him. The film is quiet because it is actually an afterlife. And the words in the film, spoken in a state of "diffusion," are arranged as commentaries on the protagonist Shigeru. This could be likened to the behavior of a person who pretends to be a corpse and listens from his coffin to the comments of mourners at his own funeral.

The actual protagonist of this film is a tombstone. Let's recall the scene where Shigeru and Takako throw away an already broken surfboard that Shigeru's enthusiastic surfing had rebroken. Feeling the sadness of separation, they seem to be bidding farewell to the surfboard, which, being too large, only fits into the rusted seaside

garbage can in a "vertical position." The surfboard's resemblance to a tombstone at this moment seems unavoidable. As long as the surfboard remains complete, with the broken-off section filled by a piece of painted styrofoam, nobody dies. It thus functions like a tombstone carved with red names for the not-yet dead.[5] During the course of the film, this tombstone called a surfboard will eventually be replaced with a complete one. Death clearly awaits the owner of this tombstone—in this case, Shigeru. His grave is visualized as pitiful, bobbing remains that have failed to achieve any kind of organic connection to this world. Shigeru succeeded at surfing the waves, but failed to participate in the world. Kitano solemnly highlights this deep sense of sorrow with unusual, almost other-worldly lighting. In the end, the film's other characters will appropriately decorate this tombstone with photographs and give it a burial at sea.

Let's examine this shot of the bobbing surfboard more closely. Because it is the film's first bird's-eye shot, it possesses the power inherent to "perpendicularity" despite being taken from an angle that is not quite perpendicular. This high-angle shot predictably shows the surfboard floating against a background of the blue, blue sea. Due to the shot's perpendicularity, and to the strength of the blue background, its composition at this moment, which recalls a snapshot, should resemble an icon. (In reality, such an impression is slightly weakened by the swaying of the surfboard.) These strengths are further reinforced by the scene's Russian-doll structure, which causes the shot of the surfboard to function like a snapshot frame within a frame. This

the quietest ocean, after death.

interjected image makes narrative sense since Takako has just released the surfboard into the ocean. However, there is only a weak relationship between this scene and the previous one where Takako's figure is shown from behind and in the center of a long shot as she releases the surfboard into the sea. All traces of sentimentality are severed in this shot of Takako taken from a distance. This should actually emphasize the sense that the subsequent shot of the surfboard on the waves doesn't belong to any particular strand of this film. (I say "should actually" because in reality, these individual images are partially linked by Joe Hisaishi's extremely sentimental music, which seems to sing "*Sa-yo-na-ra. . . . sa-yo-na-ra.*") This shot, which shows the surfboard drifting on the waves, is essentially timeless. Time has clearly passed between the previous shot and this one (as can be seen by the surfboard's distance from the coast). The scene that immediately follows is thus turned into a series of extraneous shots that function solely to show that they take place in the past tense. This liberates the shot of the surfboard from the temporal restrictions of the film. By the time we reach this shot, which is unhinged from the narrative, the scent of death should waft up from the tombstone-like surfboard. The sense of timelessness that pervades the entire film comes from the timeless vacuum implied by this shot.

© OFFICE KITANO

On the other hand, the surfboard clearly exists as a bond that connects all human beings. This can be seen in the scenes where Shigeru and Takako hold the front and back ends of the surfboard as they walk, an act that makes these scenes emotionally moving. When it becomes apparent in retrospect

beat takeshi vs. takeshi kitano

that this surfboard exudes the scent of death, we feel deep regret over our failure to recognize that "death," which appeared to be so simple, had been implied in various places throughout the film. "Death" resonates because it connects all things (an awareness of which is itself beauty). Those who do not realize this will also have missed the "death" that is fully distributed within Takeshi Kitano=Beat Takeshi himself. The epitaph that appears at the end of the film—"The Quietest Ocean That Summer"—is meant for the tomb of Takeshi Kitano=Beat Takeshi. This tombstone itself is probably the film's protagonist. As proof, the surfboard is placed in the center of the frame.

We thus come to a new awareness of how Takeshi Kitano=Beat Takeshi uses this consciousness of "death" to fully engage the world. Shigeru is an image seen from the perspective of Takeshi=Takeshi's "death." Kitano places a high value on bestiality. He "kills" the stand-in for what is presumed to be his past existence while hiding the fact that it is a "suicide." He disrupts time while inserting his "what once was" perspective into his afterlife. He thus distributes his own "death" throughout the entire film. The audience swallows these schemes of Takeshi=Takeshi, and comes to acknowledge the "traces" of Takeshi=Takeshi that exist apart from his role as director=editor of the film. Such "traces" are beautiful, provided that one has the ability to appreciate death. This "traces" and "absences" in this film are woven together like embroidery, showing themselves in the tense intervals before "death." *A Scene at the Sea* could thus be said to exist inside Takeshi Kitano. It is the quiet interlude that comes after the anomalous double-suicide of *Violent Cop*, which could be characterized as an insurrection of sensuality racing toward "death," and *Boiling Point*, which invited "death" through "accidental discharges" while at the same time extolling "diffusion" as a deterrent against it.

the quietest ocean, after death.

05

*a sonatina thrice repeated,
ending in death*

THE TEMPTATION TOWARD DEATH

In his essay "Parting Ways with Beat Takeshi," producer Kazuyoshi Okuyama recalls the advertising campaign for *Sonatine:*

> I considered myself a marketing veteran and had confidence that I could sell anything, but even I was at a complete loss as to how to market this movie. It was the most difficult to sell of them all—and worse, it was by no means a film that I disliked.
>
> I think this difficulty arose because *Sonatine* possesses a quality that is antithetical to the kind of "heat" or "buzz" normally used to sell a movie. It seems to be whispering in the audience's ear, "What are you rushing around for? Why not take a rest? Nothing much will come of your efforts anyway." This is far removed from the kind of "heat" required to sell a commercially challenging movie. It left me feeling utterly perplexed.[1]

Unquestionably, *Sonatine* is infused with a kind of nihilism and lethargy that tempts the viewer with "death." Throughout the film, a strange chill encroaches on the realm of life from the realm of death. The word *"tokatonton,"*[2] invented by the writer Osamu Dazai,[3] is supposed to awaken human beings to the reality of despair and death. Although this word may have lost its significance as an actual sound, it silently reverberates as *Sonatine*'s key note.

As Okuyama points out, this pessimism is also clearly manifested in the film's script. In one scene, the gangster Murakawa, played by Beat Takeshi, is talking with his subordinate Ken (Susumu Terajima) in a car:

> MURAKAWA: Ken, I'm thinking of giving up the yakuza life . . .
>
> KEN: We've done some pretty crazy things.
>
> MURAKAWA: Somehow, I just feel tired.
>
> KEN: You're only tired of it 'cause you finally made some dough.[4]

In another scene, Kitano seems to reveal himself unguardedly—so much so, in fact, that most critics have avoided commenting on it. The scene occurs after Murakawa has killed the "husband" of Miyuki, a woman he's picked up, after the "husband" had sexually assaulted her. (I will provisionally interpret the man who attacks Miyuki on the beach at night as her "husband" based on the line, "But this is my husband's car.") Miyuki (Aya Kokumai) gradually opens up to Murakawa on the seashore rocks:

> MIYUKI: You're not afraid of shooting someone, are you? I'm impressed.
>
> MURAKAWA: . . .
>
> MIYUKI: If you you're not afraid of killing, I guess you're not afraid of dying either.

a sonatina thrice repeated, ending in death

MURAKAWA: [Laughs]

MIYUKI: You're tough. I love tough guys.

MURAKAWA: If I were tough, I wouldn't have a gun.

MIYUKI: But you didn't think twice about shooting him!

MURAKAWA: I shot him because I was afraid.

MIYUKI: But you're not afraid of dying . . .

MURAKAWA: If you're afraid enough of dying, you want to die.

MIYUKI: I don't get it!

MURAKAWA: [Laughing]

The domination of "death" in *Sonatine* goes beyond the attraction to death that is expressed so bluntly in this dialogue. Indeed, we can probably find its origins in the very grammar of the film.

WALKING GHOSTS

According to Kazuyoshi Okuyama, Kitano first proposed *Sonatine* as a kind of sequel to *Violent Cop*. Yet from its very start, *Sonatine*'s differences from the earlier picture stand out. As if to recall *Violent Cop*, which was so much of a "walking film," *Sonatine* begins with a scene of Murakawa and Ken walking side by side down the street. However, one gets a completely different impression here than from *Violent Cop*. As I suggested earlier, *Violent Cop*'s walking scenes completely strip bare the body of the actor Beat Takeshi. Walking is part of the propulsive force that drives *Violent Cop* forward. In *Sonatine*, on the other hand, the effect of the initial walking scene could be summarized as "floating."

In this opening scene, the frame of the film cuts off Murakawa and Ken's feet so that they lie outside of the audience's field of vision. This eliminates the sense of power we get from the scenes in *Violent Cop* where the characters tread firmly on the earth. Moreover, something (in this case, the window of a café) is placed between the camera and the characters so that the walking is filmed through the window using a tracking shot. This technique, which is especially conspicuous in the work of Yoshishige Yoshida,[5] had not been used much by Kitano previously—perhaps because it gives a sense of depth to the film and, as a result, cannot help shaping a sort of "world view." Kitano shunned such effects, and the consequent directness of his films is what gives them their power. In *Sonatine*, however, the walking scenes are filmed with a moving camera. One portion of this particular scene is filmed in such a way that Beat Takeshi's body seems to be covered by the light reflecting off the glass through which it is being filmed. The resulting premonition one gets that his body will somehow turn into plastic is not the ultimate effect of filming through glass, however. What appears in this shot is alienation. Beat Takeshi makes his appearance in this film as a man alienated from the earth, a man alienated from "directness"—in other words, a man who suffers from a modern pathology.

Takeshi Kitano's staging of Beat Takeshi's walking scenes in *Sonatine* has changed greatly from his previous films. Scenes that plainly show Beat Takeshi's feet touching the ground are limited to vertical compositions in which we see him from behind as he walks away from the camera. The only exception to this rule comes near the film's climax, when Murakawa has resolved to storm a hotel and gun down the boss who'd framed him. The scene begins when he meets Miyuki for a last farewell and continues up to the point when Miyuki fires a machine gun into an open field. In it, the camera clearly shows Beat Takeshi's feet as Murakawa and Miyuki walk

a sonatina thrice repeated, ending in death

toward the screen in a vertically composed shot. Even this exception expresses the paradox that Takeshi's feet can only be filmed touching the ground when he has become absolutely conscious of "death." Other than this, however, and in complete contrast to *Violent Cop*, there are no scenes shot from the front or side in which Takeshi's feet are shown touching the ground. Takeshi Kitano=Beat Takeshi amputates his own body with the frame. He clearly and consciously constructs his own presence to resemble that of a footless ghost.[6]

This approach may result from Takeshi Kitano's participation in the editing process subsequent to *A Scene at the Sea*. For the first time, he observed human bodies cut into frames of $1/24$th of a second. The bodies fixed in each of these frames are undeniably those of ghosts displaced in time. When confronted by these ghosts, Kitano consciously transformed himself. That must have been the moment he felt the impulse towards self-amputation.

No other filmmaker has equalled Takeshi Kitano's singular discovery of the resemblance between editing and the sensation of death. Multiple types of "cutting" or "amputation" are at work in his films. Many of *Sonatine*'s scenes begin with a silent, fully frontal medium shot of one of the participants in a developing situation. (In some cases, the sequence will also end with a formalized repetition of this initial shot.) Just as symmetry can be equated with death, the frontality of these scenes, which open with a medium shot, discreetly adds a slight shock of death to the movement on the screen. Other frontal scenes, in which a group of cast members line up to face the camera, are also marked by the cold gaze of someone looking at a display of corpses. Such scenes include: the self-introductions of the yakuza visitors from Tokyo at a gang office in Okinawa; the gang leaders' meeting at a Tokyo hostess bar; and the Okinawa scenes in which the yakuza ride together in a microbus or car. (Several scenes where sleeping bodies are placed unobtrusively at the edges of the work are also evocative of a display of corpses.) Few opportunities exist for an extended give and take between two people in the dialogue sequences. In most cases, the camera is aimed at the listener, whose silence mimics death. The speaker, who is embroiled in "life" through the act of speaking, is pushed off camera—i.e. also towards the realm of "death."

In *Sonatine*, the hands of the editor are as transparent as an x-ray. To the extent that all the editing is placed in the service of "cutting," Takeshi Kitano's work echoes Bresson's in its auteur quality, but its uniqueness lies in its ability to raise this "cutting" to the level of an intense scrutiny of the body of the self. To put it another way, *Sonatine* does more than take suicide as its theme: its very expression is suicidal. It thus lacks the vitality of *Violent Cop*, where the characters fly across the screen and go into a glorious tailspin en route to the stillness of "death." Nor does it resemble *Boiling Point*, whose fascination is derived from its placement of characters at the juncture where "diffusion" coincides with reality accounts. *Sonatine*'s first point of difference from these other movies is that, while the yakuza are being wiped out one by one, the single main character to survive is Miyuki, a woman.

The nature of Beat Takeshi's physical presence also differs greatly in *Sonatine*. The persistence of his violence, so evident in the previous films, is submerged here. As I suggested earlier, the persistence of Beat Takeshi's violence demonstrates the pliability of his flesh—its ability to sustain damage. Nevertheless, this pliability is based on the basic strength and solidity of his body. One wonders if this strength and solidity is present in *Sonatine*. Take, for example, the scene in the bar's restroom when Murakawa attacks his rival Takahashi (Kenichi Yajima), who has been plotted his expulsion from the gang. Although Murakawa kicks Takahashi repeatedly, his violence does not convey the same persistence that was so conspicuous in Beat Takeshi's earlier films. After watching this scene a number of times, I noticed that when Murakawa attacks Takahashi in the restroom, he kicks him in

a sonatina thrice repeated, ending in death

the stomach exactly four times. Again, after Takahashi collapses, Murakawa strikes him in the face exactly four times. It is as though Takeshi Kitano wishes to discreetly show those who repeatedly view his film just how conscious he is of "death." [7]

It is evident that the change in the nature of Beat Takeshi's physical presence has been intentionally suggested from *Sonatine*'s very first walking scene. The action in this walking scene is negated soon after in the scene of a moving car filmed through the glass of a café. Thus the cumulative effect is zero. Murakawa and Ken are heading to where a middle-aged mahjong operator is to be executed for refusing to bring a cut of his profits to the yakuza headquarters. (The dialogue quoted earlier, "I'm thinking of giving up the yakuza life . . ." occurs just after this scene.) One gets the impression that the car Murakawa and Ken are driving in is speeding heedlessly into the depths of the night. (The lack of a soundtrack in this scene strengthens this effect.) Though there is a certain unique sensuousness to this scene, its movement forms a sort of mathematical operation with the walking scene presented just a few moments before. Here, the movement mediated by the car goes from left to right on the screen, in contrast to the earlier scene, where the movement progressed from right to left and was performed by the unmediated walking of human bodies. The "mathematical operation" that occurs between these two scenes is the addition (or subtraction) of two opposite motions, resulting in a zero. As such, it negates the "walking mythology" Beat Takeshi had established through his physical presence starting with the first movie he directed, *Violent Cop*.

ATEMPORALITY AND THE UBIQUITY OF BLUE

The use of the color blue in the film is another indispensable element in this thematization of "death." Blues are scattered throughout *Sonatine*, forming an organic chain across the film. Most of the Tokyo scenes that take place before the action moves to Okinawa occur at night, and the predominant hues are dark and subdued—mainly black, blue, and green—with the overall effect being that of a dull, bluish palette. Later in the film, this underlying blue is brought to the fore. Blue is the undertone in the Tokyo prelude, and it was clearly Kitano's intention for this tone to manifest itself more clearly as the film progressed. Before blue comes to dominate the screen entirely, it is allowed to intermittently take up portions of the screen. The scene in the microbus, just after the action moves to Okinawa, overflows with light. (See below for a further analysis of this scene, in which the Okinawan gangster played by Tetsu Watanabe faces Murakawa and the Tokyo yakuza.) The exterior of the vehicle is filmed in high-contrast lighting, producing a white that contrasts strongly with the scenes of Tokyo at night that preceded it. However, the blue of the popsicle that one of the yakuza is eating (and that serves the same function as the "spirit-offering cake" depicted in *Boiling Point*)[8] also resonates with the blue of the ice box that is carried by the assassin disguised as a fisherman, played by Eiji Minakata.

From this point on in *Sonatine*, the screen is bathed in blue. To begin with, the night is overwhelmingly blue. This signifies the presence of moonlight. Indeed, three close-ups of a full moon are inserted into the film. We should doubtless be wary of too hastily identifying this full moon with madness or lunacy. Granted, moonlight is what arouses Miyuki's "husband" to try to rape his "wife," played by Aya Kokumai, on the beach. And it is moonlight that drives Murakawa and the other yakuza to their games of "war" with fireworks. At moments such as these, the moonlight does appear to be the source of lunacy.

However, we should also note that moonlight has an additional function in the film. In each of the three close-ups mentioned above, the moon is full. It is possible that these three shots are merely a prosaic way of marking the passage of time, showing the film's diachronic progression from, say, the night of the 14th, to the 15th, to the 16th. And yet there is absolutely no difference in the appearance of the full moon on these three successive nights. Indeed, it would be natural to assume that the same cut of the full moon has been spliced into three different places in the film. If this were the case, then these shots would appear to demonstrate the complete stagnation of time— i.e. that time does not progress at all in Okinawa. Hence the film raises the theme of temporality. As soon as the action moves to Okinawa, it is harnessed into the yoke of atemporality. In this respect, Okinawa represents a kind of utopia, and it would seem that the modern realization that utopia is very close to death possesses Takeshi Kitano. To demonstrate the omnipresence of this utopia=death, the night in Okinawa is immutably, overwhelmingly blue.

This nocturnal blue transforms into the blue of the Okinawan day (as is the natural order). Nevertheless, the blue of the sky and the blue of the ocean, together with the white sand of the beach, never slip into the banality of a picture postcard. What is it that ensures that the daytime scenes of Okinawa, which on the surface resemble Seiji Izumi's *Run Southwards Towards the Ocean* (Minami e hashire, umi no michi wo!, 1986) are not merely picturesque? First of all, no aerial photography or other attention-grabbing photography techniques are used, and all scenic spectacles are resolutely avoided. The white sand and blue ocean do not serve to express scenic beauty, but rather "emptiness." Nothingness and futility—the blue sky, the blue ocean, and the white sand are employed to convey only this. If we can say that the use of aerial photography comes from a kind of agoraphobia, then *Sonatine,* which eschews any compositions that emphasize wide expanses, must be said to take an entirely different position. The vacuous space of the beach where the characters toss a frisbee and sumo-wrestle each other further exposes the "nothingness" of

the Okinawan daytime, thus casually avoiding a picture-postcard surfeit of beauty. Near the film's close, black smoke billowing from an exploded vehicle violently blots out the white sand of the beach. This seems to be a final confirmation of Kitano's intention to not allow the Okinawan landscape to be transformed into any sort of ultimate beauty."

The white shirt that Beat Takeshi wears throughout the movie becomes meaningful in relation to this blue. Before discussing this shirt, however, I would first like to recall the striking scene that reveals the film's take on "pattern."

This scene occurs in the midst of a sequence of vignettes presenting the idle games of Murakawa and his group, who find themselves with too much time on their hands. The gang has fled from an attack by their rivals to a shanty on the beach that is almost too tranquil to be called a "hide-out." After playing sumo with paper cutouts in the shack, they go outside to wrestle on the beach. The composition of this scene, with its white sand, blue ocean, and blue sky, emphasizes the sense of emptiness described earlier. Here, however, "pattern" has been inserted in the form of the aloha shirts the group received as gifts from Uechi (Tetsu Watanabe), and into which everyone except for Murakawa has changed.

With the men thus costumed in aloha shirts, the viewer cannot but be aware of the gangsters' absurdity. Aloha shirts are "leisure clothes" that occupy a completely different position from "battle dress." Hence they have the ability to completely overturn the yakuza aesthetic, represented by the black jackets and white shirts that could

a sonatina thrice repeated, ending in death

be called the basic yakuza uniform. Because the tropical-style "pattern" in these "leisure" aloha shirts is so antithetical to this aesthetic, these shirts are a type of "death," adding to the inertia of the yakuza who wear them. When this "death" makes its laughable appearance, the sense of the characters' ineptness only increases. The incongruity of the red aloha shirt worn by Murakawa's right-hand man, Katagiri (played by Ren Osugi) is particularly obvious—here we can see that Kitano is making affectionate fun of the unexpectedly endearing quality of the actor Osugi. (Kitano's affection for Osugi is also evident in Katagiri's exaggerated fear of falling into the pits that Murakawa has dug in the beach, and the scene where Katagiri clumsily rehearses the movements of a paper sumo wrestler after everyone else has left the sumo ring on the beach.) This mismatch of the yakuza and the aloha shirts, then, emphasizes the fact that the men have irreversibly stepped into the realm of an absurd death. (No matter how violent the deaths depicted by Kitano in *Sonatine* may be, their very futility means they cannot to escape the modern disease of "absurdity." This is one of the modern viewpoints expressed by Kitano in *Sonatine*.)

Intriguingly, the full-body tattoo revealed when Uechi strips to the waist to join in the game of sumo is in subtle harmony with the "pattern" of these aloha shirts. The pattern of Uechi's tattoo occupies the exact same structural position as the aloha shirts, and indeed bears a strong physical resemblance to them. When the tattoo, the most distinct symbol of yakuza aesthetics, is placed in the "leisure" position of an aloha shirt, it dies a cruel death. In order to emphasize this "pattern of death," or perhaps "death of pattern," it is necessary for the background of the scene to appear as a bare expanse. Thus, the "patterns" of the tattoo and the aloha shirts stand out marvelously against the empty white and blue of the overall composition.

At this moment, what is Murakawa, played by Beat Takeshi, wearing? Just the white shirt mentioned earlier. Indeed it is this scene that brings our attention to the fact that, in contrast to the aloha shirts, Murakawa wears a white shirt throughout the movie, though it is sometimes accompanied by a jacket. To suggest that this white shirt is Murakawa's "burial kimono" would be little more than a literary conceit.[9] As a simple first impression, this white shirt appears to express the aesthetic fatigue of the same Murakawa who declares "I'm thinking of giving up the yakuza life." Yet because Murakawa has been placed in a passive position, the white shirt also identifies his status as a man marked for death. As the story progresses, Murakawa is sent to Okinawa in accordance with a plot hatched by Takahashi and the yakuza boss. He passively accepts their orders, taking no action. Unless Murakawa were to act to reverse the course of this suicidal conclusion, the film would in essence seem to be waiting for death from its very beginning.

When completely permeated with the poison of the pale blue moonlight, Murakawa's white shirt becomes a moon and radiates blue. This is, in fact, the visual expression of Murakawa's structural position with regard to death. When, for example, Katagiri's red aloha shirt is exposed to the moonlight, it darkens to the color of dried blood; and indeed, this may foreshadow his unpleasant demise in the elevator. But while Katagiri's shirt may give a premonition of death, it is not death itself. When, on the other hand, Murakawa's white shirt radiates an overwhelming pale blue in the moonlight, it is death. (As I have suggested earlier, the full moon is death, enabling the complete suspension of time.) Murakawa is not someone who will be killed; rather he is already dead.

This blue palette intensifies in the scene when Murakawa wakes from a nightmare and casually steps outside, where he has his first encounter with Miyuki, whose "husband" is about to rape her. The moon, the moonlight, and Miyuki's "husband's" car are all blue, as is Murakawa's shirt, which is deeply stained with the pale blue

a sonatina thrice repeated, ending in death

moonlight. What are the emotions of the fatigued Murakawa when he witnesses the violent sexual interaction between this couple? On this occasion, he is utterly expressionless. It seems as if he has become an inanimate object in order to more fully absorb the blue of the moonlit scene; he is bound fast by the blue of death. Nor does Murakawa see "life" in the figure of Miyuki, who is about to be raped—unlike, for example, Muraki, the downcast character played by Minori Terada in Shinji Soumai's film *Love Hotel* (1985).[10] Muraki sees the glow of "life" in the sexual excitement of Nami (Noriko Hayami), who has a vibrator in her vagina in *Love Hotel*'s opening. Murakawa's heart does not respond; nor does he watch the interaction of the couple with an engagement that would find fault with Miyuki's "husband."

(In fact, it would seem that Murakawa in this film has something of an aversion to women. Unlike Uehara in *Boiling Point*, he is not imbued with a sensual passion that causes him to suddenly indulge in sex as he nears death. When he leaves the hostess bar where the yakuza heads have gathered to hear their boss's explanation about his assignment to Okinawa, Murakawa coolly passes through a group of the bar's women without casting them a single

glance. Although he is later attracted to Miyuki, this seems to be an attraction to her innocence rather than a heightening of sexual passion—such, at least, is the impression one gets in the scene in which Miyuki exposes her breasts to him during a sudden tropical shower.)

This is why his face is so expressionless when he shoots

beat takeshi vs. takeshi kitano

Miyuki's "husband," who comes up to confront him. In the scene when Murakawa encounters Miyuki, he decisively "receives" death in the form of Miyuki's "husband's" blue car. This is the car that will henceforth be used when Murakawa and Miyuki go out driving together. And it is this same car that Murakawa, driven by Ryoji (Masanobu Katsumura), will take to the hotel in order to kill the yakuza boss who had set him up. However, Murakawa will not return in this car for a reunion with Miyuki, who belongs to the realm of "life." While in this "blue" car of "death," he will instead put a bullet through his own head.

Incidentally, the film also begins with a blue-striped pattern. As the camera revolves and moves away, we become aware that it is a close-up of a harpooned angel fish, shot against a red backdrop. This *avant-title*, using an outtake shot by Kitano, was added by Kazuyoshi Okuyama during the editing phase. It is worth noting how well the strangeness of this image matches the atmosphere of the film. The idea of starting with the color blue is a testament the producer Okuyama's keen understanding of the power of death in this work.

THE PATHOLOGY OF DISCONTINUITY

Sonatine emphasizes the material aspect—the status as "things"—of everyone who appears in the film. This is evident from the already mentioned fact that certain scenes begin with a full frontal shot of the character's faces. It is also evident from the pitiless way in which the characters die as "things" in the murder scenes. This demonstrates Takeshi Kitano's unhesitating dramatic realization and his inclination towards speed. Such objectification also strengthens the impression of a certain kind of hard-boiledness—but this could be said of all of Kitano's "violence movies." Yet something about this film prevents its materialism from being tied to a sense of strength. If *Violent Cop* was animalistic, *Sonatine* is somehow inorganic (and this quality does not come just from its shots of the moon or the sand or the Okinawan stone walls). Something pathological that prevents violence from erupting into strength has been carefully stretched across the film.

When we inquire into what evokes this impression, we find that the work is armed with a consciousness of "discontinuity" that is contrary to the "continuity" or persistence that distinguished *Violent Cop*. (Earlier, I wrote that the cutting in *Sonatine* was as transparent as an x-ray.) This is primarily due to the shock of discontinuity that the changeover between the cuts always presents. However, this pathology of "discontinuity" actually insinuates itself into the spaces within each continuous shot as well. Due perhaps to Kitano's own malevolence, the "continuity" that should naturally exist in each span of film is thrown into doubt, burdening the characters with the pathology of "discontinuity."

This pathology first becomes evident in the scene where the mahjong junkie who has refused to bring a cut of his profits to the yakuza organization Murakawa represents is executed at the dockside at night. When the man, whom Murakawa has already threatened to kill, reappears nonchalantly in his mahjong parlor, Murakawa decides to execute him; his yakuza subordinates abduct him without a word and without a wasted movement. (In the screenplay, the name of the mahjong operator is Kanemoto, but this name does not come up in the film itself. We should note, however, that the Korean-sounding name Kanemoto was consciously applied to this character. In fact, this name is a nod to the director Nagisa Oshima. In his film *Merry Christmas, Mr. Lawrence*, a Korean army staffer [Johnny Okura] charged with homosexual activity and forced to commit *seppuku*, or ritual suicide by disembowelment, is also named Kanemoto.)

At any rate, when the "Kanemoto" of *Sonatine* is abducted, he is pushed into a car in front of the mahjong parlor, his face pressed against the car window so that it is distorted like so much "matter."

At this moment, Kanemoto embodies not only ugliness, but the pliability of a "soft object" that is at the core of his existence. Next, the film shows Murakawa and Ken arriving at the scene of Kanemoto's execution. We are shown what has happened in the meantime: Kanemoto has been brought in a car to the dock, bound with a rope, affixed to the hook of a crane, and is hanging in mid-air over the water. The true cruelty of this scene does not derive from the violence of Kanemoto's treatment, however. Rather, if we say that this scene is violent, it is because of the utter indifference to whether Kanemoto lives or dies that is apparent on the faces of Murakawa, Katagiri, and the other yakuza. Such violence is also present when Murakawa, looking at Kanemoto trussed up and hanging in mid-air, laughs, "We do some crazy shit." It is present again when Murakawa and Katagiri proceed to treat Kanemoto as no more than a guinea pig in the exchange: "How long can he hold out if we sink him?" "Usually about two or three minutes."

The violence of the indifference on the yakuzas' faces is frequently intercut with the figure of Kanemoto, who, hanging in mid-air, is gradually robbed of his sense of security. It is not just his body, but rather the very security of his existence that is suspended in the air. Murakawa mutters, "Try sinking him for two minutes," an order that is passed on by Katagiri (Katagiri's command is completely lacking in any eagerness). The crane is lowered, and Kanemoto, writhing in pain and fear, sinks into the water, disappearing from the screen. However, his absence continues to be depicted with a persistence almost akin to loyalty. Because of this, the fundamental "discontinuity" of existence is revealed.

a sonatina thrice repeated, ending in death

Furthermore, the "discontinuity" of time itself becomes an issue here. Despite Murakawa's order to "Try sinking him for two minutes," the actual time that Kanemoto is underwater on screen is about thirty seconds. (To give this abbreviation a more natural flow, a shot of Murakawa and the others watching the water is inserted here.) Such temporal abbreviation may seem like a natural strategy from the viewpoint of narrative economy, but we should note that here, time itself possesses the quality of "intermittency." Even if this abbreviation does not consciously register, it must implant a sense of rootlessness and insecurity in the viewer. Kanemoto is then raised from the water, dripping like a wet rat. From the miserable condition of his clothes, starting with the reddish-brown polo shirt that sticks to his body, we can say that the continuity of his appearance before and after his submersion has been severed. Nevertheless he continues to beg for forgiveness just as before. Even though we know it's cruel, we are likely to feel a kind of aesthetic resistance at this point to Kanemoto's continuing to plead for forgiveness though the continuity of his existence has already been severed. "He's not dead yet?" "He's really clinging to life," "It's ugly to be so attached to life," we think.

In this same frame of mind, Murakawa casually mutters, "What? He's still alive, isn't he," when he observes the results of Kanemoto's submersion. Completely ignoring Kanemoto's abject pleas, he tells Katagiri, "How about three minutes?" Again the crane is lowered, and Kanemoto sinks into the water. This time, "three minutes" is abbreviated to an on-screen time of forty-five seconds, an abbreviation that is naturalized by the insertion of talk between Katagiri and Murakawa about their assignment to Okinawa. By the time Murakawa notices that "It's been over three minutes, hasn't it?" and Kanemoto is lifted out of the water, he is already an immobile "thing." The sequence ends with Murakawa asking, "Is he dead? . . . Well, anyway. Take care of the rest." Murakawa's total indifference to

Kanemoto's death is underscored by the lack of excitement with which he utters the words "Well, anyway."

What, then, does this scene represent besides the narrative facts of Kanemoto's death and the fearsome behavior of the yakuza? It represents the anxious gaze of Takeshi Kitano seeing through to the discontinuity of existence. It is Kitano's quiet voice from the realm of death, cooling the warmth of life and declaring to those who expect continuity that they themselves are already discontinuous: life receives intermittent reflections from the realm of death, its existence flickers, and it begins to suffer from so-called "discontinuity." People (things) suddenly disappear, then return to their previous form. A distant presence amidst undulating heat waves flickers between certainty and uncertainty; it is too unreliable to put our faith in, but it is fascinating for that very reason. This consciousness of discontinuity even extends to the temporal dimension, as the periods of time concretely cited as "two minutes" and "three minutes" are betrayed by their actual on-screen time. When we consider this, we should realize that this phenomenon is not the natural consequence of the film's basic narrative, but rather of a modern pathology that has seeped into Takeshi Kitano's very core.

It should be clear from subsequent events that the above interpretation is not an overstatement. In Okinawa, Murakawa's car is often shown driving up and down the hilly open fields. Whether receding from or approaching the viewer, the car, shot in a vertical composition, disappears repeatedly as it drives along the dips of the hills. Thus the car is also placed in the position of "discontinuity." Actually, Kitano discovered this kind of shot in the film *Violent Cop*. You may recall that near the beginning of *Violent Cop*, the body of Azuma (Beat Takeshi) gradually appears head-first as he walks toward the viewer over the hump of a bridge.

The sound of the car also becomes an issue here. For the most part, the sound of automobiles in *Sonatine* is approached realistically.

For example, the sound of a car approaching the screen from far away gradually crescendoes as the car draws closer. Yet rather than understanding this simply as realism, perhaps we can say that a sound that was absent before is now present (or, conversely, a sound that was present is now absent). The unstable "discontinuity" of the sound of a car is thus capable of making an impression on the viewer. The sound of a moving car somehow disappears, giving way to the depths of silence. A mysterious "discontinuity" seeps into the film's realism and touches upon the realm of death. This is, no doubt, why the movement of cars in this film have such a visionary and gorgeous appearance.

The discontinuity of existence in this film also manifests itself in the scene where, during a moonlit Okinawan night, Ryoji, Ken, and Katagiri fall into pits that Murakawa has dug in the sand. Their falling into these pits is not set up like a sight gag, however. We can conclude this from the fact that Murakawa and Uechi take the position of spectators in this scene, laughing at the others in our place. Furthermore, when the men fall into the traps, we are not shown their chagrined reactions. Their facial expressions are lost in the moonlit night. Since the scene is captured in a comparatively long shot, the viewers are unable to identify with them. Nor can we simply term this a consciously "misfired" gag. Instead, we should examine the action here more conscientiously. Ryoji and Ken fall for Murakawa's coy "Hey! Come here. Quick!" They approach from the distance towards the foreground of the screen. Their walking forms suddenly disappear from the screen as they fall into the traps. This scene is shot in a direct and vivid way and with a minimum of pretension. In short, what creates an impression here is not an incongruity that gives rise to humor, but the "discontinuity" of people who disappear from screen in an instant.

The group of Okinawa scenes that intermittently sketch out the idle play of the gangsters, beginning with the paper sumo games, are also united by their attention to "discontinuity." Murakawa and the others, fearing an attack by their rivals, hide out at an abandoned shack by the beach. When they first arrive to check it out, their bodies are hidden in the darkness of its interior, becoming visible only when they open the shutters and light pours in. This metamorphosis is another strong example of discontinuity. Also, when Ken and Ryoji are taught Okinawan dance by Uechi in the moonlight, the continuity of their bodies is cut off by the obstruction of a stone wall. Finally, in the ultimate example, the fundamental meaning of "discontinuity" is revealed by the men's deaths. We can say that they have inherited "discontinuity" from Kanemoto's death, and it manifests itself after their move to Okinawa. (Of course, we can also find "discontinuity" in the very futility of their move from Tokyo to Okinawa.)

MISFIRING – DERAILMENT – INTERRUPTION

"Discontinuity" is likely to depress the viewer. Essentially, discontinuity is a lessening of the plenitude of continuity. There are other operations in the film that have a deflating effect similar to "discontinuity": namely "misfiring," "derailment," and "interruption." To the extent that film editing develops along a temporal axis, cinema is basically a propulsive medium. However, Kitano employs impotence to put the breaks on this propulsive force. As a result, he carefully includes the hidden themes of "misfiring," "derailment," and "interruption" among his strategies in order to produce an inexplicable sense of despair in his viewers.

Let's begin with "misfiring": all the bombs that Murakawa and his gang have gotten off the black market from America—except the one that is used in the final assault on Takahashi—suffer from this syndrome. After rivals shoot up the office in the abandoned building that Uechi has allocated for Murakawa's gang (here Kitano includes a shot of broken glass, an obligatory feature of his "violence movies"), Ryoji plants a bomb in the rival's headquarters. In the end, this bomb never explodes. The only time one of their explosives does successfully detonate is when they are playing with fireworks on the beach at night. In other words, their explosives only go off in the context of play (in this case, fireworks). In the context of their work, which begins first of all with killing, they are plagued with the absurdity of "misfiring."

A similar example takes place in the scene in front of the general store where Katagiri (played by Ren Osugi) makes a long-distance call to Tokyo on a public phone to determine Takahashi's whereabouts. The call goes through, but when Katagiri hangs up, he doesn't get back the change he was expecting. We can say that this scene contains the holds a theme of "misfiring."

Next, we can consider the theme of "derailment." *Sonatine* includes a number of scenes where Murakawa, played by Beat Takeshi, goes driving with Miyuki in her "husband's" car. Murakawa's inept driving resembles Azuma's bad driving in *Violent Cop*. Here, Murakawa manages to veer off the wide open road and gets stuck in a ditch, making it necessary for him to call his subordinates to pull the car back on the road. When Ken asks how he could drive off such a wide road, Murakawa first replies, "A snake crossed the road." Then, when Ryoji says, "You don't have a license, do you?" Murakawa answers, "She [Miyuki] was driving," excusing himself on entirely different grounds. Murakawa's inconsistency here suggests that the accident occurred because he and Miyuki were engaged in sexual play while driving. Nevertheless, Murakawa gives his excuse clearly and without hesitation, and so the car's "derailment" from the roadside is emphasized.

Finally, as an example of "interruption," we can take the sequence where Ken and Ryoji become angry because Uechi's bath has used up the water for their showers. After Ken and Ryoji begrudgingly accept Uechi's reply that "You can wash your hair when it rains," a rain shower actually breaks out. The two men happily strip to the waist and go outside to shampoo, but as soon as their hair has been thoroughly lathered up, the shower is suddenly "interrupted."

"Misfiring," "derailment," and "interruption" are each a small death. Insofar as they are concerned with the ultimate frustration of an attempt to carry something out, we can say that they each possesses a Kafkesque absurdity, even if only to a slight degree. However, each also harbors a pathogen that can bring the disease of "discontinuity" to the formerly continuous normalcy. Before turning into gags, "misfiring," "derailment," and "interruption" are inevitably united with the "discontinuity" that is the basic principle of *Sonatine*'s cinematic grammar. These secondary themes contribute to the hint of ill fortune that colors the film.

SONATINE IS THE SEQUEL TO *VIOLENT COP*

As Kazuyoshi Okuyama has noted, *Sonatine* has a mysterious power to dampen the spirits of those who come into contact with it. As I have suggested, this power can be attributed in concrete terms to: the sapping of propulsive force and the consequent floating sensation created by not filming the characters' feet; the state of alienation that afflicts the body; the consistent use of blue as the color of death; the cinematic grammar of "discontinuity," which is the inverse of "continuity"; and the secondary themes of "misfiring," "derailment," and "interruption" that contribute to this "discontinuity." These all represent the flip side of the direct sensation of power and strength that was apparent in *Violent Cop*. Indeed, they attest to *Sonatine*'s status as a sequel to or a successive development of the earlier film.

In *Violent Cop*, death was the result of life overflowing. In other words, death and life were placed in an inverse relationship. It is through this reversal that the work gains its exuberant, cinematic quality. In *Sonatine,* however, death, though taking "discontinuity" as one of its variations, is meticulously and exhaustively explored *as death.* The subject of death is brilliantly manipulated on the screen in a detailed and elaborate manner, yet since everything in the director's consciousness is subsumed towards this exploration of death, the work lacks dramatic cinematic reversals or development. Thus, it is possible to conclude that in contrast to the action film *Violent Cop, Sonatine* is essentially an art film. Rather than stopping at this criticism, however, we should consider what internal factors within Takeshi Kitano prompted such a change in his work.

Kitano carefully constructed *Sonatine* to follow up on, and to further develop, *Violent Cop. Sonatine* opens with a scene of himself that already consciously establishes the grammar of "discontinuity," clearly differentiating it from the cinematic grammar of *Violent Cop,* which was based on "continuity." He thus erases the sense of violence's tenacity, exposing instead the alienation colored by death that exists in those who carry out violence.

Naturally, Kitano's descriptive powers, already evident in *Violent Cop,* have been further refined in *Sonatine.* (Since the film is created to this high standard, the moral responsibility for *Sonatine*'s poor box-office showing should not be ascribed to Kitano.) For example, *Violent Cop* objectively conveys Detective Azuma's outsider status and contempt for the new careerist police chief by showing him reporting to work late and reading a tabloid paper while the chief is giving the staff their assignments.

In *Sonatine,* however, Kitano directs a masterful performance that conveys Murakawa's position within the organization with a single cigarette. Murakawa is in the hostess bar with Takahashi and the yakuza boss, who has probably just suggested to the gang leadership that some members of the organization to be sent to Okinawa. This

cut seems to start abruptly in mid-stream, beginning at the moment when the boss has finished his speech. The boss silently eats an hors d'oeuvre, while the gang members nervously, even petulantly, watch his hands. Murakawa, discontent, is the only one who has already begun to smoke. At last, as if to break the heavy mood, the boss tells the other men, "You may smoke," and they relax and light their cigarettes. From this one cigarette, Murakawa's position as an outsider is revealed, and the contrast between him and the other leaders in the organization—who for the time being at least are subservient to the boss—is instantly made clear. This level of directorial mastery, in which a single cigarette can speak with such eloquence, is virtually absent from other contemporary Japanese films.

The unpredictable and powerful depiction of violence in *Violent Cop*—which comes from its emphasis on right angularity—is deftly pursued in *Sonatine*, which also follows the tenet that true violence arrives from an unexpected direction. This is especially true of the scene in the Okinawan bar where Ryoji and Ken, wary of an enemy attack, are on the lookout for suspicious movements outside the bar. We are shown a strange series of interactions between the two men in parallel montage. The relationship between Ryoji and Ken, which can be seen as a variation on the one between the two young soccer players in *A Scene at the Sea*, is one of the few positive aspects in the movie, and is really quite beautiful. It begins when Ryoji brings up an extremely local, personal, and trivial subject, "Do you know the store 'Station-front Tomy's'?" he asks. As this conversation begins to

a sonatina thrice repeated, ending in death

develop "continuity," Ken gradually loosens up, and the two begin acting like close friends, even engaging in play such as a game of "William Tell" with handguns. The two men are, however, quite different. Ryoji is more introverted and, with his love of machines and bombs, something of a pyromaniac; Ken, who seems to be Ryoji's senior, is at first glance merely a tough, loyal sidekick to Murakawa. From time to time, however, he also shows an appealing humanity and affability that causes him to be chewed out for making fun of Katagiri's aloha shirt.

Returning to the scene in the bar—actually, just before this scene, to the medium shot of Katagiri and Uechi in a disco, their faces illuminated by a mirror ball. This shot is accompanied by the sound of someone being tortured, so we can surmise that they are watching the interrogation of one of the junior members of their rival yakuza gang. Murakawa's gang and their Okinawan allies have already fallen into a contest of revenge and counter-revenge, and the situation is tense and volatile. The scene in the bar, crosscut in parallel editing with the scenes between Ryoji and Ken, unfolds in this context.

Murakawa and his gang come into the bar. As they enter, Murakawa—cautious, of course—checks out the other clients. The

only customers there are three men with a rather casual appearance who are drinking and joking with their waitress in a booth. The overweight proprietress, her hair wrapped in a bandanna, comes out. When Murakawa and company order drinks, she replies, "We're getting busy now, so I'll call some girls in." If the proprietress is in

beat takeshi vs. takeshi kitano

touch with Murakawa's rivals, this call should be some kind of signal: "This is Tomiko. Send some girls over. Mari and Jun are over there, aren't they? We've got customers." With a timing that seems to confirm these suspicions, three men who look like ex-yakuza enter the bar. The men discuss what they're going to order, and Murakawa watches them suspiciously. At this moment, gunfire rings out from an unexpected direction—from the three men who were in the bar from the beginning. They are gunned down by Murakawa and his men, but not before a waiter who was bringing in beer is caught in the crossfire and the life of one of Murakawa's allies is also taken. (This man's body is thrown into the sea at dawn the next day.)

The shock when the gunfire rings out in the bar is immense. If there were assassins in the bar, it is natural for us to think that they would have been the three gangster types who had just walked in, since drama is always built upon the effect of small details. There is no reason to suspect that the other three men knew beforehand that Murakawa would be coming to the bar; they seemed to pay no attention when Murakawa and company entered. Moreover, a considerable amount of time had already passed without incident. Thus the viewer will have already dismissed these men as "safe" and paid them little attention. But it is because the gunfire comes from these men, who have already been established by the film's setup as perfectly harmless, that the shock of this scene is so severe. The extraordinary sense of "direction" that Kitano brings to this mise-en-scène is rare in contemporary film.

a sonatina thrice repeated, ending in death

In this way, *Sonatine* takes advantage of everything that Kitano had discovered in the making of *Violent Cop,* then adds something more. The grammar of death, i.e. the grammar of "discontinuity" noted above, is one of these additional elements. Next I would like to discuss one more such element and its relationship to *Violent Cop.*

GRINNING AND GOOD HUMOR

Beat Takeshi is always fatigued in his movies. His roles never require him to act lively. In *Violent Cop,* Detective Azuma does not listen constructively to his boss's admonitions; indeed he does little to conceal his contemptuous boredom. Neither does he show high expectations of his subordinate Kikuchi, or give him any technical training. In *Boiling Point,* Uehara is caught appropriating his organization's funds and is on the verge of being expelled. Yet rather than trying to ambitiously recover the ground he's lost, he merely seems exhausted. As a result, his sudden, violent, and indiscriminate sexual drive can be viewed as a kind of physical transformation brought on by exhaustion. (This sexual drive crests after he and Tamaki destroy their own yakuza organization with machine guns, and Uehara rapes a rather unattractive female office worker).

Sonatine's Murakawa, however, appears to have already passed beyond this state of exhaustion. He does not have sexual intercourse in this film, which seems to signify that he has already fallen into a state of sexual impotence. Indeed, don't his relations with Miyuki occur out of a self-awareness of his own impotence? In the context of the idleness of Okinawa, the kindness that Murakawa shows Miyuki (and the consciousness of distance that underlies this kindness) only manifests itself in un-yakuza-like pastimes such as fishing and going for drives—i.e. in "healthy" amusements. It seems as though he views Miyuki through the eyes of a man about to die,[11] and so he doesn't begrudge adjusting himself completely to her wavelength, as if he were already an old man.

In *Violent Cop*, Azuma doesn't begin to see the world through the eyes of a dying man until the climax of the film (this is why he shoots his sister). *Violent Cop* is constructed around a gradual internal crescendo that builds to the point where Azuma gains a dying man's perspective. The film's dramatic action follows along this same course, thus preserving a trajectory towards death. From its very beginning of, however, *Sonatine* is already firmly planted in the realm of death. In other words, when compared with *Violent Cop*, the distance that Murakawa must travel towards the resolution of suicide—i.e. the distance between the starting and finishing points—is extremely short. The only developments that take place in *Sonatine* come about through slight changes in Murakawa's "dying man's perspective." In this regard, *Sonatine* is a minimalist film much like *March Comes In Like a Lion* (Sangatsu no raion, Hitoshi Yazaki 1991), though the same cannot be said of *Violent Cop*.

Reconsidering *Sonatine* with a focus on Murakawa, we can say that Murakawa's smile functions as the site of a barely discernable range of concrete variations that are typical of minimalist films. Unlike the roles played by Beat Takeshi in other Kitano movies, Murakawa does not go through the entire film wearing an ill-humored expression. Confronted with the unrelenting idleness of the Okinawan scenes, Murakawa displays a good humor that almost seems to have come from lost momentum. However, since the viewer knows that this good humor surely derives from an overwhelming consciousness of death, it becomes something to fear. While *Sonatine* can be said to be no more than the story of a man waiting to die, the most thrilling aspect of the film is its depiction of Murakawa/Beat Takeshi's high spirits, which go even beyond a reconciliation with death.

a sonatina thrice repeated, ending in death

In the Tokyo scenes, Murakawa's smiles or laughs are only "skin deep" reactions such as embarassment or sarcasm that lack existential depth. For example, when Murakawa first sees Kanemoto trussed up and hoisted over the water on a crane, he laughs, "We do some crazy shit, don't we?"—a reaction that probably conceals his own embarrassment at the extremes to which the yakuza are prone. However, when the hanging Kanemoto proposes to give him a cut of his profits, the "skin" that had enclosed his expression instantly stiffens. That is to say that Kanemoto possesses absolutely nothing that cuts to the core of Murakawa's existence; his dealings with Kanemoto are purely "skin deep."

Then there is the scene where the yakuza who are going to Okinawa gather in the gang office and introduce themselves. Murakawa has the following exchange with Takahashi, whom he had recently beaten up in the restroom:

MURAKAWA: "You'd be happy if I dropped dead."

TAKAHASHI: "Yeah, it'd be safe to take a piss."

Murakawa laughs when he hears Takahashi's line. Though Beat Takeshi's laughter may appear innocent at first, there is often nothing gentle about it. His eyes do not laugh, making it impossible for the viewer to relax. Takahashi is thus reacting appropriately when his expression does not change in response to Murakawa's laughter. Since this is basically an exchange of sarcasm, one might expect Murakawa to try to put a sarcastic grin on Takahashi's face. But unlike the Beat Takeshi of TV, who tries to infect the people around him with his own laughter, the Beat Takeshi of film merely uses his laughter as a weapon in his arsenal of superficial assaults.

Murakawa's smile in the Tokyo scenes only intensifies the "skin-deepness" of embarrassment or sarcasm. The entirely different type of grin Murakawa shows next drives the audience to absolute fear. This occurs in the scene that begins with Ken and Ryoji shooting a pistol at empty cans placed on each other's heads. At the start of the scene, as Murakawa watches the two men from afar, his face is expressionless. If anything, his face might be somewhat stern from suppressing his emotion at the sight of the two young men flirting so carelessly with death. However, when he approaches them, there is a strange gentleness in his expression. Murakawa tells Ryoji to hand over his gun; he spins the cylinder, removing all the bullets but one, and fires it into the air. This is plainly preparation for Russian roulette, and Ken and Ryoji's expressions consequently begin to distort with surprise and fear. Especially noteworthy here is the brilliant timing with which Beat Takeshi's Murakawa, taking advantage of his senior status, unhesitatingly urges them to play "paper, scissors, stone." This timing, together with the direct and cheerful tone of his voice, carries an authority that Ken and Ryoji are unable to deny. Ken loses the first two rounds. Each time Ken loses, Murakawa points the gun at him and pulls the trigger. Each time, the gun fires no bullet (this scene thus corresponds in theme with the scene of "misfiring" where Ryoji plants a bomb in the entrance to the rival organization's headquarters). What makes the strongest impression on the viewer here is the difference between the facial expressions of Ken and Murakawa.

Ken pleads, "Isn't this dangerous?" and actor Susumu Terajima's face flashes realistically between strained laughter and rigid fear (this "flashing" expresses the discontinuity of his existence). By contrast, the face of Beat Takeshi, playing Murakawa, transcends the category of realism. The viewer may well find Takeshi's grin here difficult to comprehend. This grin is like some sort of existentially alien substance that expresses the sheer anomaly of Murakawa's flirtation with death. Indeed, on a superficial level, it seems that Takeshi is merely "wearing" this grin. The contorted grin exhibited by Terajima expresses the fissured judgement of someone who cannot accept the illogical position in which he has momentarily been placed, a position that threatens the very continuity of his existence. Ken's grin, then, is perfectly comprehensible to the viewer. But what about Beat Takeshi's? His grin has a strange intensity, as if to dispel any meaning in excess of the grin itself. It is not formed on the surface of Murakawa/Takeshi's flesh, but somehow manages to penetrate to his very core. Or rather, it is nothing beyond a grin, transcending the viewers' ability to judge whether it is merely a shallow grin or a laugh from the depths of Murakawa's existence that has heretofore simply been suppressed.

Murakawa loses the last round of "paper, scissors, stone." Counting from the earlier blanks, this would correspond to the gun's last chamber. Ken and Ryoji, who are released from their acute fear, jokingly ask Murakawa to confirm that he has lost. But when Murakawa, without the slightest twitch, draws the barrel of the pistol to his head, Ken and Ryoji suddenly realize the gravity of the situation, simultaneously yelling "Stop!" and attempting to prevent Murakawa from shooting himself. Thus, while Ken and Ryoji had alternated between fear and relief, in clear obedience to the laws

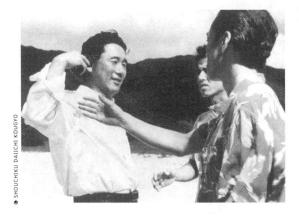

of reality, the unchanging grin on Murakawa/Takeshi's face appears to transcend reality. At this point, Ken and Ryoji, as well as the viewer, must realize that things have gone beyond a game of nerves. The scene has just the sort of "build up" required to give rise to this impression (thanks to Kitano's extraordinary editing), and has the additional

beat takeshi vs. takeshi kitano

effect of giving the viewer a premonition of disaster. Murakawa pulls the trigger at his own head, and the click of the empty chamber seems to reverberate beyond its actual sound. Then Murakawa, still grinning, exits the scene. Ken and Ryoji check the gun to confirm that there were no bullets inside, and conclude that this nightmarish ordeal was no more than a bad joke by Murakawa. With this established, the scene ends with Ryoji teasing Ken, "You were really shaking!"

But was disaster truly averted here? When this scene ends, does the viewer breathe a sigh of relief at the avoidance of disaster? The answer is no. Murakawa/Takeshi has shot himself with the empty chamber. The shock of this scene is not reduced when the viewer realizes that the gun carried no bullets. Murakawa/Takeshi has shot himself not in the realm of reality, but in that of unreality. The fearsome grin covering Takeshi's face—the "payoff" for the scene's "build up"—testifies to this fact. (In the "dream sequence" that immediately follows, the game of Russian roulette on the beach is repeated, and this time Murakawa actually does shoot himself. This dream sequence is unnecessary, however. It only dilutes the impression of uncanny fear fostered by Takeshi's grinning face, thus proving the power of this first scene where Murakawa/Takeshi shoots himself with an imaginary bullet. It would have been sufficient to show Murakawa just waking from a nightmare. It is unlikely that Takeshi Kitano is unaware of the fact that repetition can have a diluting, rather than strengthening, effect on the purity of a unique event. If this is true, then the insertion of the dream shot has serious implications, giving rise to the suspicion that, beyond a performers' penchant for repetition, Kitano is pursued by the idea of suicide on an existential level.)

Nevertheless, the grin displayed by Murakawa/Takeshi during the game of Russian roulette functions to completely alter the realistic, "skin deep" smile offered by Murakawa in the Tokyo scenes. From this point onwards, the idle Okinawan days take on entirely different qualities from the Tokyo scenes: they are both "immeasurably close to death," and exhibit "a certain lightness." After Murakawa shoots himself in unreality with the empty cartridge, he evinces a major transformation, wrapping himself in the special kind of good humor that comes before death. He laughs while playing with the paper sumo wrestlers. He laughs at the incongruity of Katagiri's aloha shirt. He laughs when he watches the slapstick sumo competition between Ken and Ryoji. Or consider the scene when he and Miyuki go for a drive:

MIYUKI: When was the first time you killed someone?

MURAKAWA: In high school.

MIYUKI: Who was it?

MURAKAWA: My old man.

MIYUKI: Why'd you do it?

MURAKAWA: He wouldn't let me fuck.

Murakawa also laughs in this scene. Whether or not this Oedipal "tale" is true within *Sonatine*'s reality, Takeshi Kitano seems to say that the exaggeration of such a "tale" should be properly met with laughter. At any rate, Murakawa's laughter seems to come from his own embarrassment at confessing a "laughable" tale that resembles the dramatic and chance-ridden *Oedipus Rex*: here, his laughter acknowledges his own high spirits.

Murakawa/Takeshi's laughing continues. He laughs in the moonlight when Ken, Ryoji, and later Katagiri fall into his traps. He laughs when talking about death and fear with Miyuki on the rocky shore. When he and Miyuki get caught in a tropical shower and take refuge under a tree, he laughs as Miyuki takes off her soaked t-shirt, and quips, "Impressive. You're not afraid of showing your tits!" When the men play war with fireworks on the beach, Murakawa/Takeshi laughs again. Murakawa/Takeshi laughs merrily as Ken and Ryoji shoot at a frisbee just before Ken is killed by an assassin disguised as a fisherman. All of this laughter seems to issue from the bottom of his heart. In no other performance in his own movies does Beat Takeshi laugh with such frequency.

Towards the end of the film, Murakawa's enemy, Takahashi, comes to Okinawa. After a gunfight in which Katagiri and Uechi are sacrificed, he is captured by Murakawa and brought to an empty field. Placed in this strained circumstance and tortured by Murakawa, Takahashi nevertheless bravely suggests that Murakawa take over Nakamatsu's territory, offering to serve as an intermediary to the boss on his behalf. Murakawa's sarcastic laugh on hearing this offer, which occurs under the rules of "reality," is in clear contrast to his wholehearted laughter in the previous scenes.

There is a general air of freedom to the group that forms around Murakawa/Takeshi in Okinawa, a group that includes Uechi, the Okinawan yakuza, and even the sudden, eccentric addition of Miyuki. The sense of Murakawa/Takeshi's respect for each member's individuality blankets the entire group. Thus, just before his attack on the hotel, Murakawa/Takeshi urges Ryoji, who is now the group's sole surviving member, to go straight. Objectively appraising Ryoji's personality, Murakawa recognizes that the young man's technophilia and knack for survival could well be applied to the straight world. This indicates both the friendship between two men who have faced life and death together, and the generosity of someone who stands at the apex of his organization towards a subordinate.

Boiling Point also features a group formed in Okinawa around the character played by Takeshi, in this case Uehara, and Tamaki, played by Katsuo Tokashiki. In contrast to the delicate balance of

a sonatina thrice repeated, ending in death

repulsion and attraction demonstrated by the group in *Boiling Point*, however, the group in *Sonatine* coheres in the simple and light-hearted manner of lost momentum. This excess of lightheartedness is critical: all scenes of Murakawa/Takeshi showing indignation at the death of his cohorts and subordinates are excluded from the film. Murakawa's uncanny kindness stems from his awareness that all of his gang members have been placed in the stratum of "death." But wasn't he from the very outset completely lacking in any positive will to resist his own death? Murakawa is a leader who passively accepts the equal dispensation of death to all the members of his gang. He feels kindness towards them because he is aware of this dispensation.

In other words, Murakawa's kindness arises from its participation in the consciousness of death; it is the obverse of death, and the viewer naturally becomes aware of this. The more Murakawa demonstrates kindness, the more the temptation of death becomes clear—hence the uncanny quality of this kindness. Murakawa/Takeshi is truly revealed. This kindness transcends performance, striking the viewer as evidence of Takeshi Kitano=Beat Takeshi's actual fascination with the realm of death. Thus the viewer will doubtless feel a shudder at Murakawa's kindness. This shudder was absent from *Violent Cop*, which at first viewing seems to be no more than an excellent thriller.

A MINIMALISM DERIVED FROM MATERIALISM

The viewer soon comes to realize that *Sonatine* is nothing less than a passage towards death. Murakawa/Takeshi's death is a given. Therefore the sequence just prior to the final credits transcends the issue of whether or not Murakawa/Takeshi will die; it only resolves the suspense of how he will die. This scene is also superb. Murakawa, who seems to be driving his blue car towards a reunion with the waiting

Miyuki, inexplicably gives up and stops the car beside an Okinawan field. The distance between Murakawa and Miyuki is made clear through the intersession of a passing yellow truck. Murakawa is then shown through the front window of the car. Any trace of a smile or laughter has completely vanished from his face, and his tense expression is stamped by the conflict of one who is concretely faced with death. He places a pistol squarely against the side of his head. Here, the viewpoint changes to a shot from the side, and we realize that Murakawa has shot himself from the blood that splatters across the window in back of him.

The camera then pulls back to reveal a landscape that abstractly represents the death that has just occurred: an overcast sky; wind (something about the scene portends cold); a wide, unpaved road; grasses waving in the breeze; a lone blue car parked at the edge of the road. All of the images collected here in a long shot—especially the eerie light from the cloudy sky—appear as true images of death. (The eerie quality of light of the sky here, in which the upper part of the sky is dark and a faint glow is seen on the horizon, strongly resembles the faint light of the sky in *A Scene at the Sea* when Shigeru's floating surfboard suggests his death). Following this long shot, we see brief paired shots of Murakawa/Takeshi's corpse, and Miyuki waiting in vain. As noted before, however, the intercession of the yellow truck has already made clear the considerable distance between the two figures (Murakawa did not go over the hilltop; nor does Miyuki react as if she heard the gunshot). Thus we comprehend that Murakawa/Takeshi has died a solitary death, and that this death has definitely not been staged for the benefit of Miyuki as a spectator.

It is in the moment of Murakawa's suicide—not only his smile, but the image of the suicide itself—that the smallest discernible degree of variation in the film is realized. The viewer will doubtless superimpose the Russian roulette scene and the dream sequence that follows it on the moment when Murakawa puts a bullet through his head. Yet the final moment of Murakawa's actual suicide does not lose its sense of singularity due to the interposition of these preparatory scenes. Rather, one has the illusion that all of the earlier suicides reverberate endlessly in this single instant. Earlier I wrote that the scene where Murakawa shoots himself in the dream was unnecessary. Reviewing this third, actual suicide, I have come to realize that this judgement was mistaken. The scenes where the suicide is merely an "empty bullet chamber" or a "dream" are filled with a strong light. In this last suicide scene, however, it becomes clear that true death is merely a material thing unrelated to powerful light.

Something else also becomes evident in this final scene of suicide: the strange sense of temporality that is possessed by *Sonatine* itself. I have already suggested that the close-up of a full moon that is inserted into the film three times, together with the overwhelming blueness of the night, indicates that *Sonatine*'s Okinawa is ruled by atemporality=death. This atemporality is reinforced by the repetition of Murakawa/Takeshi's smile, as well as by the repetition of his suicide, which is presented with minute variations.

Sonatine marks out the minimal time span required for the actual death of a man who has resolved to die. (Even the enemy lacks a clear depiction in the Okinawan scenes. The sole enemy depicted, the assassin played by Eiji Minakata, only passes across the margins of the scenes like some ominous portent. Here, unlike in *Violent Cop*, there is no organic dramatic conflict that unfolds between the protagonist and his enemy. Hence, rather than being an action film, and despite its use of yakuza material, we can term *Sonatine* a minimalist film that gives a psychological sketch of its protagonist, Murakawa.) Just as the spliced-in shot of the moon is repeated three times and then vanishes, so too the suicide scene is repeated three times and then vanishes. (This threefold repetition causes a shudder. It reminds me of the three denials by Saint Peter in the Bible, or the three repetitions at the conclusion of Jun Ishikawa's *The Virgin Conceives* [Shojo kaitai, 1970].[12])

Sonatine's minimalism spans no more than an event occurring three times and ending in death. Within this brief span, subtle variations arise in all manner of things, but after the third occurrence, everything reverts to "death." Minimalism is an expressive form that gives rise to a "small beauty" or "small pleasure." In setting the flow of the film's "minimum discernible differences" on an incline towards death, Kitano recomposes the significance of the minimalism that is at the very root of the film.

Without question, the title of the film *Sonatine* refers to the mode of a "small" work in that Kitano's vision delves into the minutiae of "small things" and finds there the ubiquity of death. I believe I can summarize the sense of temporality and indeed the worldview expressed by *Sonatine* as follows: although there are differences between each of these "small things," in a larger sense each is governed by atemporality=death; even given the vivid differences among individual things, within the span of "three times" they all face an inevitable death. According to this temporality and worldview, tranquility, gentleness, and kindness are all but a flash that illuminate the instant before death.

Thus, after completely acknowledging "reality," Kitano constructs on top of this reality not an "aestheticism," but rather a "thanalogism," or an artistic consciousness pervaded by death. And this consciousness is all the more disturbing since it is founded upon a complete acknowledgement of reality. The film then fades to black—its own perfect "death."

Finally, after the closing credits (white characters rolling upwards against a black background), a completely unpopulated scene appears.

a sonatina thrice repeated, ending in death

The boat from the scene where Ken was shot has washed up on the sand. The blue cooler carried by Eiji Minakata's assassin lies there, tattered and abandoned. In the background, a clump of sunflowers sway silently in the wind. This is an image of a firmly settled death, after the traces of the film's characters have been wiped away. Although the two scenes are separated temporally, this scene harmonizes with an earlier scene of death—the long shot of the blue car where Murakawa/Takeshi has died. This final scene tells us only one thing: that a wind is blowing over "death." In contrast with the similar moment in *A Scene at the Sea*, Joe Hisaishi's music matches the mood of this scene well. Hisaishi's synthesizer score is based on the Okinawan musical scale, which omits some of the tones of the Western scale, giving it a primitive, nostalgic, and utopian sound.

FATIGUE UNVEILED IN THE SUNLIGHT

I am reminded of Murakawa's cold gaze—as if looking at a science experiment—when the crane lifts Kanemoto out of the water for the second time, a gaze that easily penetrates to the weakness of existence itself. Such a gaze probably extends to Murakawa himself as well. In general, yakuza and sunlight are a complete mismatch. In *Sonatine*'s sunlight, Kitano takes the yakuza, who could be termed Romantic "vampires" as well as social "bloodsuckers," and uncovers their fundamental weakness. They lose all sense of direction in this intense sunlight, and have no way of liberating themselves apart from play. And in truth, there is no fulfillment in this liberation either. All the yakuza except for Murakawa wear playful aloha shirts that send their yakuza aesthetic into retreat. They die miserable deaths—particularly Katagiri and Ken—not as yakuza, but (although it may not appear this way) as weaklings whose yakuza-ness has half dissolved in the sunlight. Takeshi Kitano views the deaths of these weaklings with the detached gaze of a scientist observing experimental specimens. The Okinawan sunlight is his supplemental illumination, and the sandy beach is the slide for his microscope. Such is the stage-set that Kitano has devised for his tale of destruction.

If we recall the final scenes of *Violent Cop*, first Kiyohiro is killed by Azuma. Then Azuma shoots and kills his younger sister, who is pathetically searching Kiyohiro's body for heroin. At this point, Azuma tries to leave the scene. He is illuminated by a ray of light from the warehouse door. A shot rings out: it was fired by Shinkai, Nito's right-hand man. In a strained voice, Shinkai exclaims, "They're all crazy—every one of them!" What does Shinkai do at this moment? He turns on the light switch in the warehouse. This light coldly reveals the material appearance of Azuma and Kiyohiro—whose organic relationship had so propelled the film's drama and who together had ascended to the realm of death in such a cinematic fashion—to be corpses bathed in blood. The sunlight that bathes the Okinawa scenes in *Sonatine* is precisely the same as the dispassionate light switched on at the end of *Violent Cop*, shattering its dramatic illusion.

Returning to *Sonatine*, we might ask what position does Murakawa, as played by Beat Takeshi, have among the film's self-destructive yakuza. As I suggested earlier, he appears on the screen "already dead." A man who has resolved to die is already death itself. Murakawa alone has been clearly conscious of death, and so has already died. Unlike Azuma in *Violent Cop*, his walk does not overflow with the power of life. Even if he commits suicide at the film's climax, he cannot be called a typical self-destructive yakuza along the lines of Rikio Ishikawa, as played by Tetsuya Watari in Kinji Fukasaku's *Death of Honor* (Jingi no hakaba, 1975).[13] This is because Murakawa's role in *Sonatine* is more as a "modern man" than as a yakuza. Beat Takeshi's Uehara in *Boiling Point* is much closer to being a self-destructive yakuza of the Rikio Ishikawa-type than Murakawa.

On the other hand, the scene of Murakawa pointing a gun to his head has something in common with a scene in Eleanor Coppola's documentary *Hearts of Darkness* (1991), which reveals that her husband Francis Ford Coppola put a gun to his own head amidst the extreme chaos on the set of *Apocalypse Now* (1979). For Takeshi Kitano, film is a toy, and the shooting location is a festival. What should we make of the fact that Kitano would require a suicide at the center of this festival of his own creation? Does it not indicate his fatigue at the road he had travelled thus far under the name "Beat Takeshi"?

Kitano releases "Beat Takeshi," whose existence is so deeply intertwined with TV into his own films. That is, he shows the overwhelmingly real physical presence of his body in his films. Yet, in *Sonatine*, he also reveals the fatigue of this physical body Indeed, this urge to strip everything, including himself, bare, represents a clear act of violence against televisionesque, sugar-coated contemporary culture. The clear fatigue of Beat Takeshi's body and sensory apparatus harbors a negative magical force that invites the viewers themselves into the realm of death. It is difficult to view this invitation indifferently. Through his own very popular body, Takeshi seductively appeals to the viewers, urging, as Kazuyoshi Okuyama puts it, "Let's all die." *Sonatine* thus publicly diffuses the "pathogen of death."

The film's box-office failure was probably due to its relative lack of famous actors (and in particular actresses), and to its frequent use of cinematic abbreviation, which is ill-suited to the tastes of young filmgoers who have grown accustomed to an excess of explanation. But perhaps this film's failure to become a hit was an effective public health measure against the spread of contemporary "death" (I am of course being sarcastic). I am not sure what self-mocking comments "Beat Takeshi" may have made about the film's limited commercial potential around the time of its release. But no matter what televisionesque spin "Beat Takeshi" put on the film, the dispensation that "Takeshi Kitano" metes out to "Beat Takeshi" in *Sonatine* is nothing short of murder—the complete negation of "Beat Takeshi." Indeed, it is a pathos-filled act of negation towards all of the televisionesque contemporary culture that has embraced "Beat Takeshi."

a sonatina thrice repeated, ending in death

06

a double-header: "spirit vs. body"
and "performer vs. artist"

"HEART" AND "SUBTRACTION"

On the release of *A Scene at the Sea*, Shigehiko Hasumi published an interview with Takeshi Kitano=Beat Takeshi titled "Next time, I might just take it seriously."[1] In this interview, Takeshi Kitano gives some intriguing reasons as to why he became involved in the film's editing. Hasumi and Kitano's exchange runs as follows:

> HASUMI: In *A Scene at the Sea*, you did the editing yourself. Was this because you couldn't entrust the work to anyone else?
>
> KITANO: Yes, I believe so. You see, I thought of that movie as a space of Japanese *noh*,[2] and I was the one who saw it when we were filming. At that time, I was more or less conscious of my own heartbeat, and so I saw the picture as my heart beating and the blood circulating through my body. It's most comfortable to watch the film we shot with my own heartbeat and pulse. It would be hard for me to have it cut to the rate of someone else's heartbeat. This was a really selfish film, and so I cut it to fit me comfortably. If I had turned the material over to someone else, they would have cut it to an entirely different pulse.

One gathers from Kitano's remarks here that, through his editing, his films move at the same tempo as his heartbeat. To put it another way, his films are his own "heart" itself; to this extent, his films move in conjunction with his own body, even if he does not appear as an actor in them, as is the case in *A Scene at the Sea*. (Kitano's films, which are directly tied to the "body," are full of surprising ellipses and a sense of speed; they are united by a methodology that aggressively rejects anything extraneous, dramatically amplifying the sensation of "death." But this is a separate question.) From first to last, what Kitano depicts in his own films is the "body"—principally his own "body."

Another thing that becomes clear in this interview is how Kitano's directorial technique of using "subtraction" makes this "body" more prominent:

HASUMI: In *Violent Cop*, there is a large white room used by the syndicate boss. Was that a set?

KITANO: We borrowed a newly constructed building for that. Of course the art directors and set designers want to do their jobs, so they tend to add a lot of things. They never take things away. If you say, "This doesn't really seem like a syndicate boss's room," they'll say, "Okay, how about putting some lockers over here," making the situation worse with more unnecessary things. So one time we just had to take everything out of the room. We put in one table and called it quits. So it may seem like the art directors aren't doing their jobs, but maybe they're doing a big job by having the courage to do no job at all.

One thing I always say is that in manzai you've got to keep talking. But with something like a picture, the picture

a double-header

tells the story, so if you try to explain it verbally, it somehow turns false. If you try and symbolize that picture with words, you end up giving unnecessary information to whoever's looking at it, so I think that should be avoided.

. . . I often make my art directors cry. They'll make a two or three million yen set, and then I won't go there at all. When they ask, "What should we do with it?" I'll tell them, "Why don't you break it down." It seems it's quite a shock for them. (Laughs) But if I didn't do that, it would ruin the film. When I look at it, and it doesn't look right, I don't use it—you have to have the courage to eliminate things.

Kitano's words here raise a lot of difficult issues. On face value, it would seem that this attitude severely limits the area of set design, but the main point is that he places a high value on "subtraction" in his directorial arithmetic. The secret of his technique as a director is that, when every unnecessary element has been eliminated, what becomes visible is the actor's body. However, if a director were to build a two or three million yen set and then never once use it, he would inevitably receive strong criticism from the production staff, who would wonder why he had asked them to build the set in the first place. Thus, although Kitano's directorial gift is for "subtraction," when given free reign, this gift itself becomes a threat that the producer must seek to eliminate. From the realistic perspective of contemporary filmmaking, one hesitates to lavish praise on Kitano's unique directing talent. If a set comes out contrary to Kitano's intentions and cannot be used, the very fact that it was built in the first place indicates a problem in communication between the director and the art director.

beat takeshi vs. takeshi kitano

At any rate, there is no doubt that Kitano's "subtractive" directorial technique is bound to provoke the ire of his producers. Furthermore, this "subtraction" is directly connected to the "grammar of death" in Kitano's films. Just as he takes away from his sets, he "kills off" his characters. In the same way that he "takes away" from his sets and makes unwelcome suggestions to his producers, he shoots unwelcome films in which people die off, one after another, further compounding the ire of his producers. Such is the cursed cycle that Kitano finds himself in. Yet just as Kitano's elimination of unnecessary objects from the set accentuates the bodies of his actors, so do the deaths of the characters.

However, we should also note that televisionesque contemporary society generally avoids this type of fully-revealed body. That is to say that contemporary society, which is composed of a mass of viewers with televisionesque sensibilities, treats bodies with a strong existential presence as objects of loathing. The fact that Kitano's anti-TV films, which use the representative TV star Beat Takeshi, have failed to become hits attests to the fact that the sensibility of moviegoers has already become televisionesque. In fact, the tendency of a television sensibility to avoid Kitano's films is a measure of the overpowering nature of Beat Takeshi's body in these films.

This was first evident in *Violent Cop*, in which Beat Takeshi's body became the agent of overwhelming violence. His violence in that film has an astonishing persistence, and its endurance creates a magnetic field that concentrates the negativity inherent in his flesh. Although this body tends towards negative emotions, it embodies a thoroughgoing strength, so it is not afflicted by any sort of pathology. In his performance as Detective Azuma in *Violent Cop*, Beat Takeshi's emotional intensity gradually increases despite his efforts to suppress it. If we observe the pathology of Beat Takeshi's work, however, we see that the power of his presence gradually decreases over the course of the roles he plays in his films. First of all, in contrast to the sense of concentration demonstrated by Azuma in *Violent Cop*, Uehara begins to suffer from "diffusion" in *Boiling Point*. Although this accurately reflects the "diffusion" that afflicts contemporary society, Uehara/Takeshi's body is difficult to accept. Unlike most members of society who suffer from "diffusion," Uehara in *Boiling Point* has a violent power that bursts forth unexpectedly in several different directions. However, by Beat Takeshi's next appearance in *Sonatine*, this violence has been repressed, and Murakawa is enshrouded by the gloom of death. For those viewers who are unable to experience fear when confronted with this body, this must be simply and irredeemably depressing.

Takeshi Kitano's movies are all movies about death. If we observe their flow, we will see that they begin to approach closer and closer to death. From a producer's point of view, it is not necessarily unwelcome for movies of a certain unwholesome type to give off the scent of death. Basically, people enjoy watching death. However, it is unforgivable for a film to truly approach death, halting the Brownian motion that stirs the film's very particles so that it comes to rest on death itself. "As you yourself admit, you killed the artistic director. You killed the scriptwriter. This was all the fault of your directorial technique of 'subtraction.' In order to bewitch people with the 'death' in your films, you killed the very staff who were your biggest sympathizers. Don't you realize this?" The frightening thing is that any producer admonishing Kitano with words such as these would not be guilty of misreading the situation, but would instead have struck at the very essence of Kitano's films.

THE BODY AS A BULWARK AGAINST DEATH

Amidst this cycle of films dealing with death, Kitano's "heart" becomes discouraged. In the interview with Shigehiko Hasumi mentioned earlier, he relates the following words of "death":

I think I should quit when the time comes to quit. But I wonder where I'll get the insight to know when the time has come. All of the work I'm doing now, comedy or whatever . . . I wonder where I'll find the end to it. There'll come a time when I'll just have to say "I have no more talent left." The people around me will doubtless be nice and say, "You can still do it," but I've got to make the judgement myself. If my own judgement goes bad, then it's all over. You know, there's no reason to feel sorry for an old man who's gone senile—he probably doesn't even realize he's senile. So someday I won't even know when I don't have any talent—that's why I should go ahead and decide in advance. I can still do it now, but when I start to slip, I probably won't realize it. So I think I should quit in about five years. But basically I'm just a dirty old man, so I'll probably keep on "doing it" anyway. I really have no shame—I'll probably say, "Well, I'll still do some acting."

In an interview with Yoichi Shibuya, Kitano speaks even more clearly about his disillusionment:[3]

As for comedy, it's become quite tough, for what—five or six years now?—it's been tough. I guess comedy is really more about being a good talker than having talent. Especially talking in front of other people, it's more like a nervous reflex. Now that reflex is getting dull, so even while I'm talking I get irritated. You see, it's possible for your ad lib to be really on target, but lately I feel like it's a little off. I felt it was a little off from about five years back, and I told myself I was getting worn out. When I go to see young manzai comedians perform, though, I feel a little relieved. I can see that they're just rearranging material I used to do in the old days, and I tell myself I can still get by doing the same thing. But then again I think, "No, I can't do it!" and it's really quite painful.

To put it plainly, what Kitano says here comes from the disillusionment that accompanies the self-knowledge of age. If we focus on the words "nervous reflex," however, we realize that all of his words are bound together in the territory of the body. Indeed, Takeshi Kitano's speech (as opposed to that of Beat Takeshi) is always steeped in the rhetoric of the body, and thus comprises an "ideolect" whose strength is different from that of conventional speech. At any rate, it would seem that his disillusionment arises from his own body.

The circuit formed by Kitano's spirit and body is indeed circular; the spread of disillusionment from one to the other does not by any means cut off this circuit. This is clear from another part of Kitano's interview with Yoichi Shibuya:

SHIBUYA: In your films, the protagonist always and without fail dies. When I watched your new film *Sonatine*, it occurred to me that actually you can't die in real life, so for now you try to take care of this by dying in your movie. (Laughs)

KITANO: (Laughs) Yeah, someone like Yukio Mishima could really die. I've thought about why Mishima was able to die, and you see, his body was never able to keep up with his spirit. Apparently, he had a problem with his motor nerves, and he really struggled to bring his body up to the same strength as his spirit—doing karate, kendo, body building, boxing, and so on. But his body was never able to reach the same level. So, in a certain way, death was the highest price that his spirit could ask his body to pay. In my case, if I tried boxing, my body could probably manage it. So instead of the spirit doing away with the body, the body is able to respond, and this kind of puts the brakes on things. If I had a problem with my motor nerves, I'd probably do what Mishima did, too.

Kitano's words here speak volumes, regardless of what one thinks of Kitano using Mishima as a comparison. To paraphrase, "suicide" represents the victory (or something like the humiliation) of the spirit over the body, but in Kitano's case the "body" is stronger than the "spirit," and so the suicidal impulse is naturally repressed. With the exception of *Sonatine,* where Murakawa seems completely exhausted, the life-force implicit to the roles Kitano plays in his films is the saving grace that prevents viewers from falling into the depths of hopelessness, despite the fact that his films are permeated with death. In other words, Beat Takeshi is the "star" of the films in the true meaning of the word, and the full implications of this are what make Kitano's words in this interview so powerful. "The body is the bulwark against death"—if we use this simple truth to scrutinize Kitano's films, in which the "body" is always revealed, we will be close to discerning the secret of the aesthetic that unites all of his films.

Shifting the focus onto Kitano himself, however, it seems to me that his "body" is not the only thing preventing him from suicide. Obviously, the dualism of "body" and "spirit" underlies the words of Kitano's interview. It occurs to me that this very dualistic way of thinking functions as a way of preventing Kitano from taking his own life. Such dualism pervades Kitano's thinking across an entire range of subjects: life and death, sex and love, men and women, words and images. Kazuyoshi Okuyama's essay on Kitano suggests what lies at the roots of this dualism.

I remember what he said one night at a bar in Akasaka, soon after we first met. As we were drinking, our conversation drifted to private matters. He told me, "Even while I feel love for myself, there's another me who's always looking at myself with detachment."[4]

The dualism of one's self and another self-who-observes-one's-self-dualism of Beat Takeshi and Takeshi Kitano—is another vital force that prevents Kitano from suicide. In this case, the paradoxical modifiers "self-love" and "detachment" (literally "sobriety") are taken from the basic vocabulary of existentialism. Staving off death through "self-love" alone would be no more than pointless vanity. But if this self-love is undergirded by "detachment," then throwing off the self would be to set another self free—such, at least, seems to be the philosophy of Beat Takeshi=Takeshi Kitano.

In the previously cited interview with Yoichi Shibuya, Kitano refers to his filmmaking as "letting off steam." In other words, if he couldn't make films, his freedom of spirit and his body, which has been alienated by television, would be completely bottled up; perhaps, this suggests, he might even have chosen death. Just as his body is a salvation for his most sincere viewers, his films have become a way to restore his own body—i.e. they are a salvation from death. This is not the pride or indulgence of a man privileged enough to make films into his "toy." Even if we detect a certain arrogance here, we can hardly pass judgement after seeing a man recover from the crisis of suicide.

Actually, there is not a trace of self-absorption in Kitano. Proof of this can be found in his interview with Yoichi Shibuya:

SHIBUYA: What I thought was really funny when I watched [the television show] *Heisei Board of Education* was when the show became controversial, and you were asked about the ending animation. You didn't understand the question. You hadn't been watching the show, had you? (Laughs)

KITANO: (Laughs) Yeah, I hadn't watched it at all. I'd ask "What's 'The Diligent Student'?" and they'd say, "We do that for the ending," and I'd say, "Oh, that's the kind of show it is." I hadn't seen my own show. Just because I'm in it, does that mean I have to watch it?

SHIBUYA: You don't watch any of your shows, not just *Heisei*?

KITANO: Almost never.

SHIBUYA: From the very beginning?

KITANO: Yeah. Well, you're assuming that I'm at home when my shows are on. If I were, I'd watch another channel for sure. You see, I've already done those shows.

Here, we can glimpse Kitano's preference for speed. Thus he is instantly able to overcome the stagnation of self-consciousness. Considering the ubiquity of his own image, one cannot help but be amazed at the power of Kitano's intellect to grasp his own self-image without ever looking back on it contemplatively. However, since his intellect is indeed such that he can objectively view his own self-image, he can easily avoid the modern pathology of loss of self. If one understands that Kitano, who possesses such an intellect, is seeking after suicide, then one must also realize that this death wish is not an issue unique to Kitano alone, but must be considered from the wider perspective of contemporary society. Actually, the self-portraits that emerge from Kitano's interviews are not those of a special public performer, but of a contemporary man. The following exchange can be found in the same interview with Yoichi Shibuya:

SHIBUYA: You weren't allowed to watch *anime* when you were a child?

KITANO: No—I couldn't read *manga* either. That was absolutely not allowed at our house—our mother was an "education mama." So now I'm really interested in the kinds of things that kids do in kindergarten.

SHIBUYA: What sort of manga or anime do you look at?

KITANO: Well, for anime, *Sailor Moon R*. (Laughs) I really look forward to that! That's on Saturdays at 7—the same time as *Heisei Board of Education*. (Laughs) I'm such a pushover—I even buy Sailor Moon goods! "That one's coming out in June"—I'm really quite knowledgeable! (Laughs)

SHIBUYA: You watch it by yourself, not with your children?

KITANO: My kids are already past that—they spend all their time on computer games.

SHIBUYA: What kind of manga do you read?

KITANO: Lately I've been reading erotic manga, kind of like sex-education manga.

SHIBUYA: Do you mean "ladies" comics'?

KITANO: Those are pretty good, too! (Laughs) I watch adult videos, too.

SHIBUYA: Weren't you a fan of adult videos a long time ago?

KITANO: Lately, I've been making my assistants go out to get me the ones where they really show pubic hair, where they're really doing it. So I'm able to kill time pretty well when I'm at home.

beat takeshi vs. takeshi kitano

SHIBUYA: Watching *Sailor Moon R* and adult videos—you're really spending some quality time at home.

SHIBUYA: As far as your [home] environment goes, aren't these things you were through with ten years ago?

KITANO: What are you trying to say? That I'm getting senile? (Laughs) I'm getting more and more like a kid—next they'll have to put diapers on me. (Laughs)

Kitano's consciousness completely mirrors the "decadence" and "regression" of contemporary society. Without the slightest attempt to conceal it, he states the pathology of contemporary society, himself included. And this becomes a sort of code in his films. What is the code held in common by Takeshi Kitano, and, for example, David Lynch, Peter Greenaway, the Jonathan Demme of *Silence of the Lambs* (1991), and Quentin Tarantino? It is an aesthetic of the "display of corpses." Not only is this a question of aesthetics, it is one connected to a type of ethical disposition that does not hide the cracks in reality, but instead envisions corpses there. Takeshi Kitano directs Beat Takeshi as if he were the ultimate corpse. The fact that he himself, and indeed his own body, becomes an issue in his films marks a subtle difference between Kitano and the other filmmakers just mentioned. But it is hard to deny that the regressive self-portrait that emerges in the interview above also has something in common with the character of his films.

THE HISTORY OF THE PERFORMING ARTS AND *MANY HAPPY RETURNS*

Beat Takeshi's oddity also exists in this same dimension. That is, his oddity exists on the same plane as contemporary society. However, Takeshi Kitano＝Beat Takeshi uses a different word to describe this oddity. In the interview above, Yoichi Shibuya returns to the point that Kitano does not review his own performances, which causes him to lose sight of his manzai roots; he recalls Kitano's words that he "had the feeling about five years ago that the response [to his comedy] was dampening." When Shibuya suggests to the actor/director that these are very dangerous signs, Kitano replies as follows:

> At first I was at a real loss about what to do. I tried quitting smoking and drinking, or making my body more flexible. (Laughs) But doing such idiotic stuff was no good at all. Because after all I'm just a freak, from the perspective of television. I'm like a freak, so the question is how I'll wind up in the end—will I end up totally wasted or not? Will I go to waste when my talent runs dry? Or can I make money by showing off what a sad state I'm in? Maybe I'll give that a try. (Laughs)

It is likely that Kitano's use of the word "freak" here is connected to his occupational consciousness as a "performer" or "riverbed beggar."[5] According to his historical view of the performing arts, the performer is actually a "freak" who is able to overturn some elements of contemporary society. Furthermore, his "oddity" also functions as a line of defense, warding off an effusion of literary praise. Only one person has been able to mold this historical consciousness of the performing arts into a film. This person is none other than Toshihiro Tenma, who for some time has served as Kitano's faithful and commonsensical assistant director.

Tenma's film *Many Happy Returns* (Kyoso tanjo, 1993) includes an original screenplay by Takeshi Kitano, who produced and performed in it as well. If we can say that this film has an ethical beauty, it is because it completely understands and adheres to Takeshi Kitano=Beat Takeshi, though in fact the production of the movie carefully avoids Kitano's filmmaking techniques. With its cautious and moderate spirit, it illuminates Takeshi Kitano's films and Beat Takeshi's body from an entirely different angle. It is indeed lamentable that so many commentaries (particularly in magazines and entertainment guides) blindly identified the film's technique as having been inherited from Kitano.

Although *Many Happy Returns* does not have much uniqueness with regards to story, if we focus on the character Beat Takeshi plays, Daisuke Shiba, we will see that this role hides a mechanism that has the dangerous potential to overturn the film as a whole. The main theme of the film is the strangeness of the creation of new religious cults, and the strangeness of a contemporary society that encourages this creation. Daisuke Shiba/Beat Takeshi, however, functions as a hinge that opens this theme up in a totally different direction. By placing Takeshi Kitano=Beat Takeshi in this position, Tenma shows his love and respect for Kitano.

In contrast to the establishment of new religions in the past, the formation of religions in today's information-driven society lacks a firm footing in artistic innovation. In the past, the tales of holy signs and miracles that were used to propagate new religions were often set to the melody of a *sekkyobushi* narrative song.[6] This was one source for the development of the arts.

In *Many Happy Returns,* Masami Shimojo plays the founder whose miraculous ability to "walk on water," "stay underwater for over ten minutes" (consider this against the death of Kanemoto in *Sonatine*) and to "heal the sick" is proselytized by Shiba. As the story progresses, however, Shimojo is chased out of his position as the cult's founder. The narration that Shiba uses to establish the founder's credentials does not refer to modern or contemporary society, but rather pre-"modern society"—in other words, the realm of the "performing arts." Thus, in the last scene we are shown brief vignettes of the founder, who has already been chased out of his position, reuniting with Shiba, who has just killed the fanatical, ascetic believer Komamura (Koji Tamaki); the two put aside their past differences to resume proselytizing on the banks of a pond. This scene, which is not found in the shooting script published in *Scenario* magazine,[7] is not intended as a gag. Rather, it effectively impresses upon the viewer the fact that Shiba and the founder have belonged to the realm of the "performing arts" all along.

NEARER TO GOD

Shiba, played by Beat Takeshi, sticks out from the others in the cult, since he ultimately has to place himself in the realm of the "performing arts." Thus Beat Takeshi=Takeshi Kitano's position as an artist is demonstrated by Toshihiro Tenma, the man who understands him best. Actually, the foundations of this cult are highly dubious, and the "diffusion" of its members due to this fundamental weakness can represent the diffusiveness of the "world" itself. (Tenma must have learned this from *Boiling Point*.) The single-minded pursuit of profits; the fabrication of miracles; the concealment of sexual relationships in order to preserve the group; the inflexibility of people who can't adapt to reality; the ambition to rise to the top of the organization; failures in communication; affairs; death—these are nothing other than the phenomena that inevitably arise in a world that suffers from "diffusion." In order to set up such a "world," all the figures within the cult are carefully placed so that they can maintain their positions in a "diffuse" manner. (In this respect, *Many Happy Returns* is as much of a "theory of baseball" as *Boiling Point*.)

Among the film's "diffuse" characters are the protagonist Kazuo (Masato Hagiwara), who enters the group as a shady outside element and advances to the position of "new founder," rapidly transforming his unreliable sense of reality into a strange fanaticism. The other characters are: Go (Ittoku Kishibe), who thinks the purpose of the group is the pursuit of profit, and so disingenuously enters a friendly alliance with Shiba (Beat Takeshi), while secretly harboring ambitions of supplanting his superiors in the organization; the pitiful Komamura, who finds value only in spiritual training through poverty and abstinence, and whose fundamental inflexibility makes him a heretic within the group, eventually leading to his sacrifice when he falls into a romantic trap; and the original founder, a lonely old drifter who is placed in the position of "founder" as a matter of circumstance, but who nevertheless falls into an alcoholic rapture and begins to believe in his own miraculous powers, with the result that he is chased out of the group as a dangerous element.

Finally, there are Hisae (Yoshie Minami), a good-natured old woman who becomes a sincere believer when she miraculously regains the ability to walk on her shrivelled legs; Yoko (Miyako Yamaguchi), a middle-aged woman who seems to be a true believer, but whose main concern is her secret affair with Shiba; and Yoko's good-natured but slow-witted daughter, Tomoko (Aya Kokumai), who lacks the willpower required to pursue the possibility of pleasure outside of the religious group, and instead tries to seduce Shiba, her mother's lover, despite the fact that she lacks the necessary craftiness. These differing character traits represent nothing other than the nature of "diffusion" in today's world. Beat Takeshi's Shiba stands out in this crowd—and in particular contrast with Go—as the only character who suffers from real emotional and spiritual conflicts.

The first half of *Many Happy Returns* follows these characters as they move from place to place in provincial Japan trying to spread their religion. In fact, in some respects, the film calls to mind the time-tested plot of such pure road movies as Wenders' *Kings of the Road* (1976). This road-movie appeal, together with the dramatic provocativeness of the depictions of the on-screen "miracles," flicker in the gap between truth and falsehood, permitting us to rank this as a successful work.

a double-header

That does not mean, however, that the film is an overwhelming master-piece. Since the inner conflict of Beat Takeshi's Shiba is never fully expressed, the film climaxes with shouted lines that seem to echo Jean Genet. The film's ultimate underachievement comes from the fact that it is unable to capture the depth of this dialogue in cinematic terms.

The dialogue is instead shouted at Shiba by Kazuo, who has usurped the position of "founder" and has begun to take on a strange dignity. Komamura, who has fallen into a sexual trap devised by Shiba and Tomoko, begins to fight back like a cornered rat attacking a cat. In the midst of their struggle, Shiba ends up killing Komamura. For the first time, Shiba is faced with the realization that he has killed someone. (Beat Takeshi infuses Shiba with a physical presence com-pletely different from that of all the roles played by Beat Takeshi in Takeshi Kitano's films; for the first time, he gives a completely natural performance as a man facing the fact that he has killed. Just before he kills Komamura, who has fallen on the floor, Shiba repeatedly and "obstinately" kicks him. However, perhaps because he is not wearing shoes in this scene, Takeshi creates a different sort of physical impres-sion than in his other films. It is as if the actor Takeshi has a voltage switch embedded in his body, and can vary the proportion of "strength" and "weakness" or "positivity" and "negativity" with infinite precision. In this scene, Shiba/Takeshi projects a very subtle physical-ity—say, seventy percent "weakness" and sixty percent "negativity." Undoubtedly, part of the fascination of *Many Happy Returns* is the revelation of Beat Takeshi's "body" in this particular scene.) At any rate, Shiba is faced with the reality of having murdered Komamura, and the oscillating expressions on Shiba/Takeshi's face reflect the many troubling thoughts passing through his mind. At this moment, Kazuo, played by Masato Hagiwara, utters coldly, "So, Shiba, God has finally punished you. Is this the only way you could get closer to God . . . by sacrificing Komamura?"

The idea that one can approach closer to God by killing someone is connected to the philosophy found in the words of the medieval Buddhist priest Shinran:[8] "The good man will certainly attain rebirth in paradise. Yet all the more so the evil man!" In such a case, however, the evil perpetrated by a murderer must leave its traces on his or her inner conflict. Within the "real world" of *Many Happy Returns,* Shiba has slipped into the reality of murder after having been torn between the contemporary world and the divine; traces of this tragic fate must remain. (Needless to say, the above lines of dialogue are also a criticism of the crowds of bodies that have accumulated in Takeshi Kitano's previous films. If we can say that these films are filled with a spiritual strength, it is due to the mediation of a Genet-like mythology governed by the contrary fantasy that the yakuza of these films are "holy men" anointed by their taking of human life.)

Nevertheless, the traces of inner conflict that we would expect from *Many Happy Returns'* Shiba are actually quite faint. For example, just beyond the midpoint of the film, Shiba reads the notes for the group's newsletter written by Kazuo, who has just become the new "founder." The two exchange the following lines:

KAZUO: Do you think Komamura will okay with these "notes from the founder"?

SHIBA: Who cares? Just write "This is the word of God" at the end.

KAZUO: How could I do that!

SHIBA: Why not? God is something you can't explain. That's the whole reason for God's existence.

KAZUO: I don't think I'm cut out to be founder.

a double-header

SHIBA: A founder is just a sacrifice. He's like a human sacrifice to God by the believers. There's no need for him to understand God.

KAZUO: ...

SHIBA: Religion and reality don't mix. It's because they don't mix that we've got religion and God. That's why religion is a comfort for people tired of reality.

In this film, Shiba is constantly expressing the view that the true nature of salvation is that "the believer believes," rather than that "God exists." (Another example occurs in the train scene where Shiba approaches Kazuo, who has not yet joined the sect, and tries to dispel his doubts that the lame old woman [Yoshie Minami] whose legs have been miraculously healed by the founder is actually a fake.) Since we learn from Komamura's fond recollections that Shiba had been quite enthusiastic about the sect's rise in the old days, we can say that Shiba's conflicted consciousness is implicitly expressed in the film's "present," when he and Go are consumed with amassing huge profits through donations. However, such a conflict is nothing more than an interpretation based on the script, not a conclusion based on the actual film. As Makoto Shinozaki argues, Takeshi Kitano's films are the farthest thing from explication, and are therefore a true rarity among contemporary Japanese films. In this sense, *Many Happy Returns* does not attain the level of Kitano's own films.

A QUESTION WITHOUT A DEFINITIVE ANSWER

To explore further Takeshi Kitano's conflicted consciousness with regard to God, we can return again to his interview with Yoichi Shibuya for the July 1993 issue of *CUT*:

SHIBUYA: Everyone thinks about death, and no one faces it in a happy mood. People feel gloomy about death, and most people facing death will try to escape it a little more than you. They'll take a religious or mystical tack, or they'll try to repress the issue altogether. Didn't you ever try this yourself?

KITANO: That's why I've read so many of those types of books. But they're all pretty dubious, aren't they?! Anyway, I just can't accept them myself. Dying is a kind of insurance—isn't the world after death a new world for everyone? I have no idea if the soul survives or not—it might just be nothingness—but wouldn't simple nothingness be something new, too? It's different from the way things are now, after all. So I'm interested in what death will be like, and I don't feel it's such an unpleasant thing. It's possible that we have some sort of out-of-body experience after death, where we're looking at our own body—that'd be pretty interesting too. So this is a kind of insurance. But I don't think we should try to cash in on this insurance right now. When I die, I'll enter this strange world that I've been so curious about, so it's really something to look forward to, not something to be afraid of. That doesn't mean that I'm going to die right away—I'd rather wait for the insurance policy to mature a little. (Laughs) Life itself is pretty sketchy—we don't really know what it's all about. I don't know why I'm talking here like this. Sure, you could say it's just chance, but it's pretty exasperating to sum up everything with the simple word "chance." So I want to find some reason for it all, I want to be able to give myself some reason for the fact that the earth is here, and that I was born in the year

Showa-something[9] and am now wearing a suit and talking like this. I still don't understand these things at all, or I don't understand all of it, and so I guess it's a good idea to think these things over like we're doing now.

SHIBUYA: Haven't you ever felt a strong fascination with religion, as one supernatural approach to these questions?

KITANO: Yes—very much so. I've got a tremendous interest in religion. But—to start with the question of God—it doesn't really matter if he exists or not. Of course, I'd be happy if he did. But I've never heard the voice of God, and I've never recognized something God was trying to say in my own consciousness. And when I read religious tracts, I always feel like they're a lie, so I guess my own head or heart just doesn't go along with it. My conclusion is that there's an overwhelming difference in power between human beings and God, and there's no reason why humans should be able to understand the words of such a different being. So even if God was present for someone, who'd be able to receive his message? To give a rather childish explanation, if you said "I am God" to a frog and began to make all sorts of complaints, there's no chance that the frog is going to say "Oh, I see what you mean." I think it's about as impossible as that. But after death, the conditions change, so if people retained some kind of consciousness after death, I'd say there's about a fifty-percent chance that we could understand [God's message], so I have some hope in this possibility.

We could summarize Kitano's comments here as follows: "It would be more interesting to believe that there's a world after death";

"therefore, I am also interested in the existence of God"; "on the other hand, from the vantage point of the afterlife, 'reality' is extremely uncertain"; "even if God does exist, the realm of God and the realm of humans are completely different"; "therefore, God continues to be unknowable for mankind." Since these arguments are consonant with the views of many people in contemporary society who join new religious cults out of a half-baked sense of reality and a vague desire for self-betterment, they can thus be deemed a revisionist realism. Kitano's comments show glimpses of the conflict within a man drawn towards death who tries to resist this temptation. As arguments, however, they are actually quite commonsensical and boring.

As I suggested earlier, Takeshi Kitano's body is superior to his spirit when faced with death, and this body tries to escape death. Therefore, his spirit (or mind), which is inferior to his body, has nothing to say to us about death or God—such, at any rate, would be the most unflattering interpretation. But actually no one has a definitive answer to questions about God or death. Such questions are different from the self-questioning that occurs on television, since no one can avoid their unanswerability. (Thus, to make a film that squarely confronts the subject of death is itself a rebellious betrayal of televisionesque culture.) This is why Kitano's novel *Many Happy Returns* (Kyoso tanjo, 1990) upon which the film is based, is incomplete. I suppose it would be perverse of me to wish that Takeshi Kitano's views of God and religion were closer to the side of evil (e.g. that he would proclaim "Death and God are nothing other than themselves, but the body, in its treachery, can overcome even these.") Since Kitano's interrogation of religion is confined to this dimension, the film *Many Happy Returns,* based on his own novel, also remains limited to the scope of a "caricature of contemporary life."

Nevertheless, the line "Is this the only way you could get closer to God?" harbors a fearsome depth that momentarily surpasses these limits. Evil is a means of approaching nearer to God; divinity resides not in thought or prayer, but in action. We can glimpse here a fearsome quality that has the potential to overturn traditional religious values. But this is ultimately a subjective interpretation—there is no solid evidence of a sustained philosophy that we can trace throughout the film.

The last scene, however, impresses quite a different feeling upon the viewer. This feeling stems from the recognition that Takeshi Kitano=Beat Takeshi's historical understanding of the performing arts, going as far back as their origins in premodernity, is directly connected with his own body. Indeed, this leads to the realization that, although he may have stepped back momentarily from the front lines, Takeshi Kitano=Beat Takeshi can overturn commonsensical reality with his loutish performer's face, liberating "reality," clothed by death and religion, into a state of anarchy. This realization occurs in a dimension that transcends his works—it is sufficient for the viewer to experience it directly and emotionally. "He has understood himself not as an artist but as a performer." Confirming this strengthens my confidence in Takeshi Kitano=Beat Takeshi, who I have always perceived to be a man not of the spirit, but of the body.

07

*finally, transcending
"beat takeshi" . . .*

MATERIALIZING THE OTHERNESS OF THE BODY

It is time to answer the question of how Takeshi Kitano has directed
Beat Takeshi. First, as I have argued in detail, Takeshi Kitano rigor-
ously treats Beat Takeshi as a "body." As suggested in chapter six,
even though this body is definitely pregnant with "death," it also
possesses a force that resists suicide. Thus he has been able to
reclaim the life of his own body from the repression of television.
This is why he calls the movie set a "pressure valve." However, pro-
gressing from his directorial debut to his most recent film, this body
has become increasingly shrouded in an air of fatigue, and thus has
become more and more foreboding. Even so, we should not forget
the simple fact that this body retains the strength to frustrate the
spirit's suicidal pressure.

With a sure and prophetic power, Kitano's films point the way
for the films of the future. Insofar as the films of the future also reject
the pathological "complexity" that increasingly afflicts American
movies, then Kitano's films can surely be deemed a post-American
cinema. That is, his films express the beauty of "simplicity" to a
remarkable extent. However, this is but a result. I must emphasize
here that it is unwise to try to evaluate Kitano's position from the

point of view of film history. Rather, it is better to approach this task with the knowledge that Kitano is the person in Japan who has best employed the strategy of "anti-television."

When considering the duality of television and film, it goes without saying that television has developed out of a thoroughgoing realization of what is cinematic. Nevertheless, while television is governed by "homogenization," as if adhering to a magnetic field, Kitano's films are governed by the field of "otherness." Various phenomena of "pure cinema" arise in the midst of this field. Indeed, these phenomena have been the subjects of my previous discussion in Chapters 2 through 5.

By way of recapitulation, the various phenomena of pure cinema can be grouped into three aspects: time, space, and the body. The aspect of the "body" in Kitano's films entails a materialization of an "otherness" that is completely unique in contemporary Japanese film (Junji Sakamoto's *Tokarev*[1] would be the only possible comparison). This "otherness" arises, of course, from Kitano's critical disposition towards televisionesque homogenization. However, the majority of viewers fail to assimilate to this "otherness." Instead, they simply feel repulsion. The phenomenon of Kitano's works being avidly praised by a few while failing miserably at the box office arises from this misprision.

Kitano has incorporated extremely heterogeneous elements into the aspect of "place." In *Violent Cop*, with the help of cameraman Yasushi Sasakibara, he realized "place" as the concrete location for continuous "action." From there, he went on to realize the abstract space of "diffusion," "absence," and "void." It is plain that his mania for "subtraction" was the driving force behind this transformation.

We could venture that Kitano's treatment of "time" is the most remarkable of all. His ability to continually realize pure time rather than narrative time is extremely rare among film directors. In his first film, he captured the most fascinating cinematic time, that of "continuity

finally, transcending "beat takeshi" . . .

itself" (this was realized not merely by long takes, but as a result of the circulation of power enacted by the way the characters are edited). Subsequently, he introduced an experimental filmmaker's radical sense of decentered time punctuated by "diffuse explosions" *(Boiling Point)*, and then a tragic sense of time, in which everything has already occurred, leaving only "traces," yet which is replete with the possibility of reversal *(A Scene at the Sea)*. Lastly, by pushing the editing function to the fore, he successfully realized a different type of cinematic pure time, that of "discontinuity" *(Sonatine)*.

Of course, Kitano's treatment of time stands in an organic relationship to his treatment of space. Furthermore, this treatment of time and space is reinforced when he fuses them with his own (Beat Takeshi's) flesh and body. One wonders if there has ever been a "physical movie" auteur as strong as this. What is truly surprising is that this has all been achieved within a framework that the average viewer can appreciate as "simplicity." Moreover, by taking on the theme of "death" or "suicide," Kitano has positioned himself directly opposite the mainstream of Japanese filmmakers such as Shinji Soumai, who endlessly return to the theme of "rebirth."

Kitano's body has thus travelled through the following trajectory: an anxious body, climbing step by step towards a multivalent suicide *(Violent Cop)* in his films; a tentacular body, thoroughly infected with the modern pathology of "diffusion," which, experiencing a tinge of euphoria, "diffuses" even that moment of concentratedness on the path to suicide *(Boiling Point)*. The trajectory then passes through the body that camouflages itself with its own anticipation of death, embellishing itself with its own afterimage amidst the great "thereafter" that is reality, to the point where it can no longer be called a body *(A Scene at the Sea)*. And finally, the trajectory finds in the space of absence the body that martyrs itself, as if in order to present the audience with a microscopic view of a body plagued by "discontinuity" and fatigue—

though paradoxically this body can be seen as no different from that of an ordinary "modern man" *(Sonatine)*.

With the exception of *A Scene at the Sea,* these bodies are thrown on the screen with an overwhelming accuracy that stands up to the most minute scrutiny of metabolic functions, muscle structure, perspiration, and analysis of movement. Although I use the expression "thrown up on the screen," it goes without saying that Kitano does not resort to close-up shots to illuminate these bodies. Rather, just as the "body" impels the formation and composition of the film, the "body's" formation and composition are made manifest through the very movement of the film.

At any rate, the cinematic "other" known as Beat Takeshi is thus materialized as a truly breathing "other" that rises up autonomously, full of life, at a point far removed from the viewers. Its very ferocity is awe-inspiring. Indeed, Kitano's imagination has dissected the divine—but perhaps we can now state counterintuitively that only that which can be dissected is divine.

THE SELF-DESTRUCTION OF THE TELEVISIONESQUE BODY

Takeshi Kitano is living out a double life with "Beat Takeshi," and "Beat Takeshi" is none other than television. This is Kitano's second method of directing "Beat Takeshi." Television is the air in which "Beat Takeshi" floats, and undoubtedly "Beat Takeshi" has experienced a floating sensation with regard to his own televisionesque body. However, for Takeshi Kitano, this body is the other. The true other is not the body of "Beat Takeshi" realized in his films, but his own televisionesque body, which is deprived of gravity and exposed in television's homogeneity. This is why his activities on television have caused him such fatigue.

finally, transcending "beat takeshi" . . .

Of course, "Beat Takeshi" is that rare person who can express alterity with his own body. TV viewers have probably been drawn to Beat Takeshi the TV personality by an unconscious faith in this fact. However, ever since Takeshi Kitano=Beat Takeshi distanced himself from the extreme physicality of manzai comedy, there has been no doubt that no matter how much he is praised for being poetic, he has been troubled by the question of whether or not this televisionesque body called "Beat Takeshi" is identical to himself. From Takeshi Kitano=Beat Takeshi's perspective, film directing should have been a way to capture this self-identity. At a fundamental existential level, the "otherness" of the "acting" body was essential to being able to escape the closed circuit of "questioner=respondent." Thus acting could be sublimated to true pleasure. For example, it is well known that as soon as Kitano appeared on the set of *Boiling Point* as an actor, his role was generated by his tremendous creativity as a director, since he was working without a script. Following his own pleasure, he was compelled to imprint his own otherness on the movie screen. This was an issue not of self-revelation, but of salvation.

In this, he succeeded. Looking back, we realize that the seed for such a realization of alterity had already germinated in TV, the "home of Beat Takeshi." From time to time, amidst the inescapable "floating" of television, he surely became aware that the otherness of his own body was hiding in ambush, indistinct though it may have been. The film performances of Beat Takeshi expanded the traces of the alterity that already existed on TV as if tearing open a wound.

However, the question remains of whether Takeshi Kitano=Beat Takeshi was truly able to dispel the essential rootlessness of his own body that existed amid the flotation of televisionesque homogeneity. If he had, his film performances on screen would have been joyous affairs. This does not explain why he imprinted himself on the screen as a "suicide."

To imagine that in contemporary society one can happily travel back on forth on the circuit between TV and cinema is a fantasy. The film body would necessarily blur when transferred to TV, and so it is in fact natural that, with each circuit back and forth from TV to cinema, the body will increasingly be plagued with vacuity.

Moreover, the realization of the otherness of Takeshi Kitano=Beat Takeshi's body, which has been his personal salvation, is of absolutely no consequence for "TV" itself. (Only a lover of film can embrace this aspiration towards the body's alterity.) The viewers' self-love is spread across TV like a net; indeed, television is nothing beyond a giant illusion formed from the warp and woof of this net. Someone who travels willfully along the circuit between TV and film will not be supported by cinema, which has already lost nearly all of its status in society. Nor will he receive anything but malicious interference in the form of shallow criticism from TV to the effect that thematizing the body is too "heavy." This is only natural, given that TV shamelessly claims the right to define itself as "contemporary culture."

In this respect, attaching a cinematic body to "Beat Takeshi" is itself a kind of "self-destruction." In film, he directed himself completely as a body=thing. On a basic level, he did so to establish this body, but on a secondary level, he did so to bring about the "self-destruction" of this body. There can be no error here—this "self-destruction" is definitely factored into Takeshi Kitano's technique of directing Beat Takeshi. Hence the subject matter of his films: "self-destruction" vividly materializing into his theme of "suicide."

Not only the film set, but everything "outside" of television takes on the property of alterity. The televisionesque body incorporates the body of TV viewers, which is coated with the fantasy of homogeneity. When this body is exposed to alterity, it is inevitably placed on the path to "self-destruction." The "other" is something that homogeneity must not be allowed to meet—this is truly a universal problem.

finally, transcending "beat takeshi" . . .

Here we see that the suicidal death wish, which began as a personal matter for Takeshi Kitano=Beat Takeshi, merges into a death wish for televisionesque "contemporary culture." Beat Takeshi's problematic position in contemporary culture centers on this point. He is trying to realize an impossible circuit between film and TV.

This is a cursed proposal from the point of view of televisionistic contemporary culture (and yet how much longer will this culture exist?). Unlike Clint Eastwood, Takeshi Kitano is unable to realize the time-honored dream of the actor-director with a sensation of joy. Rather, he traces a path of inevitable defeat (although this defeat may be a glorious one). Kitano is clearly of a post-Eastwood generation. He demonstrates the fierce retaliation of a man uniquely close to TV who takes TV for his enemy.

Nearly everyone believes that so long as Takeshi Kitano is committing "suicide" in his films, he will not do so in reality—he is acting out "suicide" in order not to commit it in life. And they are more or less correct to argue that no one has the right to question this personal method of salvation. Be that as it may, it will be a Sisyphian labor for his filmography to continue in this same manner. This is what I mean by a path of inevitable defeat. Straddling the mutually estranged media of film and TV, Kitano repeats his circuit of "death" and "rebirth." Yet even if this personal narrative is elevated to the level of a myth about the impossibility of contemporary culture, it will ultimately amount to nothing more than vain heroism.

Each of Takeshi Kitano's movies to date has been a masterpiece of the first order, and each can easily become the object of unreserved devotion for film buffs. Yet no matter how much Kitano defies televisionistic contemporary culture by introducing his violent body into its midst, televisionesque culture will only suck these bold experiments up into itself. No one can be reborn into a new future from out of televisionesque contemporary culture, and it is likely that televisionesque contemporary culture will continue to extend its pernicious homogeneity into the indefinite future. As long as this is the case, anyone affiliated with television is unlikely to be able to escape this homogeneity through actions or even through "death," as the death of Masataka Itsumi illustrates. It is thus a logical contradiction to imagine that those who cannot escape "contemporary culture," even through "death," could bolt away and be reborn into a new "future."

The task at hand is of a different nature: Kitano's filmmaking strategy must break through to a new level. He must embody televisionesque contemporary culture and stake a position completely within it so as to transform cinematic "pre-contemporaneity" from the inside. This is my hope for Takeshi Kitano. Otherwise, he will never be able to break free of this cycle of impossibility. Undoubtedly, he has the potential to make many more thoroughly cinematic masterpieces suffused with impossibility. Nevertheless, I believe that this would be of no fundamental benefit to cinema. The trajectory of his films thus far has demonstrated his many strategies for avoiding suicide. Even if this arouses the moral sympathies of his viewers, however, it only serves to humor their weaknesses and does nothing for the future of cinema.

The task is thus to efface the dualism of "homogeneity" and "alterity" in order to avoid providing more fuel for its continuation— to neither be simply the "questioner" nor the "answerer," but, while on the surface establishing the structure of "questioner=answerer," to reveal the "differential" between "questions" and "answers," and to show the fissures of "otherness" within the "homogeneity" of contemporary culture. As a "man with a body of otherness," the manzai comedian Beat Takeshi has already been flickering across televisionesque homogeneity. All that is required of him now is to expand these flickers musically. If "Takeshi Kitano" wears the mask of "Beat Takeshi" in the context of homogeneity rather than alterity, his work will then indeed enter a new phase, and the dualistic battle of

finally, transcending "beat takeshi" . . .

"Takeshi Kitano" and "Beat Takeshi" can be resolved. It is thus not a question of which of them will emerge triumphant, but that the battle will be fought and resolved only by removing the difference between these two extremes. One may wonder how those who watch this battle will be able to distinguish between "homogeneity" and "alterity." But the means for initiating this battle are at hand.

ABOUT THE NEXT WORK [2]

Takeshi Kitano has been relatively frank about his plans for his upcoming works. (For example, the idea for "Okinawan Pierrot" that Kitano described to Shigehiko Hasumi in the third issue of *Représentation* took shape with no major differences as *Sonatine*.) In interviews with Hasumi and Yoichi Shibuya about the "crisis" in his filmmaking, he also talked about his ideas for his next movie after *Sonatine*:

SHIBUYA: If you're making a comedy, your stance towards the film must be entirely different. Up till now, your films have been a sort of pressure valve, but isn't this one going to be more stressful?

KITANO: Not really. You see, in this comedy I'm not afraid of shooting really bad jokes. Some filmmakers today put in material that's extremely refined, but I'm ignoring that sort of stuff altogether. I'm putting my shit right out there, so people will say, "Ooh, that's the worst!"

SHIBUYA: (Laughs) Like a parade of bad humor.

KITANO: That's right. Like people showing their balls and making fun of gays. And it should be pretty funny, since it's a "period drama."

SHIBUYA: A period film?

KITANO: Yeah. If it's a contemporary comedy, word will get out that it's a piece of crap. But I can retreat by saying that after all, it's a period film. Come to think of it, I'm always looking for a way out. (Laughs)

SHIBUYA: (Laughs) You're always competing in television, aren't you—throwing yourself into competitiveness.

KITANO: Not really.

SHIBUYA: But wasn't that the way it was from the beginning. Especially with your manzai?

KITANO: Well, maybe with manzai . . .

SHIBUYA: That type of total competitiveness was what led the way for everything to follow.

Or, we can look at the following exchange:

HASUMI: You've made three films now. The next one is "Hideyoshi"?[3]

KITANO: Well, now I'm trying to get "Hideyoshi" made somehow.

HASUMI: You're going to be actor-director?

KITANO: Yes. I'd like to shoot the flooding attack on the castle— was it Takamatsu Castle?—if I could do it right. It'd be hopeless if it looked like a composite shot. I'm planning to look for a pond and building the set of a castle right in the middle of it. Then it'd look more or less like the scene

finally, transcending "beat takeshi" . . .

after a flooding attack. Even if there wasn't a pond there to begin with, I'd like to find a place that would turn out that way if you put in water. We probably won't be able to start from scratch with sandbags and the like. But anyway, as a picture, I have an image of the lord of the castle coming out and committing seppuku. But I guess that's a pretty hackneyed image, so maybe I'd have someone suddenly attack him, and he has to react. I've got that image, and also I've got the idea that Hideyoshi should be really childish. There'd be someone like Sen no Rikyu,[4] and Hideyoshi would get angry and just slice his head off. He'd set up Rikyu's decapitated head across from himself and have a tea ceremony. He'd have that kind of cruel streak, but he'd be capricious—sometimes he would send out presents of tea implements to people around him like Kanbei Kuroda.[5] When the lord of the castle pleads for forgiveness and says he'll commit seppuku, Hideyoshi will suddenly kick him, or he'll rape his wife. But then, he'll forgive the lord. I have this idea of a real volatile character, so I think it could be pretty interesting.

If we're able to film it, I just may take it seriously this time. I feel like something has clicked in—to tell you the truth, up till now I haven't worried over the films so much—I took them pretty lightly, but this time I'm really going to put myself into them. But I'm also afraid if I put myself into it too much, I'll screw it up. (Laughs) I'll wind up in trouble if I get too smitten with it. (Laughs)

As I suggested in the first chapter, Takeshi Kitano as a subject does not philosophically create "Beat Takeshi" as an object. Rather, it is more often the case that the object="Beat Takeshi"=the "body" momentarily or transcendentally creates a philosophical statement. Thus, I feel certain that any sight gags he might create with his body in the realm of film, even those that incorporate masochistic scatology, would resemble a type of ballet or music, at least to the extent that they were formed out of the philosophy of the body. At such a time, the bodily rhythm of "continuity" that has propelled his films, or the quiet but disturbing rhythm created by the "cutting" of the body, will give rise to an entirely different meter.

This in turn will result in an entirely different trajectory from his previous films—one that has passed from the display of bodies with a strong sense of being to the display of their alienation. At such a time, the rehabilitation of the body that Takeshi Kitano=Beat Takeshi has attempted in the face of televisionesque contemporary culture will finally be completed. This rehabilitation of the body is the answer Takeshi Kitano has been forming from his youth in the '60s the present day.

Undoubtedly, the hope for a comedy film from Takeshi Kitano=Beat Takeshi is actually a prayer for the salvation of those who live in televisionesque contemporary society. The variety-show performances by Beat Takeshi and Akashiya Samma can create a state of bliss for their viewers that is unsurpassed by traditional manzai comedy. A sort of spark passes back and forth between the bodies of Beat Takeshi and Akashiya Samma in their roles of "cut-up" and "straight man," and this gives off a rich sensation of movement, like a momentary judgement that confirms their bodies. When combined with the floating sensation of the placement of their bodies in the space of television, their relationship is truly musical. In fact, it often reminds me of a jam session.

In shooting his comedy, Takeshi Kitano=Beat Takeshi could jettison the provisional sitcom grammar that comedy fans have internalized, creating instead an elusiveness that is, in its utter novelty,

finally, transcending "beat takeshi"...

closer to the realm of evil. He could, moreover, take the floating, musical sense of movement that he has cultivated on television and transfer it to the framework of cinema, an act that might have a self-destructive effect for cinema itself, and that could even transcend the genre of film. This "variety" embodied in film would take its lead not from Kiyoteru Hanada's unclear and idealistic "Theory of the Arts of Sight and Sound," but from Eisenstein's "Montage of Attraction." The placement of "attractions" in a "montage" could be considered a fault or even a kind of heresy from the perspective of film, which strives for conformity. But isn't this at base what we expect from "performance"? The sense of editing would itself be comedic. The brilliant editing talent demonstrated by Kitano in *A Scene at the Sea* and *Sonatine* inspires our trust, and insofar as the rhythm of his editing was based on his own heartbeat, viewers can expect his body to manifest itself through his editing in addition to appearing before them in the form of sight gags. The editing in a comic film by Kitano would probably not manifest as the kind of "cutting" that fiercely slices the viewers' perception in *A Scene at the Sea* and *Sonatine*. But even if this patchwork of "attractions" is shaded by the consciousness of "cutting," it could form a wider current that would be buoyed up by the richness of that line-up of "attractions."

Beat Takeshi's slight twitch, where he tilts his head towards his shoulders, is, I believe, an expression of his uncomfortableness in the space of TV, and as such is quite appropriate. Placing this kind of spasm at the center of his future comedy would be a safeguard against overindulgence, bringing a new element to film comedy. Kitano can begin to transcend the tautology of televisionesque contemporary culture by using the negative mediation of televisionesque contemporary culture, a not especially difficult process. Furthermore, by completely embodying the monstrosity of televisionesque contemporary culture—and therefore denying it—he would return to the enjoyment of disguise, hence avoiding the closed circuit of "questioner=answerer." He would also be spared the madness of "suicide." What we can hope for is not that "Beat Takeshi's" body will be anticlimactically revealed to be Kitano's own, but rather that this body will be liberated as a "performer" in a free-spirited jam session.

As a result, Takeshi Kitano=Beat Takeshi's strategy will change. While he proclaims on the one hand that the TV in televisionesque contemporary culture is indeed TV, he will probably also pursue making films that are personal expressions and that try to overcome the pretentiousness of switching from the self-assertively televisionesque to the self-assertively cinematic. By so doing, he can tear down the previous structure of his work, which had cast a pall over all of televisionesque contemporary culture, whose central axis is self-love. Compared with his previous work, where he placed his own televisionesque body in a cinematic space intended to break it down, this will not be difficult. He has called his own films "toys," as if to mock the difficulty of his own position in them. But he will probably not call his coming film a "toy." His statement that he will get "serious" with his next film should be understood in this context. The comedy he should shoot next will test the limits of his ability to be directly himself. And being himself should not, after all, be such a difficult matter.

The problem for the coming film comedy will be how to organize his "words," which are so volatile on television, in contrast to his terseness in film. What makes him so effective on TV variety shows is his volatile language, which can turn any given subject on its head—in other words, his verbal wit. However, even on variety shows, this kind of language is only used for brief periods of time. If he were to transfer that language to film, his viewers would become thoroughly fatigued. The contemporary significance of the Takeshi/Samma routines comes from the way they play with the various topics at

finally, transcending "beat takeshi" . . .

hand. Yet we must admit it will be extremely difficult to separate these various topics from their specific Japanese contexts and bring a musical continuity to this verbal play.

Will Beat Takeshi really play Toyotomi Hideyoshi? The critical spirit that he brings to his stiff clowning on variety shows is derived from the self-mocking spirit of the emperor's new clothes. In this sense, Hideyoshi is a good match for Takeshi. I wonder if he will draw nose hairs on himself—those anti-Chaplinesque, Asian-style nose hairs that look like they're drawn with a magic marker. By shooting a "period film," he will undoubtedly recover something that has been lost in contemporary films and the films of televisionesque contemporary culture—that is, the spirit that would overturn the present through a commentary on the past. Thus, for Kitano, a "period film" would not be a way of glossing over his inadequacies, but rather a framework for exposing his critical consciousness in a way that's different from his previous films.

I can say no more about the film Kitano is likely to make in the future. So, based on my previous remarks, I will conclude this essay with a prayer. In his next movie, may "Beat Takeshi" be a fervent talker. May his next movie be a comedy. May it exceed two hours—no, may it be a two-part movie exceeding four hours (with a change in its box-office fortunes, too). May it overflow with primary colors. May it flow to the accompaniment of bright music. May it not be simple, but rather filled with details, impossible to take in fully with a single viewing. And may it be televisionesque throughout, may it vie with televisionesque contemporary culture in speed and win. May it thus transcend both "film" and "TV." May it transcend even "Beat Takeshi."

section 2
articles

the long journey of the melancholy king

ONE

"Action exposes an illusion quicker than contemplation." In the days of the "Two Beats,"[1] when Beat Takeshi mounted an invasion of the space of television from Asakusa, he seemed to overflow with vitality and destructive force, a realization that comes to mind based on his furious torrent of phrases such as "Discrimination against old hags," and "Go to hell!"

The greatest "illusion" that Takeshi sought to dispel was that of the television space where he himself existed. Takeshi exposed the instability at the very foundation of television. However, we must inquire why this act of exposing never amounted to a decisive attack.

First of all, we can make the general observation that people who "expose" something derive their own form from the fissures that are subsequently created, and simultaneously obtain a type of strength from it. The movement of this exposure, which has a kind of thrusting-up quality to it, is naturally oriented towards the "outside." This movement of quickening and birth is necessarily violent. Subsequently, the one doing the exposing "separates" from the object of exposure.

The framework of "television" is formed by an agreement to "not say something." We can be sure that Takeshi sees through this agreement, and moreover realizes the indefiniteness of this "something." He is thus able to steal the "dignity" from falsehood (for example, the falsehood that television performers are "representatives" of the viewers). When Takeshi stirs up the falsity of the false with his own performance, television itself is inevitably transformed, and the space of television becomes "playful." At these moments, the heightened falsehood of television guarantees the actions and movement of Beat Takeshi the TV personality, and Takeshi's actions and movement in turn heightens the falsehood-shattering playfulness of the television space—thus creating a relationship of mutual reflection and reinforcement.

This mutually reflective relationship between the performer and television's own framework stipulates television's high level of "interiority." Thus, Takeshi does not "move to the outside" through his act of exposure, but rather "enters" even deeper into the falsity of television. This, in turn, ultimately serves to strengthen the "interiority" of television. This is the mutually reinforcing condition of television and Takeshi: insofar as television gravitates towards Takeshi, television increases its interiority; insofar as it deepens its solipsism, it gravitates further towards Takeshi. This (to return to our original question) is why Takeshi's method of exposing television's illusions lacks the quality of a decisive attack.

Needless to say, someone who is capable of heightening the interiority of television will have all the more value as a television performer. The taboos that Takeshi breaks in his speech (for example, by using the word "omanta") are not in themselves taboo, but rather exist on the margins of taboo (at a very close distance). Nevertheless, it is thrilling to watch television's pretenses being shaken. In the process, television as a whole becomes richer. As it territorializes its margins (and the margins are always being enfolded into the interior), its interiority only increases. This movement of renewing the interior is itself "Takeshi." The viewer undoubtedly breathes a sigh of relief that this movement towards the interior is actually a friendly one. (So for some malcontents to say that they have gotten close to Takeshi's aggressiveness would be mere delusion).

Of course, television is encompassed within the terms "contemporary culture" and "Japan." As a result, Takeshi has naturally extended his range of critique to include "contemporary culture" and "Japan" as well. Consider, for example, one of his trademark observations: that "Red lights aren't dangerous if we all cross them together." With this observation, he takes aim at the Japanese temperament with deadly accuracy. Yet rather than devising a wide-ranging, derisive "theory of Japaneseness" as seen from below, his expression is closer to being a simple "sign."

In other words, since Takeshi does not destroy the space of television, which is expanding homogeneously into its periphery, he can only maintain the position of a gadfly for a moment at a time. The Takeshi that exists subsequent to these moments is merely a "trace," and so he must increase both the frequency and speed of these momentary flashes. He becomes, in fact, a flickering existence (e.g. by wavering between being an introvert and a wiseguy)—a "sign." His "words," such as "Discrimination against old hags" and "Go to hell," also become signs.

This flickering existence comes with its own type of "pathos," as if Takeshi were merely a yardstick for the majority, or as if, in taking an advocacy position, he ended up being marked for sacrifice by the majority. This "pathos" is that of someone for whom "speed" is readily translated into "sensitivity;" it is the "pathos" of a person whose "warnings" occupy a position somewhere between sincerity and performance, and thereby cease to truly be warnings. In other words, it is the pathos of one whose efforts yield "futility." However, because of Takeshi's endearing childishness, this "pathos" easily transforms into a sympathetic "familiarity." This is the greatest reason for his popularity. It is said that "elegance is the quality of conduct that transforms the greatest degree of being into appearing." In Kitano's case, however, "elegance" is nothing more than this "flickering." And appearance or "exteriority" for him has become to equal "the body."

If Takeshi is someone who uses "action" rather than "contemplation" to dispel illusion, does "contemplation" follow the whirlwind of action, giving him a sense of plenitude? Despite his seeming self-confidence, doesn't he fear that contemplation following after the body will only slow him down? It is here that Takeshi's melancholy arises. Wouldn't his "flickering" mode of being predetermine a "manic-depressive" psychological condition?

In his book *TV Exhibition Notes* (TV hakubutsushi, 1996) Hiroshi Aramata writes the following:

> . . . According to Akira Yokozawa, the television program *Go Ahead and Laugh!* (Waratte ii tomo!) was an unprecedented experiment in every sense. . . . For Yokozawa, however, pressing conditions made such a show necessary. Before *Go Ahead and Laugh!,* they were broadcasting a studio variety program called *It's time to laugh!* (Waratteru baai desuyo!). The genesis of this show's title was groundbreaking, since it had been chosen not on the basis of how it looked in print, but on how it sounded when spoken out loud. Nevertheless, the comedians who had come to the show from the manzai boom never rose above slapstick, and when backstage, they never talked about anything beyond women and money. The performers' personalities were dragging the quality of the show down. Faced with this situation, Yokozawa discontinued the show and tried to bring Beat Takeshi into the program that would replace it. Takeshi declined the offer, however, explaining

that "As a manic-depressive, I really couldn't host a daytime show every day."

Takeshi was thus able to avoid the fate of the TV personality Tamori, who lost his "nighttime subversiveness" to "daytime mundanity." "Manic-depression," in addition to "flickering," has helped to create the value of Beat Takeshi.

Even if they don't talk only of women and money, comedians degenerate: they lose their speed. As a case in point, many of the people behind the manzai boom are now reduced to hosting travel programs for stations like TV-Tokyo.[2] They show exaggerated surprise at what ordinary people are doing. Or they become experts at showing hyperbolic relish at eating regional cuisine and pronouncing it delicious. This is, of course, extremely "fake," but what these comedians don't realize is in fact the most important point—that such exaggerated surprise undermines the speed necessary for television.

Takeshi has no such blindness. He is almost certainly aware of the fact that "melancholy is contained in such dignity as is concealed in sublimeness, but this quality is lost as soon as it becomes the consequence of some sought-after emotion or some 'sentimentality.'" Takeshi possesses nobility, and this nobility is derived from his contemplativeness. This is why he often touches his face with his hands when he occupies the space of television; by doing so, he calls into play "the chin, the nose, the forehead, the finger, the hair"—i.e. the tools of contemplation." Thus, even before his motorcycle accident, his outward appearance often indicated melancholy.[3]

How shall we define television in this instance? Such a definition is indeed difficult in a case like Takeshi's, where the performer does not consider performing on television as a "privilege," but rather as an experience that leads to "boredom and fatigue." Likewise in the case of the "bored, fatigued" viewer who sees the "interiority" of television as merely the constant repetition of televisionesque qualities and not as the productive and harmonious result of television's practitioners.

Let us hypothesize some possible models for how television operates: 1) as a "court"; 2) as a [literary] "salon"; 3) as a "room" or *intérieur*; 4) as a "mirror"; and 5) as a "utopia."[4]

1. "The precept of joy is an integral part of the court: 'Truyen—being sad—is possible only insofar as the individual segregates himself from his community of feudal peers.'" Here, Takeshi, who possesses the "tools of contemplation," would be considered a deviant.

2. "The system of the salons originally developed as a second-tier 'world' alongside that of the court; the same behavioral ideals prevailed in it, and melancholy was the emotional state of a group, not of individuals. The greater the flight from the world, the greater the significance of the individual: bourgeois psychology emphasized the individual's emotions, which could at most be intensified via the agency of a friend, acting as a mirror for them." If Takeshi feels boredom and fatigue with the homogeneity of television, it may be because television operates according to the model of the salon as described here.

3. "[Gloom] is part of the *intérieur* to which 'mood'—the constellation of the material contents—binds it." This is probably the viewer's way of thinking. The viewer can take the scene of a room projected from a television to be an extension of his or her own home. There is nothing more dreadful than the "melancholy" that arises when one realizes that the "arrangement" of, say, television personalities Hiromi, Akira Nakao, and some forgettable

the long journey of the melancholy king

station announcer is a product of the agoraphobia and stereotyped consciousness of the show's production staff. The melancholy intérieur described by Kierkegaard in the nineteenth century has been amplified by the wretched state of contemporary housing conditions, and further reinforced by television.

Alternately, television could, as is commonly thought, be considered "society's mirror." (There are probably more than a few people who have viewed Takeshi—who never minces words as a social critic—as a proxy or mirror.)

4. "It is nothing to talk the needy out of his need. Rather, one must do just the opposite: need must be set up all around him, like a mirror of his existence that has deviated into the insanity of the flight from life. . . . The mirror in this case represented the reconstitution of the lost relationship to society; but it was the duplication of the ego, which was intended to feign sociability, that allowed the illness to be deduced." The use of television as a mirror invites this type of idleness. This is because television only reflects the viewer's own pathology.

5. "Utopia takes shape as a compressed space." Isn't this the definition that most resembles television? Such a "utopia" naturally tends towards "atemporality." "Emptiness and monotony may stretch the moment and the hour and make for 'boredom,' but they shorten and dissolve the larger and largest masses of time to the point of nullifying them." Doesn't this speak to television's atemporal tedium? I will touch upon this again later, but after his motorcycle accident, Takeshi said that he could remember

neither riding the bike nor having the accident. Why was his memory wiped out like this? Perhaps Takeshi's everyday time, typically regulated by his extremely busy television performance schedule, suddenly lost its form when confronted with a "large expanse of time," that reservoir of a vast atemporality. Such a mundane sense of the everyday would almost certainly be displaced by the external pressure of a motorcycle crash; perhaps this is how his memory was erased.

At any rate, when considered in this light, it is clear that "television" is a supratemporal (or atemporal) "interiority" that comprehends all these historical forms of "interiority"—the "court," "salon," "intérieur," mirror," and "utopia." Having taken this historical detour, then, we can state that television's interiority is indeed the interiority of contemporary society itself—that is, one that enfolds its own deviant symptoms within its homogeneity so that the "deviant's" body is also arranged within its "interior." This "interiority" is thus transformed into a distasteful space that propagates facsimiles of itself that include the "deviant." Even time cannot accumulate here. Takeshi's role in television has been to make viewers aware of the encroachment of this contemporary "interiority"—not directly, but by suggestion, through the symptoms of uneasiness he displays in television's interior space. Thus Takeshi's melancholy can participate in the viewer's melancholy as a kind of premonition.

But isn't this an ill omen for Takeshi? Here we can recall the words, "The eighteenth-century bourgeoisie began to lay claim to the attitude of resignation that had once been reserved for the ruler." In this way, the ruling class finally toppled.

For some time now, we have been hearing people who say, "the age of Takeshi is over." Of course, those who make this claim also have the subtlety to prepare an alternative. They might say, for example, "now is the age of Downtown,"[5] or "now is the age of Ninety-Nine."[6]

Granted, Team Downtown's Hitoshi Matsumoto does possess the stature necessary to be a successor to Takeshi. Matsumoto mobilizes the feelings of the age in which the "disgusting" can be laughed at; while slowing the pace of Takeshi-style "flickering," he heightens its absurdity. Compared with the machine-gun delivery of Beat Takeshi and Beat Kiyoshi's manzai, Matsumoto's comedy creates a space of drama and an odd sense of stagnation. In this regard, the gravitational pull of Team Downtown's performance space could be deemed stronger than that of the Two Beats. (Of course, the outstanding comic sense of Masatoshi Hamada is working in the background of both of these teams.) However, the spongy physical presence of Matsumoto, which can produce a sense of languid melancholy in his viewers, is quite unlike Takeshi's. Takeshi can oscillate between a momentary death (such as a display of malice) and a momentary rebirth (such as the habitual twitch in his head and shoulders), and finally, with an embarrassed smile, arrive at a sense of despair (all out of breath). The strange impression he gives of a purity of intention that is always just a hair's breadth short of melancholy, can indeed be overwhelming.

Takeshi and Matsumoto each give life to their own originality. As such, Matsumoto is not trying to usurp Takeshi's sphere of action. While Matsumoto has of course been "influenced" by Takeshi, he has not "surpassed" him. To read the appearance of Matsumoto in relation to Takeshi in this way would be to take an excessively narrative approach vis-a-vis the atemporality of television that was discussed earlier.

This "atemporality" naturally denies maturation. Takeshi himself has reminisced as follows:

The worst thing about the manzai in the days of the Two Beats was that we gave priority to the jokes. Up until the time of Yasu–Kiyo,[7] it was half about "performance," and W Kenji's manzai was all performance. We couldn't do that, so we gave priority to the jokes. We wrenched our brains trying to do something different, but jokes, after all, were jokes, and not performance. After I turned thirty-five, the times changed, and it was the younger guys' time, and it got harder. With performance, it doesn't matter how old you are—the older you are, the more polished you get. [That's how it was for people like Kokontei Shinsho][8] in the old days.

We must realize here that Takeshi is not relating his chagrin at being surpassed by the younger generation, but rather describing the atemporality of television, which makes no provisions for maturation. These are the words of a man who has awakened to melancholy. "In melancholy being-in-the-world, that which is being-in-the-inner-world reveals itself in a spatiality characterized by pure presence—directionless and nontopological remoteness—and finally in a spatiality characterized by the arbitrariness of the punctual." Takeshi himself presided over a brief high point when the "interiority of television" was heightened through the mobilization of "the arbitrariness of the punctual." This high point came in the show *We are Jokers!*,[9] which was produced by Akira Yokozawa. (While this show could be described as a mix of *Saturday Night Live* and the Japanese show *Bubble Holiday*,[10] it is in fact worthy of the highest possible consideration on par with the films of Takeshi Kitano.) Let's return to Yokozawa's words from Hiroshi Aramata's book:

> There was no chance that we could make anything that was polished, so we might as well give free reign to our creativity. On the set, we'd have a brief planning session, and then we'd roll the cameras, without even a camera rehearsal. So we'd get

the staff and the cast to just have fun on the show. And we'd broadcast to the audience that "we're just having fun," like a kind of signal. If, for example, Samma blew wind during the show and was rendered speechless, or if Takeshi farted on the set, we wouldn't cut it as NG—we'd just put it in as it was. This was what was most novel about our show, I think. The Drifters[11] would cut these outtakes or the backstage banter. But *Jokers* would put its mistakes right out there like a confession, and this would create an atmosphere of fun . . . . In *Jokers*, "Takechanman" and "Black Devil" would have a . . . competition where they'd change shape, or they'd fall in a pond, and if it didn't go well, there was no way we could do it over. We'd create the kind of situations where there'd be nothing but a first take.

This was not a utopia since "the abhorrence of chance is the order of the day in a utopia." The lack of utopianism in *Jokers* meant that it also lacked melancholy, which shares with utopia the sign of the "atemporal." Rather, this program summoned up a different value from melancholy—that of "camp," as described by Susan Sontag: "The dandy held a perfumed handkerchief to his nostrils and was liable to swoon; the connoisseur of Camp sniffs the stink and prides himself on his strong nerves." "Camp is a further attempt to deal with boredom by means of an aesthetic approach." "Camp eludes boredom because all things can become important to it and because their arbitrary interchangeablity and replaceability offer the guarantee of constantly changing pleasure."

Joker's exaggeration of television's interiority was not the result of its encroachment on "insider" spaces. Rather, its television interiority expanded simply because, with its dramaturgy of (idle) "repetition," "enduring humiliation," and "childishness," the energy exhausted in this program's "changes" was huge. However, if you took a good look at Takeshi, who was supposedly increasing television's interiority, you would realize that he was standing outside of television. His face as "Takechanman" was filled with sexual ecstasy. Of course, the etymology for "ecstasy" is "ek-stasis," or "standing outside." In this way, *Jokers* impressed its viewers with a kind of joy.

TWO

Late at night on August 2, 1994, Beat Takeshi had a motorcycle accident in which he avoided sudden death by the margin of a few seconds. Takeshi's own book, *Facial Paralysis* (Ganmen mahi), describes the circumstances of the accident in detail. This books confirms above all else that he is a thinker who consistently takes his own body as the starting point for his thinking. Thus he reacts with a kind of fresh energy against his own flesh, which has been robbed of its freedom and strength; in the spiritual crisis of death, he experiences fear of the "treatment" that would swallow up his body itself. (Thus the book completely avoids the self-congratulatory tone of those who relate their "near-death" experiences.)

This confirmation of the body as a starting point must have spurred his decision to hold a press conference immediately after his release from the hospital, thus laying bare his "face" that had so obviously been transformed by nerve damage. There was something about the press conference, including his joke, "Ganmen Mahina Stars," which made people want to cry out in pain.[12] The asymmetry of his face—particularly in his gaze—destroyed its sense of direction (thus giving the impression of a dispersion of volition). Then there were the successive transformations of Takeshi's mouth, cheeks, and jaw. Though the face is the primary locus of frontal engagement, in his case it gives the impression of being a site of "incontinence." Later, when the highlights of this press conference were broadcast on

the long journey of the melancholy king

television, the television editors emphasized those moments when Takeshi's face looked particularly miserable. Anachronistically, they wanted to highlight the shopworn television-drama scenario of a libertine who takes one too many liberties and brings his world crashing down around him.

In contrast to this, those who watched the entire press conference were viscerally struck by the theme that emerges from Takeshi's subsequent account of accident. The flesh of Takeshi's face did indeed seem on the verge of breaking apart with the effort of each independent action, and yet there were also hints of a return to directionality and frontal engagement. (This was, in other words, "flickering" on the largest possible scale.) His movements, which seemed like a "desperate struggle," were so valiant that they made viewers want to cry out in pain. The press conference could thus be called "camp" in the true meaning of the word. At the same time, the "interiority of television"—whether described as a "court," "salon," "intérieur," mirror," or "utopia"—was destroyed by the luminosity of Takeshi's own face.

This press conference was Takeshi's finest "work" as a television performer. But surely he was more aware than anyone that this conference was enacted in a domain that, as the script of *Kids Return* (1996) would have it, was indifferent to "beginning" or "end."

Since then, as those who witnessed his will to recover during the press conference would have predicted, Takeshi has recouped much of his facial expressiveness. However, his greatest moment of "flickering" has turned the everyday flickering of his subsequent television performances into mere "traces." Furthermore, by showing the way towards a destruction of television's "interiority," he also diluted the chance of a confrontation between the cinema auteur Takeshi Kitano and the television performer Beat Takeshi. It was because of Beat Takeshi's very dependence on the interiority of television that Takeshi

Kitano was able to use the "exteriority of film" as a weapon in the battle against Beat Takeshi. It seems to me that Takeshi Kitano and Beat Takeshi have begun to meld together after the motorcycle accident. And in contrast to schizophrenically breaking apart, melding together is undoubtedly a quieter and happier type of movement.

In an interview with Makoto Shinozaki in the November 1997 issue of *Studio Voice*, Takeshi recalls that "After my traffic accident, I began to perceive colors more intensely." We should not read this, however, as the narrative of someone who recovers from ennui and faces the world with fresh eyes. Rather, in Takeshi's case, we can trace this intensification of colors to the the press conference during which, bathed in the light from the flashing cameras, he was barely able to blink his eyes, and even his tears were dry. The daggers of light he experienced at that time are what is being reflected in his words "I began to perceive colors more intensely."

When Takeshi gazes out directly, using his body as a starting point, he inevitably gazes at his own melancholy—a melancholy that has increased dramatically since his return to television. Hence he has come to claim a position in proximity to television instead of within it. That is, this notion of being "in proximity to television" is not about being in the central space produced by television's interiority, but rather about being in an incidental, unrelated position. Moreover, the "proximity" here corresponds to the tangle of self-abandonment and attachment. In other words, this "proximity" is neither directly touching nor completely removed from a painful space. This, in turn, reflects the desire not to fall away entirely, even though the "adhesion" has come undone.

Needless to say, this bears upon melancholy as well: ". . . melancholy remains in 'proximity to the world,' despite the loss of a world, if only in order for the individual to maintain the communicative principle, which the human psyche cannot be easily persuaded to relinquish."

the long journey of the melancholy king

Therefore, as he stands impassively at the "side" of Guadalcanal Taka, who is presiding over the well-known "boiling water commercial" sketch, Takeshi no longer exudes an active person's potential for melancholy, but manifests instead the immediate melancholy of "one who doesn't act." Indeed, it seems that he has changed from one who portends melancholy to one who demonstrates it. Thus, for example, his appearance on *Takeshi's Genesis of Everything* (Takeshi no banbutsu soseiki) reminds us of the words ". . . the flight from 'society' into nature . . . is what remains of the world when one ascertains that it is no longer the world."

But what are the implications for television's "world" if "the world is no longer the world"? Perhaps this is the condition that arises when every aspect of television fuses together. Such is the case with the "boiling water commercial," which Takeshi coolly observes from the sidelines. (Given the prohibitive nature of television, it's hard to believe that this sketch would continue after the Aum Shinrikyo incident.)[13] This sketch is based on the violent "fusion" of television's self-serving power, which is then used for self-promotion—e.g. the viewers' pleasure in watching torture, and the vulgar hope that a woman's breasts will fall out of her swimsuit.

There are countless variety shows that operate on the principle of fusion in this way: *Quiz: The Devil's Whispers* (Kuizu: akuma no sasayaki) ties together the advertising system and the viewers' sense of superiority over the suffering of others; *Hit Parade in the Night* (THE yoru mo hippare) ties together the public karaoke of vain singers with a pop-chart countdown; *Iron Chef* (Ryori no tetsujin) combines a cooking show with a live sports broadcast; *Please! Ristorante* (Onegai! risutorante) combines an erudite cooking show with cheap drama. All of these shows exemplify "fusion" under the standard that proclaims that "combination variety shows are a hit!" When visual desire, gastronomic appetite, and competitiveness fuse inextricably together, however, won't viewers become complete slaves to televisionesque desire?

In this respect, television variety shows are now truly "shameless." The funny lines of the "talent" appear in subtitles on the screen, and are obstinately repeated through editing. Given the current combination of televisionesque redundancy and temporality, the "naked exposure" that had previously exemplified televisionesque temporality begins to seem excessive. Thus we can no longer hope for the rich transformations of an overdressed show like *Jokers*.

Takeshi seems to be attempting to unravel this variety-show excess and fusion simply by placing himself "near" it. Undoubtedly, the simplicity of his current screen presence is connected with the simplicity of his films and his manzai. At any rate, his role seems to be that of one who unravels or untwines. In this respect, Takeshi wears a surprisingly aristocratic mein: "It would be impossible for the nobility to 'work off' its boredom . . . As a result, a form of meaningless work emerged that served no other purpose than to kill time. The French court set an example for the fashion of handicrafts: since '1770 the ladies occupy themselves with "parfilage," untwining gold tresses.'"

Earlier I wrote that "the opportunity for a confrontation between the cinema auteur Takeshi Kitano and the television performer Beat Takeshi has necessarily been diluted." This will in turn probably contribute to the impossibility of bridging television and cinema. (That is to say that in order to construct a bridge between the two poles of television and cinema, the two must exist for Takeshi as distinct and opposing poles.) Yet rather than being merely a question about just Takeshi Kitano=Beat Takeshi, it seems to me that it has bearing on the cultural condition at large. The impossibility of such a bridging between the two media has increased after Takeshi's motorcycle accident.

the long journey of the melancholy king

It may seem like a rather contradictory example, but after Takeshi Kitano's *Fireworks* (Hana-Bi, 1997) received the Golden Lion Prize at the Venice Film Festival, I was twice interviewed on television about it. At the time, the biggest question was, "If Takeshi's films have been so well received in Europe, why haven't they been successful in Japan?" Television doesn't recognize that the axis of this question is skewed. Films like Takeshi's, with their intense depiction of violence and their anti-Hollywood minimalism, are unlikely to attract more than a limited audience "both in Europe and Japan." But they have received enthusiastic critical response "both in Europe and Japan." This question is itself a manifestation of the directionless "stitching together" that takes place in television. Therefore, the only way to answer this question is to "unravel" it (which takes time).

Actually, this is no more than a clever rewording of the question "If Takeshi is so exposed on television, why aren't his movies hits?" Thus the question itself cannot escape from the syndrome of endlessly returning to "television-centrism." (But aren't questions supposed to be at the "center" of questioning or discourse?) Such a question altogether dismisses the "condition of film," and thus of Takeshi Kitano—only "Beat Takeshi" exists in this question. Film directors are hardly household names in Japan. Even when a female announcer reading a newspaper article mispronounces the name of Taiwanese film director Hou Hsiao-Hsien as Hou Hsiao-En, no one sees this as a problem. This perhaps is evidence that the Japanese generally don't give respect to cinema as a whole.

Television and cinema are diverging from each other at an accelerating pace. To tell the truth, for television (in other words, for "Japan"), Beat Takeshi and Takeshi Kitano are completely different people. Thus in order for the struggle between Takeshi Kitano and Beat Takeshi to maintain its effectiveness, it is no longer necessary to set them apart from each other with a "vs." Rather, it is necessary to meld the two together and annihilate the ground of conflict between them. Surely Takeshi has announced a new phase in this struggle (a struggle that can no longer be called a struggle) by melting all of his television melancholy into *Fireworks*. That is, it has become necessary for him to aim at "synthesis."

I remember that Takeshi, in a educational television show on writer Kenji Nakagami,[14] once said something to the effect that "Just as Nakagami has dual residence, living in both Kumano and Shinjuku, I have dual residence in Asakusa and on television." This could also be called a dual residence in television and cinema. Such a division of residence would lead whoever it affected to "boredom and fatigue." This is a kind of mutual annihilation of opposites that erodes the "melancholy of the land" and dilutes the "melancholy of the sea." What can it be replaced with? If melancholy is required of Kitano, then it must be a new, supraterritorial melancholy of strength, one where everything has melded together.

THREE

Melancholy of strength is not too different from "weakness." Indeed, it would be correct to say that melancholy of strength is a spirit of weakness that has been exchanged for something radical. The idea of multifaceted praise for weakness calls to mind Seigo Matsuoka's novel *Fragile* (1995). In fact, it was quite a shock to discover that Kitano's *Fireworks* trembles with the same fragility and delicacy that was indicated in Matsuoka's book. *Fireworks* and *Fragile* are united by the same themes: "the lacking king" (Nishi, played by Takeshi in *Fireworks*, is almost completely lacking in words); "journeying" (Nishi takes off on a desperate flight with his terminally cancer-stricken wife, played by Kayoko Kishimoto); "hooliganism" (Nishi is alarmingly violent); and "twilight" (after dispatching the yakuza who

are chasing after him, Nishi's trembling, wretched silhouette melts into the "blue," snow-like ink dissolving in water—surely this must be a special effect).

Such signs of weakness are not just piled one on top of another. Instead, they are deepened as they permeate the film, ending ultimately in silence. Horibe, played by Ren Osugi, also loses the power of words midway through the film—thus he too, like Takeshi's Nishi, is a double for Beat Takeshi=Takeshi Kitano. After this silence, Kishimoto's last two sentences, and the last two gun shots, should function as a final moment of strength that substantiates the whole of the silence that came before. (Unfortunately, however, the music by Joe Hisaishi that blares throughout this scene interferes with such an effect.)

It is difficult to find an apt comparison for *Fireworks*. The delicacy of its editing, which contributes to its silence, means that its viewers have no choice but to respond to it with the insect-like feelers that lie dormant in their own archaic depths. On this point, the only contemporary Japanese films that can compare with *Fireworks* are the works of the documentary filmmaker Yasuo Matsukawa.[15] Matsukawa, who always includes the image of a butterfly in his works as a kind of signature, organizes a type of "shared perception" through his editing, which functions like the fluttering of a butterfly's wings. A similar type of "shared perception" can be found in Kitano's work.

However, *Fireworks* differs from Matsukawa's *Hands* (Te, 1974), which depicts a symphony of workers' hands. In *Fireworks*, the character Horibe, whose wife has deserted him, becomes an amateur painter. Only then does Kitano finally show his hands. However, Kitano's depiction of Nishi's "trials of the hands" is more powerful. When Nishi stops his van in the snow to put chains on his tires, his colleague, Kishimoto, in the driver's seat, mixes up drive and reverse and runs over Takeshi's hand. Later on, when Nishi's yakuza pursuers hold him at gunpoint at the inn where he has been staying, his finger is bloodied when, as if by accident, Takeshi inserts his finger between the gun's hammer and cap to stop it from firing. (This scene is unquestionably the high point of the film's realization of violence.) Thus *Fireworks'* symphony of hands is very different from Matsukawa's *Hands*. In this way, Kitano presents us with a bitter commentary on the words of Rimbaud, who optimistically predicted that this would be a "century of hands."

As the example of the use of "hands" in *Fireworks* demonstrates, the movie possesses a truly symphonic structure. Moreover, just as Takeshi's previous films have corresponded to his own physical states—for example, "fatigue" or "weariness"—this work begins at the singular starting point of his own bodily condition, then "symphonizes" it. We should not overlook this point.

It is quite likely that Kitano conceived of this film on the basis of his persisting facial "paralysis." First of all, the story features Ren Osugi's Horibe, who is "paralyzed" from the waist down. The basic set-up of the film is one in which few words are spoken, though the violence speaks volumes. Yet this violence is always depicted indirectly. There is, for example, Nishi, who falls into debt caring for his dying wife and who becomes a wanted man in the processs. There is also Beat Takeshi's own slightly skewed facial expressions, which capture a sad bestiality that, out of all the leading roles in Takeshi's other films, had previously been displayed by Claude Maki. Each of these are marked by "paralysis." Once again, despite the numerous instances of such "paralysis," the effect is not one of mere repetition.

the long journey of the melancholy king

It is a well-known fact that melancholy and collecting go hand in hand. We should note, however, that collected items form a constellation of their own, and that the twinkling of such a constellation makes a kind of music. In *Fireworks*, the different examples of "paralysis" create a polyphonic music of "sadness." We can conclude, then, that the physical state presented by Takeshi Kitano=Beat Takeshi is one of "sadness," and is thus utterly different from those in evidence in his earlier films.

This "sadness" does not stop at Takeshi's private condition after the motorcycle accident. Instead, through the strength of the film's exposition, it "permeates" into a more universal condition. Hence melancholy here departs from a private "loss of the world" and develops into a positive resource for constituting a "world." The function of melancholy here with respect to the "world" is not robbery (thus it forms a constellation without "twinkling"), but rather recovery. (This is the same trajectory traced by Kitano's facial expression after his accident). To quote from Benjamin, "If melancholy emerges from the depths of the creaturely realm to which the speculative thought of the age felt itself to be bound by the bonds of the Church itself, then this explains its omnipotence. In fact, it is the most genuinely creaturely of the contemplative impulses, and it has always been noticed that its power need be no less in the gaze of a dog than in the attitude of a pensive genius."

So whether or not *Fireworks'* creator is a "genius" is unimportant. The more fundamental point is how the movie causes its viewers to be led into the archaic strata of a dog, to use Benjamin's word, or that of a butterfly, to borrow from Yasuo Matsukawa's films. The viewing subject, who has become a dog or a butterfly, is then captivated by the force of melancholy that fills the world to overflowing. From here, the world melts into weakness. In this case, "the world" and "fireworks" are identical in value. Kitano has never before shot a film like this.

beat takeshi vs. takeshi kitano

Fireworks starts off with a close-up of the face of a pushy little boy, and ends with the face of a young girl. If we are to say that *Fireworks* is a sparkler, pointing at the sky, then realize that this sky is the "future."

Incidentally, the implications of the film's title, *Fireworks—Hana-Bi* in Japanese—are complex. The press release for the film suggests a binary opposition of "*hana*" (flower: symbol of life) and "*hi*" (fire: gunfire, hence a symbol of death). Actually, the film itself transcends this binary opposition. An example of this is Kitano's own paintings, which are used in the title credits, as decorations in various settings within the film, and as the works painted by Osugi. These paintings are as elaborate and colorful as "hana-bi"—fireworks—themselves. Yet when the camera closes in on the details, we realize that the paintings are accumulations of momentary inspirations, or "hi" (fire/flames/sparks). Thus we are presented with "a flower composed of fire."

Another example is the use of flashback—a first for a Takeshi Kitano film. (This is one of many techniques Kitano uses for the first time in this film. Others include: the use of many colors to compose the screen image; the clear marking of locations; overlaps; and shots that initially pan across a scene to explain the location.) The scene where one of detective Nishi's colleagues (Makoto Ashikawa) is killed and another (Susumu Terajima) is gravely wounded by a small-time gangster (Yasuei Yakushiji) in a station complex is shown three times, as if in a series of enlargements. (I've argued in the past for the significance of the number three in Kitano's films.) This movement of memory, seeping in from a single point and suddenly expanding, itself resembles "fireworks". And "sadness" appears yet again at the point where the workings of memory become identical to the movement of "fireworks."

Finally, there is the scene where Takeshi and Kishimoto actually play with fireworks during their trip. This moment flawlessly captures

the long journey of the melancholy king

the themes of "interruption" and "explosion" that run throughout Kitano's earlier movies, which in turn suggests that such "hana-bi" (with their vigorous cruelty) may represent the "breath" of all of Kitano's films.

Incidentally, the two young faces that bookend *Fireworks* are enfolded within two of Takeshi's paintings of angels, which are shown during the title credits and after the ending credits. These "angels" reflect yet another Benjaminesque theme. In a passage on Paul Klee's painting *Angelus Novus* (1910), Benjamin describes his sense that that this angel was staring fixedly at the "wreckage" of a catastrophe and simultaneously moving farther and father away from it. With a fierce wind at its wings, the angel in Klee's painting is described as being carried towards the "future." In *Fireworks*, the angel of the title credits (drawn as a winged Buddhist nun) is depicted as being in the midst of a strange tumbling-back motion. This motion, it seems to me, establishes the entire film as a kind of "wreckage."

What should be noted in this regard are the many ways that *Fireworks* demonstrates "simultaneity." In the stakeout scene, all the detectives are chattering away "simultaneously" except Nishi and Horibe. The "wreckage" is not formed out of the teleological "flow" of time from past to future, but rather exists in the thickness of a "simultaneity" that is invaded by all possible times. Undoubtedly, this realization was the basis of Benjamin's *Arcades Project*, which describes the arcades of nineteenth-century Paris through an exhaustive array of contemporary documents. Of course, in *Fireworks*, we find the literal "wreckage" of the junked car lot, whose owner is played by Tetsu Watanabe. The "space" of this film, then, points to the "arbitrariness of the punctual," a fact that is also emphasized by the inclusion of Takeshi's own paintings.

In melding together "the journey of Nishi and his wife" and "Horibe's painting," Kitano purposefully robs each scene of its independence. (Noteworthy here is not the additive property of scenes, but their parallelism: Kitano has never before used parallel montage in this way.) He does this in order to capture the effect of "weakness." Then, at the film's conclusion, he argues for the "simultaneity" of life and death through his two "doubles" of Takeshi and Osugi. (In this way, he eliminates the overwhelming "pressure" of death that is so evident in all his films through *Sonatine*.) Kitano thus devotes his full attention to the complexity of a technique that is both fragmentary and "simultaneously" parallel. While this type of jumbled film structure was probably somewhat impromptu, a sure aesthetic hand "simultaneously" lurks behind it.

I should mention in passing that the painting of an angel after the final credits is missing a wing. Needless to say, it is thus the complete universalization of the "paralysis" that occurs throughout the film and because of which this painting is allowed to appear.

Unlike *Violent Cop, A Scene at the Sea,* and *Sonatine,* which were all single lines pointing towards death, the structural condition of *Fireworks* is no longer a single line. Rather, it is a widening of time and space that prepares for the exercise of arbitrary choice. A tendency towards this type of "plurality" has been evident since Kitano's fifth film, *Getting Any?* (Minna-yatteruka!, 1995). Each of these films, however, has shown its own unique take on this kind of "plurality." In *Getting Any?*, it was the piling-up of anecdotes; in *Kids Return,* it was the portrayal of life=time; and in *Fireworks,* it is the film's very structure. In other words, the plurality in Kitano's works since *Getting Any?* should not be conceived of as a single unit.

the long journey of the melancholy king

Instead, each film works on a different level, forming a "plurality" within Kitano's filmography. This very lack of attachment to a single approach is itself remarkable (though the seeds of this plurality was evident in his second work, *Boiling Point*).

The issue is one of sensibility—i.e. whether or not this pluralism is able to recognize "the strength of weakness" as opposed to "the value of weakness." Hence, as Makoto Shinozaki argues in the previously mentioned *Studio Voice* interview, to say that *Fireworks* represents a "compilation" of *A Scene at the Sea*'s silence with the violence of Kitano's other movies would be too crude an analysis. The sense of time and space that are woven together in *Fireworks* differs from his other films. Kitano must also be conscious of this. The puzzle that Nishi and his wife silently work on together in the film shows precisely such a consciousness of self and other—even if the parts are the same, the structure of the whole will be completely changed depending on how they are put together.

By dint of the fact that no scene can stand on its own, this time and space of plurality/arbitrariness prepares the way for "salvation." Regardless of their degree of technical facility, the paintings by Takeshi that are inserted into the film, with their primitive eccentricity reminiscent of Kiyoshi Yamashita[16] and their suggestion of dangerous eroticism recalling Sonnenstern,[17] are remarkable for the way they bring an emotionality to the fore. (I'm especially fond of the group of "animals" with flowers in place of heads.) The emotional desolation of these paintings seem to be redeemed by virtue of being placed in the film. Moreover, all of the actors in the film are similarly redeemed. This is true of the scene in which Takeshi robs a bank, which seems to be missing logical details. It is also true of the luke-warm quality of the gags involving Takeshi and Kishimoto on the road; the very fact that they lack precision contributes to this atmosphere of salvation. We should note, however, that far from wiping out the film's "melancholy," such salvation beautifully amplifies it.

Perhaps it would be helpful to consider the origin of this aesthetic attitude. It seems to me that it is related to "relinquishment"—specifically, Japanese-style "relinquishment." I got a hint of this recently while watching an educational television special on Kitano's Golden Lion award at the Venice Film Festival. The special showed old footage of Kitano paying a visit to Akira Kurosawa. In the course of their conversation, Kitano said something to the effect that his film technique, which experiments with very terse depiction, is tied to a consciousness of *iki*.[18]

Shuzo Kuki's *The Structure of Iki* (Iki no kozo, 1930) is a work whose powerful argumentation, by virtue of its brilliant insights, seems more violent than elaborate. Its central arguments tie "iki" to a sense of "relinquishment": "The third attribute of iki is resignation, an indifference that has renounced attachment and is based on a knowledge of fate. Iki must be urbane. It must be a well-formed and elegant disposition with a good grace."

Takeshi's color sense, which until *Fireworks* had been dominated by cold, dull hues, also corresponds strikingly with Shuzo Kuki's intuition that "blue" and "gray" are the colors of "resignation." Furthermore, in the days of the Two Beats, Takeshi could encompass himself and his entire audience through his method of accumulative enumeration. He would say, for example, "And something like X doing Y-or-another." This had the ultimate function of cultivating a "resigned awareness" in both self and other.

Similarly, the "disinterestedness" shown in the aforementioned scenes where Takeshi robs the bank or where Takeshi and Kishimoto are performing gags is also related to "resignation." In fact, Takeshi and Kishimoto are the film's ultimate embodiment of "relinquishment" and "resigned awareness."

Journeying, one of the signs of weakness enumerated by Seigo Matsuoka, is also recast as "iki" in Shuzo Kuki's work: ". . . In other words, iki has its origin in the 'World of Suffering,'[19] where 'one's body drifts in the light swirl of things without floating free.'" Thus the "Japan" that Takeshi and Kishimoto wander through in their flight is superimposed upon by the "World of Suffering." While Shuzo's "World of Suffering" is a Buddhist term, for Takeshi, the "suffering" of the "World of Suffering" is transformed into something more positive. It is transformed into something in realm of the melancholic.

When viewed in the light of *The Structure of Iki,* the "double suicide" of Takeshi and Kishimoto at the end of the film loses its importance. Instead, we realize that the essential point is that all along Takeshi has made a "lover's pledge" with Kishimoto and his colleagues. A "lover's pledge" occurs when, for example, a courtesan refuses to kiss other customers in order to preserve her fidelity to the man she loves, or when she exchanges her love for "resigned awareness" by getting a tattoo of "XX forever." One can glimpse a tattoo also on the heart of the "hooligan" Nishi.

Indeed, it seems that the heart tattoo=melancholy has become a creative principle for Takeshi Kitano=Beat Takeshi in all his works since *Getting Any?,* where "multiplicity" has "flickered" in all its different forms. Each "fulfillment" has brought about a "disillusion of fulfillment" that has served to propel him onward to the next film. We can compare this with these words on Proust: "The conclusion that, in the Proustian utopia, the individual recovers the world by looking backward, must, however, be modified. For the site of fulfillment (Proust speaks of the "disillusion" fulfillment" [. . .]) is a system that takes possession of past reality by means of memories, but in its satisfaction at having done so, it can then exclude the reality of the present."

By fixing his "work resembling life"="system," at the very end of his life, Proust lost his "life." "Disillusionment" was the final phase of this. For Beat Takeshi=Takeshi Kitano, however, disillusionment is just a stage. His "minimalist" method of expression is a major force in restraining this type of systemization. Therefore Takeshi—who is the most conspicuous "melancholy king" in contemporary Japan—will undoubtedly continue his long creative journey. *Fireworks* serves us notice that he has reached a new starting point.

getting any?

ORIGINAL RHYTHM

Takeshi Kitano's film *Getting Any?* is by no means as "ridiculous" and "scandalous" as its advertising campaign claims. Watching it over and over again, I came to realize that it is a precisely calibrated film—indeed, a masterpiece unequalled in Japanese film history. (Kitano is said to have prepared the script himself: we can be sure that this contributed to the film's precision.) Compared with the slapstick films of the early Ozu, Ko Nakahira's *Beef Shop Frankie* (Gyunyu-ya Frankie, 1956), or Yuzo Kawashima's *If Humans Walk* (Hito mo arukeba, 1960), this work can boast a more complex structure and a busier sensibility. I watched the film on its premier on February 11, 1994, taking notes on the margins of the scenario I had bought (published by Fusosha Bunko) to recall the details. It was then that I became confident of my above appraisal. (Despite its ads, which called it "the first work directed by 'Beat Takeshi,'" "Takeshi Kitano" was the name on the scenario's title page, as well as in the opening and closing credits of the film.)

Getting Any? is essentially a Hollywood movie. The protagonist, played by comedian Dankan, decides to buy a car in order to get girls and engage in "car sex." When this plan is frustrated, his desire roams further afield to fantasies of "riding executive class in a jumbo jet," "making guns to get money," "robbing a bank," "becoming an

actor," and "becoming an invisible man." Insofar as its story is propelled by the shifting fantasies of its protagonist, the film employs the same devices as certain Hollywood movies, such as Preston Sturges's *Unfaithfully Yours* (1948) and Norman Z. McLeod's *The Secret Life of Walter Mitty* (1947). We should note however, that the film's story and space are unfailingly advanced by the "correct order" of lines of dialogue in each sequence, no matter how minor, and by the convincing abbreviation of time through adventurous jump cuts. Where necessary, the cutting is subdivided for maximum efficiency. The placement of cuts is especially precise in the scene after Dankan fails to score with a girl at a bus stop, and his car is overtaken by a bus filled with the other people who had been waiting at the stop and who are now yelling insults at him. (The framing of this shot is also precisely calculated.) Another outstanding scene occurs at the home of the yakuza boss, played by Chambara Trio's Tetsuya Yuki. Hung on the wall is a series of "ancestral portraits" of successive generations of yakuza bosses going back to a Sharaku-style actor print[1] and concluding with a hanging scroll that looks like Shotoku Taishi.[2] Rather than being left as a simple gag, the progression of portraits is dexterously grafted onto the camerawork, which shows the yakuza members climbing the staircase. This results in a nimble shifting of attention. It seems to me that the narrative economy in evidence here reaches the level of cinema from Hollywood's Golden Age. Thus it is impermissable to regard this work as a TV-style variety film such as Monty Python's *And Now For Something Completely Different* (1971).

getting any?

As far as the pattern of gags goes, the film strictly denies any actual connections that the cast might actually have amongst themselves. As such, it is unlike the TV program *We Are Jokers!*, which effectively utilized such connections to create gags. (*Getting Any?* does, however, contain some parody of actual events.) Rather, it leaves all the actors (including Masumi Okada,[3] who has a cameo) completely exposed. (As in *Boiling Point*, Dankan's body is particularly believable. It appears as if he's actually being slapped in the Cessna by the hit man Joe Shishido.[4]) Time after time, the cast captures the abundant humor of "contradiction" on screen. When Dankan, who's training to play a medicine salesman extra, jumps onto a small ferry, the actor playing Zatoichi, the blind swordsman,[5] flies off the other side of the boat. Strictly speaking, this see-saw motion is a physical impossibility, but through the magic of temporal abbreviation, this "contradiction" does not appear to be one.

Another example occurs in the scene where Dankan holds up a cash-transport vehicle using the same method used in the so-called "three-hundred-million-yen incident."[6] The hold-up is successful, but he cannot extinguish one of his sticks of dynamite, and the cab of the truck bursts into flames. As the flames shoot up, day turns to

night outside. While this is merely a way of making the flames more visible, it is certainly another "contradiction." We can thus say that the film grammar that permits such contradictions is the dream-like grammar of early cinema.

Moreover, the gags themselves resemble the gags of early cinema. There are the repetition

beat takeshi vs. takeshi kitano

gags, such as the subtitles "translated by Natsuko Toda"[7] that appear a total of five times throughout the film (twice in Persian, the first of which is absurdly long compared with the amount of dialogue being conveyed). Next are exchange gags, such as the time Dankan mistakes a manure scoop for a cane-sword or, in the Zatoichi sequences, a water barrel for an oil barrel; or when Dankan is himself confused with the assistant of the "Society for the Promotion of the Invisible Man," played by Makoto Ashikawa. Also present are gags resulting from the confusion of cause and effect, such as the scene where Dankan appears before his enemies with a violin case, causing them to cringe in fear because they think it's a machine gun. Contrary to the viewer's own expectations, when the case is opened, it actually contains a violin. When Dankan begins to play the instrument, however, his enemies begin to writhe in pain at the sound. Finally, there are the meaningless gags, such as the two occasions when Dankan lets down a rope to try to break into a building.

Getting Any's structure is precisely calibrated. The scenes of Dankan trying to rob a bank to get money to impress girls with are especially well constructed. There are a total of seven of these short scenes (all of them take place at the same bank). 1) Dankan enters the bank, but a burglary is already in progress, so he exits dejectedly. 2) Dankan says, "Hand over the money!" but the bank employee calmly tells him to take a number, and he unthinkingly complies. 3) When he enters the bank, the bank employees, unbelievably, are all police officers. 4) Dankan directs the teller to close the outside shutter after handing over the money. He expects the shutter to come down behind his back, but instead it descends between him and the counter, so that the space he occupies becomes part of the city sidewalk. 5) Dankan disguises himself as a guardsman and tells the employee, "I've come for the regular safe inspection." The employee returns to tell him unequivocally that the director has not heard of any such inspection. 6) Dankan dresses as a homeless man and asks "Please give me some money," but is again turned down. 7) Copying the method used in the so-called Teigin Incident,[8] (or in Kei Kumai's *Teigin Incident: Death Row Prisoner*), he dons the white uniform of a health worker and is about to have the employees drink poisoned medicine when a garrulous man appears and says, "Let me be the one to make a toast!" Momentarily carried away, Dankan himself drinks the poison.

These scenes may at first resemble a TV-style succession of skits, but judged in terms of the propulsion of the whole work, they are closer to the dream grammar of early film. It should be noted that scenes 1, 2, 3, and 6 are not in the original scenario, and that they are actually more effective than the scenes that were originally included. (There are numerous differences between the scenario and the actual film. In general, the scenes that were added during shooting are the funniest. This is doubtless an indication of how the set functioned as a creative springboard. Nevertheless, it is regrettable that in the scene where a rival yakuza spy is being tortured, the film substitutes the simple physical comedy of S&M torture for the "information society"-style torture described in the scenario, in which a spy is tortured when his TV is switched off in the middle of a program, leaving him desperate to know the outcome of the show.)

The fourth of the above gags takes after Luis Buñuel in its transformation of space (such as the startling scene in *The Discreet Charm of the Bourgeoisie,* when a curtain is lifted and a dining room transforms into a theater stage). In another scene, Dankan is mistaken for the hit man Joe Shishido and importuned by a group of yakuza to demonstrate his shooting ability in a field. This absurd atmosphere is conveyed by the boss, Tetsuya Yuki, who fails to notice his underlings milling pointlessly around the field, and again during the demonstration of Dankan's shooting, when all of the yakuza are again compelled to wander pointlessly around the field. This space, subjected to an absurd magnetic field, resembles the mansion from which no one can exit in Buñuel's *The Exterminating Angel* (1962). Another example can be found in the scene where the president of Jonan Electronics (played by the actual president of the company)[9] walks from his shop to the parking lot holding an attaché case full of cash. Though it appears at first that Dankan is the only one trailing him, we then see behind him people who look like desperate salarymen in loan trouble, and finally Indians, Goemon Ishikawa, Jirokichi Nezumikozo,[10] and Zorro. The impression this gives resembles the scene in Buñuel's *Andalusian Dog* (1929), where tugging on a priest pulls up a piano and even mule carcasses.

However, if we have gone this far, we must also admit that the nonsensical scene where the hit man is given a shooting test (a quick-draw artist who can kill even germs and molecules!) resembles Atsushi Yamatoya's *Lupin III*.[11] Moreover, there is the scene where Dankan and an old prospector dig in a cave for hidden Tokugawa gold: Dankan says "We'll split this fifty-fifty;" the old man says, "I've worked on this for so long, I should get seventy percent," and Dankan replies, "Okay, seventy-seventy." The playful logic of this scene calls to mind Lewis Carroll, or, in cinematic terms, Monty Python's *Holy Grail* (1975). So many gags are organically tied together in *Getting Any?* that searching for their origin would be meaningless.

In the same way, it would be inaccurate to call this movie a "banquet of parody." True, *Getting Any?* quotes from countless other films in addition to the ones mentioned above: David Cronenberg's 1986 remake of *The Fly* (or perhaps the original 1958 version); the Godzilla series; Toei yakuza films;[12] American new cinema in the scene where Dankan imagines being gunned down by police; Kiriro Urayama's *Cupola no aru machi* in the scene at the Kawaguchi cast-metal factory; Nikkatsu "Romance Porn" flicks[13] in the sex scene with Ezawa Moeko as the cast-metal factory matron; Banmei Takahashi's *Tattoo* (Tattoo ari, 1982) in the bank-robber scenes; Junji Sakamoto's *Tokarev* in the shot where Dankan follows the women in Japanese sandals and summer kimonos into the public bath; Kinji Fukasaku's *Double Cross* (Itsuka giragirasuruhi, 1992) in the scene where the guardsmen are shot from the armored car; and the ending of *Silence of the Lambs* in the invisible man scenes where the protagonist can only be seen with special glasses. Alternately, the cheapness of this last scene is a tribute to the low-budget science fiction imaginativeness of Godard's *Alphaville* (1965), and the boldness of the broken-down car scenes could be read as an homage to Godard's *Weekend.* In *Getting Any?*, quotations are collected and melted down as if to proclaim that this is the nature of contemporary society. Hence their origins lose their meanings.

Dankan's fantasies about riding in a Cessna undeniably summon up the world of Ko Nakahira's *Crimson Wings* (Kurenai no tsubasa, 1958). However, just as Dankan is not Yujiro Ishihara, the flight attendant in the fantasy Cessna is not Sanae Nakahara; when Dankan actually rides in the Cessna, the hit man on the plane does not bear the slightest resemblance to Hideaki Nitani.[14] Characteristically, the tenor of the scene changes, degenerating into the lewd mambo of the pilot-cum-flight attendant, Guadalcanal Taka—a dance that resembles Helmut Berger's in *The Damned* (Visconti 1969) or Charlotte Rampling's in *The Night Porter* (1974). These quotations are not embedded into the work: instead they slide willfully across it like Dankan's nomadic sexual desire. The "quotation" violently blurs the territory of the "quoted." Kitano's work here approaches the dismemberment of the "rhetoric of quotation" technique that has been developed since the 1970s. The emphasis here is not in the "act" or "technique" of quotation, but in demonstrating its ever-expanding "movement" or "reference."

This sliding movement is typical of the entire film. The scene of shadow pictures represents a desire-laden movement back towards a pre-cinematic time; the parade of "world defense vehicles," where the parade sergeant advertises a reduction in the rental fees for a "Hibino no Astro High Vision" TV, carries an indirect jab at the tie-in commercialism of current-day film production. As for the adult video media that goes hand in hand with cinema, the "mosaic" filter that always blocks only Dankan's private parts seems to express staunch support for the sex scenes of "Romance Porn" films (could this really be true?). Most of all, the fundamental movement of the film, where images embody the materialization of the protagonist's desire must derive from Kitano's "meta" consciousness of film itself.

Kitano's own films also show up in this work. In the "High Vision" scene mentioned above, the amateur baseball scene is a reprise of *Boiling Point;* the game of "William Tell" on the placid beach in *Sonatine* is transformed in this film into a scene where a real apple is placed on someone's head, but, in a typical incongruity, the weapon being used is not a pistol but a Japanese sword. Innumerable actors from previous Kitano films, such as Hakuryu and Eiji Minakata also appear, but here again this does not give the impression of a solemn engagement with Kitano's previous works, but rather of a continual atavistic chain reaction. The rule in Kitano's hard-boiled films that gunfire will always come from an unexpected direction reappears in the scene of Dankan's shooting test as a hit man, where he aims at a coin thrown into the air, and shoots the yakuza right in front of him in the back of the head. However, the crucial point here is that this does not give rise to the shock of Kitano's previous films, but rather to laughter. This laughter arises from the "lightness of the body" produced by such slapstick sound effects as the clang of a hammer ringing on someone's head.

In this film, the sense of being or presence in the characters is slight. The role Makoto Ashikawa plays is typical. Why are Dankan's

getting any?

cells transformed so easily, even pathetically, into oxygen in the Invisible Man Machine? And why does the now invisible Dankan float a wan smile, as if unconsciously realizing that he will never become a true sexual agent? Such a sensibility does not exist in Kitano's previous films. Moreover, the thoroughgoing decentered-ness of this film, with its endless accumulation of small details, was also absent from his earlier work. This is thus a new permutation of Kitano's vision of "contemporary culture."

The repetition gags in the film contributes to a sense of decline as well. Actually, when I first saw the film, its continual forward motion somehow gave an impression of "stagnation," similar to the addition of zeros, as in $0 + 0 + 0 + \ldots$ A number of other elements also recalled the negativity of previous Kitano films: the physicality of the portion of the film featuring the "Chambara Trio"; the way the yakuza lose their sense of direction (not only in the shooting test scene described earlier, but also in the scene where the yakuza, led by Tetsuya Yuki, face the wrong direction while awaiting a gun duel). Cold colors predominate in the location shots: the cars Dankan buys are all shades of the same blue as Beat Takeshi's car in *Sonatine,* no doubt amplifying the sense of the film's coldness. Moreover, the watchwords of Kitano's films—"the temptation of death" and "the temptation of self-punishment"—also proliferate here. The license plate of the yellow car that Dankan first receives, together with a gun, from Susumu Terajima reads "4 4 4 4," repeating the homophone for "death" four times; the self-punishing gag in the Kawasaki baseball stadium where a festival drum player strikes himself with a mallet is more pathetic than funny. Or there is the scene where Dankan visits the Cessna airline office and finds Taka about to hang himself. Finally there is the sequence where Hiro-o Oikawa receives a cake with a time bomb inside and naively brings it home. When the cake explodes, he and his family are singed, cartoon-style, after which he clumsily climbs on the railing of a bridge to throw himself into the water. After Kitano's motorcycle accident, he said in an interview that he had been "completely on the edge" prior to the crash. The scenes in *Getting Any?* described above suggest that this work is actually an ominous report on Kitano's mental condition at that time.

The topical satire in *Getting Any?* is also dark and destructive. For example, in the scene where Dankan brings a bag of white powder to Dr. Chin, played by Higashi Sonomanma, Sonomanma gives it one trial taste after another, and eventually dumps the entire bag over his own head. While the immediate implication of his action is that the bag contains the real thing, the scene emphasizes the paradoxical results of overconsumption. Another essential point is the large extent to which the written word is foregrounded in the film. I mentioned earlier the subtitles "translated by Natsuko Toda." Elsewhere, on the billboard for the "American-style" topless pizza,[15] the restaurant's name "Ultra Satisfaction" is written in big letters. In this way, Kitano constantly abuses the power of naming.

It's not until the end of the film that we learn that Dankan's character in the film is named "Asao" (this is because much of the beginning of the film was cut out in editing—the original rushes of approved scenes ran almost four hours); "Asao" is probably a reference to "*asadachi*."[16] Moreover, "cash-transport vehicle" is written on the cash-transport vehicle in big characters. While this is of course a gag, it also raises a serious issue for contemporary culture.

According to Walter Benjamin's *Collected Writings Vol. 3: Language and Society*,[17] the act of naming was originally permitted to God alone. As names began to separate from the true nature of things, human speech fell into the confusion of sin. Names began to float meaninglessly—this is the slippage of signifiers without signifieds. The label "cash-transport vehicle," then, is a manifestation of the sin of "excessive naming." In this case, for words to convey only something slightly beyond themselves deprives us of thought itself. The result is that the characters written on the side of the transport vehicle make us strongly conscious of the white noise of contemporary culture.

It is certain that we are being deprived of thought when told a meaningless narrative. However, what if such a narrative generates its own rhythm. . . ? Wouldn't our thoughts then be reconstituted under the magnetism of this rhythm? Such talkativeness can only be excused when transformed into music. Other "intermittent" rhythms (such as the scatological jokes) are woven into the basic beat of *Getting Any?*, resulting in a complex rhythm. (In the Kawasaki stadium scene, the musical exaltation produced by the combination of the festival drum and an organ playing blues chords is a direct representation of this process.) This kind of complex polyrhythm is essentially that of a film that is not, after all, suffering from a pathology, as I came to understand viscerally after watching *Getting Any?* numerous times.

In the past, Kitano has stated in interviews that he edits his films in accordance with his own heartbeat. In *Sonatine,* "death" was unquestionably a part of this heartbeat. In *Getting Any?*, the heartbeat seems at first to be something dark, but if you listen closely, it transforms into a bright rhythm. Viewing the press conference of Kitano's release from the hospital after his motorcycle accident, anyone would have been stunned by the transformation of his face. However, this reaction was primed by the "contemporary culture" represented by TV news shows that edited together the most shocking views of his face. After watching the entire conference several times, however, I was able to detect a kinetic expression of renewal on Kitano's face, which had at first seemed so inorganic. My final impression of *Getting Any?* is the same.

The central theme of this film is clearly "love=death." Dankan becomes the Flyman because of the sexual fantasies he has authored, and is fated to die by the flyswatter. Covered in manure, his final words are "Ah . . . sex . . . ," thus tying love and death together. As Dankan is dying, Beat Takeshi and Makoto Ashikawa hold up signs saying "The Flyman is an intelligent mammal!" and "Save the Flyman!" (Here again is the intrusion of written language.) If the film had ended here at the Kawasaki stadium, we could give it the pat appraisal of being a comedy about a man who lets his desire run free on the sea of contemporary information. Yet this is not the case. As in *Sonatine*, images return to the screen after the final credit roll. In a parody of *E.T.*, a black shadow flits across a full moon. Dankan is heading towards Tokyo Tower as the "Grasshopper Man." Hopping down, he is skewered on the top of Tokyo Tower. Dankan's movement here approximates the logo used in the film's ads composed of a conjunction of the symbol of maleness (circle/arrow) and the female symbol (circle/cross), in which the masculine arrow penetrates the female circle. The meaning here is, of course, "ultra satisfaction." Tying together love and death, Dankan expires. Thus the film transforms a tragedy into a good laugh. From this we can understand that the friendly encouragement of the title also refers to the sexual act.

I have neglected to comment on Beat Takeshi's role as the scientist of the "Society for the Promotion of the Invisible Man." Needless to say, his performance here is a familiar one, in which he lightly and cheerfully slides across "contemporary culture."

getting any?

kids return

In his landmark essay on Godard, "The Catastrophe of Slow Motion,"[1] Shigehiko Hasumi focuses on Jean-Paul Belmondo's lines in the second half of *Breathless:* "Informers inform, robbers rob, killers kill. This simple dogma, recalling the saying that 'a woman is a woman,'[2] is the central issue for Godard." This simple proposition comes to life as movement in Godard's films. Viewers of those films "have no choice but to register bewildered surprise at on-screen phenomena that are difficult to explain as either causes or effects." Hasumi identifies this as the experience of Godard's viewers. Hasumi's essay came to mind while watching Takeshi Kitano's *Kids Return* because of the lines spoken to a young athlete by an older one in the boxing gym: "Strong guys are always strong . . . weak guys are still weak, even if they quit drinking." This proposition eventually collapses, however, into the realization that "strong guys are not necessarily always strong." Nevertheless, viewers of Kitano's film will undoubtedly also "have no choice but to register bewildered surprise at on-screen phenomena that are difficult to explain as either causes or effects." In other words, if Godard boldly exposed human action in *Breathless,* then Takeshi Kitano unpretentiously, and without sugar-coating, projects the tactile sensation of "life" in *Kids Return.*

beat takeshi vs. takeshi kitano

Of all Kitano's films, *Kids Return* will probably remind viewers most of *A Scene at the Sea* in that it belongs to the same genre of "coming-of-age films," and also because Kitano himself does not perform in it, though he was responsible for directing it, writing the script, and editing it. Another resemblance between the two movies is the way temporal structures are created by the circulation of the "pairing off" of "couples." *A Scene at the Sea* features two couples: the deaf-mute male and female protagonists, and the two boys who switch from soccer to surfing after observing the deaf-mute couple's fascination with surfing. The way the actions of these youths reflect those of the couple can be described as a ripple of "love" that infuses the film with a keen lyricism. However, no split takes place in either of *A Scene at the Sea*'s "pairing offs." In other words, the two kids remain together from the beginning of the film to its end, and the deaf-mute protagonists are separated only by the clear intercession of "death," not by such indistinct factors as differences in ability or direction.

In *Kids Return,* even more "couples" take the stage: the two protagonists; a second pair who observe the growing strength of one of the protagonists as he trains to be a boxer, and who subsequently change allegiance from their gang to boxing, much as the kids in *A Scene at the Sea* change from soccer to surfing; and a third pair who hope to become manzai performers. All of these pairs are high-school students when the film begins. However, although the film's protagonists—Masaru, played by Ken Kaneko, and Shinji, played by Masanobu Ando—are clearly a "couple" from the start of the film, an

kids return

imbalance hangs over their relationship. Since Shinji calls Masaru the diminutive "Ma-chan," we can guess that the two have been friends from childhood. However, their relationship seems to be predicated on Shinji's dependence on Masaru, a volatile and selfish delinquent. We could say that the film represents a threat to the stability of the world's couples, insofar as it narrates the birth of subjectivity in Shinji, who begins to free himself from his dependence on "Ma-chan."

In concrete terms, the fissure between the two begins after their regular shake-downs of fellow students are interrupted by the reprisal of a boy who's been training at a boxing gym. Masaru makes up his mind to take revenge by learning boxing, too, and Shinji tags along and also begins to learn. In contrast to Masaru, who only sees boxing as a way of winning fights, Shinji approaches the sport with his natural seriousness and makes rapid progress. At this point, Masaru forces his "sidekick" Shinji to spar with him, and is knocked down repeatedly by Shinji's naturally accurate, blistering counterattack—an event that decisively creates a rift in the self-evident nature of their relationship. At this decisive instant, Kitano wisely avoids the mistake of cutting to a close-up of Masaru's stupefied expression. Instead, the two leave the gym and go to their habitual Chinese

restaurant, where Masaru hands both his meal and the ring name he was considering over to Shinji. Although this show of generosity keeps Masaru's vexation and disappointment from showing, the scene is all the more moving because we know that his careful control of his facial expressions only indicates the extent of his disillusionment.

beat takeshi vs. takeshi kitano

At this point, the "couple" of Masaru and Shinji breaks up. Masaru disappears from the film for a while, and the next time we see him he's become a yakuza recruit. The two meet again by chance at the coffee shop where they used to hang out. No longer able to indulge in the same friendship as before, they carefully exchange glances, sizing each other up. Their realization that what they see in the other cannot be expressed in words is profoundly existential. Subsequently, Masaru begins moving up rapidly in the world of the yakuza. This ascent is developed in parallel to Shinji's rise as a rookie champ in the boxing world. Just as Claude Maki was "chosen" to be a surfer in *A Scene at the Sea*, it would seem that Masaru has been "chosen" to be a yakuza and Shinji to be a boxer. But the film answers, "No, such is not the case," to this assumption.

Shinji's expulsion from the boxing world is painful to watch. The person who serves as a catalyst for the degeneration of Shinji's ascetic spirit is a former rookie champ, Moro Morooka, who belongs to the same gym. He is the person who tells Shinji, "Strong guys are always strong . . . weak guys are still weak, even if they quit drinking." Morooka demonstrates with his own body that you can eat and drink as much as you like and still maintain your weight by throwing up afterwards. Eventually, Shinji adopts the same philosophy. When he is then unable to lose enough weight, he uses a laxative at Moro's urging, and his peak-performing body looses its sharpness. One could well say that Moro, who corrupts his gymmate's talent in this way, is a kind of devil, but the fact that this devil is no more than a dull-witted factory worker reflects Kitano's realistic view of humanity.

It seems I have regurgitated much of the film's "story," but what's important to keep in mind is that this story takes shape through bold cuts from scene to scene that leap over large periods of abbreviated time. The lengths of time that the camera remains

© OFFICE KITANO

fixed on the objects of the story are also short. This is because Kitano has adapted a strategy of looking at all his characters from multiple perspectives during any given scene. For example, in addition to the aforementioned Moro, all the other characters at Shinji's gym—including the gym's top prospect, a fellow with the ring-name "Eagle"; the gym manager, played by Hatsuo Yamaya; and the trainer, played by Takekazu Shigehisa—are given screen time on par with Shinji's. Similarly, in Masaru's yakuza gang, the gang leader, played by Ryo Ishibashi; his subordinate, played by Susumu Terajima; and even the skinhead and the boy who used to work at the Chinese restaurant, are all given equal treatment. Rather than following the lead of television drama, which centers on its main characters, Kitano seeks to capture the texture of the diffuse contemporary world.

Because each scene has its own gravity or pulling-power, nothing essential is omitted or dispersed, even though the story is advanced by extreme jump cuts. The "whole life" of a daydreamer protected by Masaru and Shinji named Hiroshi (played by Michisuke Kashiwaya) is described: from high school, to graduation, to his employment as a salesman, to his marriage to the coffee-shop waitress he had always had a crush on, to his second job as a taxi driver, to his overwork and death (perhaps) in an auto accident. This "whole life" is sketched through seemingly split-second shots, or through the indirect remarks of the other characters. Likewise, the film sketches out the rise of a team of would-be manzai comedians, and even the metamorphosis of a juvenile delinquent into the manzai performers' manager. This telegraphic style is one of the reasons why the film is able to evoke "bewildered surprise." Certainly, abbreviation has also been a distinction of Kitano's previous films. However, the stories that he told all consisted of a single line—for example, the arc from the appearance of his protagonists to their deaths. This film diverges from his prior work by experimentating with multi-layered character development.

Kitano has not lost his realistic gaze, which views people as things, but this time he has filmed a "screeenwriter's movie." This differs from his earlier works. By manipulating subplots and the reciprocal reflections of his characters, he creates an extremely subtle, multi-layered work. The effectiveness of the jump cuts here is doubtless an extension of what he learned from his previous movie, *Getting Any?* In hindsight, we could describe *Getting Any?* as an experiment in abstractly depicting the twists and turns of a man's (Dankan's) "whole life." As in *Getting Any?*, most of the gags in *Kids Return* are passed on to the viewer after their inefficacy as comedy has been established. (In *Kids Return*, we have the comedy routines of the manzai performers, the running gag of the high-school students trying to sneak into an adult movie, and the lewd "teacher doll" with private parts constructed of light bulbs, a flashlight, and yarnthat Masaru and Shinji dangle from the roof to the classroom window.)

At any rate, the temporal arc describing the lives of the characters in *Kids Return* has definitely lengthened. In this sense, the film represents the first time that Kitano has actually observed the "time" that transforms the world of people's lives. And yet a sense of "timelessness" pervades the film as well. This effect, we should stress, is a confirmation of Takeshi Kitano's talent as a filmmaker rather than as a screenwriter. It is clear from the way that the high-school gang is depicted, including their way of rebelling against teachers, that *Kids Return* is not set in the present. However, there are no signs indicating the actual time frame of the film. It is not even clear how many years after the students' high-school graduation the film covers. This is a deliberate strategy for Kitano. In one scene, we see Masaru and Shinji riding a bike through the school grounds. Later we see Shinji riding on the same route, taken from the same camera angle. Similarly, we see the two boys jogging across a certain overpass, and again we see Shinji and his trainer on the same route. The repetitions are not identical, since they do not follow the same people, and yet the scenery does not change. Thus a muted sensation of cruelty—a cruelty that will inevitably follow the characters for their whole lives—seeps into the film. *(A Scene at the Sea,* by contrast, was composed of long series of more equal repetitions.) The cruelty of this film is due not only to Masaru and Shinji's failures in the yakuza and boxing worlds, or in Hiroshi's death by traffic accident. Rather, its true cruelty lies in the sense of "timelessness" that Kitano has consciously prepared for these "kids who won't grow up" as they

encounter the cruelty of the adult world. (Of course, their facial expressions do pick up a certain seriousness as time progresses in the film). Despite the film's overarching temporal structure of present day/flashback/present day, this sense of "timelessness" gives rise to the contradictory impression that somehow the film never really "returns" (though the actual passage of time is clearly indicated by the white hair that gathers on the brow of their homeroom teacher, played by Leo Morimoto).

When the two protagonists go back to their high school, circling on their bike in the schoolyard as before (the title *Kids Return* clearly derives from the scene), they exchange the following

beat takeshi vs. takeshi kitano

dialogue: "Ma-chan, it's all over for us, isn't it?" "What are you talking about? It's not even started yet." Nevertheless, in depicting this "return," the film seems to circumscribe the shape of a zero. The difficulty in distinguishing between "beginning" and "end" foregrounded here is indeed the contradictory way of the "world"; and such indeed are the contradictory circumstances under which Masaru and Shinji must continue to live. The film's cruelty is amplified by the fact that its protagonists do not die.

kids return

fireworks

THE BEAUTIFUL WANING OF BEING

Takeshi Kitano broke many of his own filmmaking rules in *Fireworks*, which once again combines skillfully directed action scenes with a spare storytelling style. Techniques he uses for the first time include flashbacks, dissolves, and starting scenes with moving shots that serve to identify the space. He also uses shots that include identifiable landmarks such as the Rainbow Bridge, a Shinjuku intersection sign, and Mt. Fuji. In previous Kitano films, the scenery always captured an anonymity and universality by remaining stubbornly nonspecific. In this film, he abandons that strategy; shots impressive for their picture-postcard scenic beauty appear repeatedly. Takeshi Kitano, the visual artist who had in the past insisted on gray, overcast exteriors, does not shy away from shooting bright and sunny exteriors here. As a result, *Fireworks* is the first of his films that could be characterized as "colorful."

This does not imply that it lacks the characteristic "restraint" of Kitano's work, merely that its "tendency toward plurality" has been strengthened. The films up to and including *Sonatine* were characterized by their unitary construction. Every shot was independent and pared of impurities. As a result, tension increased as the films approached their conclusion—"death." In contrast, the films after *Getting Any?* have a pluralistic construction. In *Getting Any?*, the episodic structure itself was pluralistic, and *Kids Return* focussed on capturing the multifarious lives of several people. Speaking of *Kids Return*, the main character here is again a "couple." Like Masaru and Shinji, both of whom quit high school to pursue different paths, *Fireworks* depicts the different trajectories of Nishi (Beat Takeshi), an ex-detective forced into retirement, and Horibe (Ren Osugi)—(one could see this film's Takeshi/Osugi pair as Masaru/Shinji years later). But there is a difference. In *Kids Return*, the similarity between Shinji and Masaru was the transitional arc in which Shinji, through boxing, and Masaru, through being a gangster, each reached their peak before falling from grace. In *Fireworks*, a different cruelty is carved out by the way the lives of Takeshi and Osugi are unable to come into alignment with each other. During the stakeout of a murderer, Osugi is shot and paralyzed from the waist down. He retires from the police, is abandoned by his wife and daughter, and spends his days in despair at the beach until he discovers painting. While in pursuit, Takeshi sees the killer who got away with shooting Osugi kill another police officer. Takeshi loses control and brutally retaliates. He is, as a result, dismissed from his job. Prior to this, Takeshi had already lost a young child, and his wife (Kayoko Kishimoto) was diagnosed with terminal cancer. He plunges into debt to raise money for his wife's treatments and to help support the widow of the murdered officer. He thus shares with Osugi a distinct feeling of paralysis. Takeshi's character is expressionless, as if competing with Kishimoto, who, aside from laughing, never even speaks until the very end of the film. Although this expressionlessness creates a feeling of paralysis, it is also true that Takeshi's post-accident face is in fact slightly paralyzed. The moment he removes his sunglasses at the opening of the film, his face reveals a sorrowful beastliness that we have never seen before (it evokes the expressions of the best leading character in a Kitano film,

238 / 239

fireworks

Claude Maki in *A Scene at the Sea*.) Takeshi is no longer emanating fatigue, he is emanating sorrow.

The film's elegiac tone heightens as it progresses towards its dénouement. Osugi sheds tears as he looks at a flower. To make money, Takeshi robs a bank, takes off in a van with his dying wife, and is eventually pursued by his former colleagues (Susumu Terajima etc.). Takeshi's escapades and Osugi's painting process are positioned in a parallel relationship through editing. They are unified by their shared condition of silence with respect to dialogue, and by the editing techniques used in the film. Also of note is the fact that the paintings created by Osugi in the film were actually painted by Takeshi. This film is filled with Takeshi's paintings: under the opening credits, in the hallway of the hospital, in the loan shark's office, on the wall at the bar, etc. All the paintings are detailed and colorful and have an unabashedly childlike quality (thus the feeling of paralysis exists here as well). They depict angels, animals with flowers in the place of heads, and fireworks. Filled with primitive painterly impulses, they are like a cross between Kiyoshi Yamashita and Sonnenstern.[1] In one painting, thin white characters meaning "snow" appear against a black ground as snowflakes. Yellow charac-

ters meaning "light" create sparkles on the canvas as the camera pans to a large character for "suicide" that looks like a fallen figure on a snowy field. Each painting is a momentary carving of "fire." Therefore, even if the painting as a whole may look like a "flower," it contains "fire" in its details. The title *Fireworks* (literally, "fire-flower"

beat takeshi vs. takeshi kitano

in Japanese) seems to imply not the opposition of "flower" (life) with "fire" (death), but rather a mutually inclusive relationship. The colorfulness of the film's scenery thus synchronizes with the paintings. This is evidence that the film was created primarily from images in Kitano's brain. In other words, he executed, in his own unique and simple way, the same approach to filmmaking as Tim Burton.

Takeshi Kitano is omnipresent in this film. His alter egos are the paintings, the character he plays, Osugi, the young girl at the end who runs around with a kite that will not fly, and Kayoko Kishimoto, who is the embodiment of "despair" smiling. Hence, this is a film of plurality. Osugi continues to live through the wings of his creative spirit, and Takeshi commits suicide with his wife—this represents the two sides of Takeshi's mental state. What flows throughout is "the feeling of paralysis" that is stamped on the film with finality when the painting of a one-winged angel appears after the end credits. However, this "paralysis" is more a general state of our times rather than a personal one for Takeshi Kitano. That is, more than the feeling of paralysis itself, what is probably being probed here is the beautiful "waning" of being, in which the feeling of paralysis makes the world appear more colorful. Of course, the audience experiences this waning as much as the filmmaker. So it is not something we censure, but rather something we yearn for.

fireworks

kikujiro

I occasionally reflect on Takeshi Kitano's restless intellectual movement as he conceives of a film, writes notes and a scenario, endlessly revises these while shooting, then further rearranges the order of the scenes while editing. What he is probably calculating in his imagination are the various effects of the combination and collision of "fragments." These fragments accumulate while still clearly retaining the vestiges of their singularity. Thus the autonomy of these fragments is conspicuous within each completed film. While such fragmentation indicates Kitano's personal sense of time, the arrangement of the fissures they form also expresses the depth of history. This methodology strongly recalls Walter Benjamin's theory of allegory, in which things are gathered together from the opposite shore of forgetfulness, and what has been collected is then endowed with temporality. The film *Fireworks* first brought Benjamin to mind in the context of Kitano's works, as it is replete with Benjaminesque symbols: angels, melancholy, ruins (the junked car lot), and finally, the temporal arrangement of disparate fragments that have been collected.

As Kitano himself has admitted, his film *Kikujiro* (Kikujiro no natsu, 1999) takes *3000 Leagues in Search of Mother* (Haha wo tazunete sanzenri, 1976)[1] as its narrative model. Still, it is not so simple an affair that it can be reduced to that narrative alone. If the film were a travel chronicle with only a few digressions, it could be classified under the road-movie genre. Actually, though, I did not get this subjective impression from the film. First of all, the little boy and the gangster, who are strangers to each other, are introduced to yet more strangers in a series of encounters, and are thus repeatedly exposed to the pattern of "appearance/disappearance." Various "types" that can be fairly said to be imprinted with Japanese cultural ethnicity[2] appear throughout: the two waiters who aspire to be tap dancers; a child molester played by Akaji Maro; a juggler and a mime traveling as a couple; street-stall vendors such as Taro Suwa; two bikers; and finally a couple of Japanese goblins or "*tengu*."[3] Even more than Takeshi's yakuza character, it is the little boy who seems reconfirmed as an ethnic type through these encounters. The face of this child (played by Yusuke Sekiguchi) took my breath away when it was first fixed in the frame. Unlike the faces of his classmates, which are marked by familial happiness, his face is clearly marked with the loneliness of a parentless child. His thick eyebrows and protruding ears seem somehow Buddha-like, but when Takeshi paints his face with clumsy—perhaps we could say ethnic—make-up, he seems to exude the spiritual power of Shinobu Orikuchi's "little god."[4]

Actually, the true core of this movie is not Takeshi coming to the aid of the boy, but rather the opposite: the journey of a yakuza who is led and aided by a "little god." An ethnic (or folkloric) panoply of characters is temporialized in a completely folkloric manner—a structure that betrays Takeshi Kitano's unique intelligence, thus surpassing the run of previous road-movie filmmakers. As a result, thrilling, kinetic scenes are completely excluded from the film. The journey, which begins with Asakusa,[5] takes us through locations as follows: 1) completely commonplace, man-made spaces, 2) desolate landscapes whose cinematic qualities are sharpened by the darkness of night, and 3) anonymous spaces of play characterized by extreme marginality. The third of these recalls *Sonatine*'s scenes of idle play in Okinawa. I will omit an inventory of the scenes in *Kikujiro* that correspond with those of his previous films, but it is important to recognize the methodology of "inheritance/transformation" used by Kitano and made possible by "using scenes that resemble previous ones" and "altering the overall effect." Thus he is able to spontaneously achieve the wonder of preserving simplicity in each film while increasing the complexity of the overall effect.

Let me attempt some iconographic analysis here. Kitano's imagination is waiting for the temporalization/mobilization of his own painting of an angel that appears during the title sequence, and of the tattoo on Takeshi's back, both of which are shown at first in a colorful but motionless state. Their mobility will be activated by sound (in this case, the sound of the bell). At the beginning of the film, the local color of Asakusa is established through the sequence of several tinkling wind chimes for sale in a shopfront, a Chinese lion and peony tattoo insignia on a t-shirt for sale to foreign tourists, and the sound of a bell from a passing bicycle. If we say that the overall image of the film is the static pattern of a "tattoo" felicitously made mobile by the sound of a bell, then this opening sequence clearly foreshadows what is to come.

The child has nightmares twice in this film. His first is the transformed memory of almost being raped by the child molester played by Akaji Maro. This dream is triggered by the image of the tattoo seen on Takeshi's back as he sleeps in the hotel room. The second nightmare occurs in the scene where the child waits in back of a Shinto shrine for Takeshi, who for the first time on-screen becomes a victim of violence. Two tengu intrude into the boy's dream, pressing in on him with a sinister intensity. This scene begins to overlap with an elevated shot of a tall black tree's silhouette as it blows in the wind amidst the magical lingering light of festival-booth lanterns. These

images of festival lanterns and the restless motion of the tree also resemble tattoos. The effective insertion of incongruous images such as these nightmares is undoubtedly a legacy from *Fireworks,* but from another point of view, the impetus to put a still picture in motion is a new discovery for Kitano. The focus here should be on the process of putting things in motion. Hence these scenes, while bearing the meaning of nightmares, are also scenes of escape from nightmares.

Benjamin was the first to see cinema as an example of the loss of aura, not in a negative sense, but as a "space of motion." He organized within himself the motion-amidst-rubble of walking in the city, and of children's play. Currently, Kitano, like Benjamin, sees the contemporary world as an accumulation of rubble, and intuits motion as the true meaning of film. The traffic in things, captured almost incidentally, is what develops this sense of motion to the highest degree. Kitano's attention to this traffic resembles Robert Bresson's eye for the flow of money in *L'Argent* (1983), and yet Kitano takes it to another dimension. At first, Takeshi's yakuza only gives the child capitalist commodities such as a bicycle-racer outfit and a ten-thousand-yen note. But this changes during the course of the film. The orange given to Takeshi by Fumie Hosokawa's juggler transforms into the rice ball that he steals from Beat Kiyoshi and gives to the boy. Takeshi presents the "angel bell" from the Great Gidayu's bike to the boy under the pretext that it represents a token of his mother's love. The handmade sunshade-hat made from a giant leaf is undoubtedly also a gift from Takeshi, but since both he and the boy

kikujiro

wear them, it becomes a kind of offering which the two make together. After Takeshi is beaten up by the yakuza who operate the summer festival, it is the boy who buys medicine and gives it to him. Thus the traffic in items between Takeshi and the boy gradually becomes indirect, spiritual, and mutual, taking on a kind of magical transmutability/mobility. At this time, the "experience" of visiting one's mother is transferred abstractly to Takeshi, giving rise to the pathetic scene where he visits his mother in the nursing home. (I shuddered at Kitano's expressive power, which is able to convey the loneliness and stubbornness of Takeshi's mother in one short scene.)

Kikujiro creates these moments filled with mobility in a dimension removed from the directness of a road movie. The theme of something being repeated three times, inherited from *Sonatine*, reappears here in the scenes where someone falls in a hole and flails his legs around. But this gag is performed twice by Takeshi and then handed over to the Great Gidayu. The subject carrying out the action shifts in this process of "putting things in motion," and thus the repetition doesn't materialize in the realm of fear, but rather serves to spread good humor. What, then, is finally temporalized through the process of making things mobile? At the film's close, the

boy asks "What's your name, Mister?" and Takeshi answers, "Kikujiro, you idiot!" Of course, "Kikujiro" is the name of Takeshi Kitano=Beat Takeshi's actual father. Takeshi Kitano uses the drama about a yakuza, played by himself, and a child to show the relationship that he wishes he'd had with his father long ago. Therefore we can understand

beat takeshi vs. takeshi kitano

this film as an "imaginatively possible" emotional exchange between Takeshi and his actual father, projected onto the "real life" of kids today. The indirectness of the structure becomes a kind of modesty, which resonates with the Japanese understanding of modesty as a virtue. However, because this is merely the realm of imaginative yearning, of "the possible," a fissure appears in the lonely depths of the director's personal sense of time: the past explosively overflows into the present the instant Takeshi makes "Kikujiro" his own character's name. This mysterious process, when skillfully evoked, has the power to move us to tears. In response to Benjamin, who saw cinema's comedy as an explosion of rubble, Kitano gives us an additional gift: the explosive power of tears.

brother

Takeshi Kitano has made a Hollywood film—this evaluation of his new work *Brother* (2000) is undoubtedly correct. The volume of bullets and shells expended in the movie certainly surpasses Kitano's previous efforts. It might even seem that the director's estimation of Hollywood is so low that he thinks its true essence is volume alone. Moreover, this film embodies the warped consciousness with which Hollywood treats Japanese characters. In other words, a Japanese person has taken on the mantle of Hollywood, intentionally making a film that will be a national embarrassment.

There are a number of shocking scenes in *Brother* that, in their deadly impulsiveness, will surely bring a shudder to anyone familiar with the "kamikaze spirit" of former times. These include the scene where Susumu Terajima, playing Takeshi's subordinate, takes his own life in order to persuade the Los Angeles Little Tokyo crime boss to join Takeshi's gang. Equally shocking is the scene where Ren Osugi, playing Takeshi's yakuza "brother," commits seppuku at a gang banquet to demonstrate his loyalty after breaking the code of honor by joining a rival yakuza organization.

Takeshi plays a yakuza who has lost his base of operations in Japan and takes over a gang of black drug dealers in Los Angeles that includes his own brother (Claude Maki), who has adopted rap culture.

The artless manner in which Takeshi expands his power in the American black community is, in a word, reckless. The depiction of Takeshi's rise in Los Angeles, together with the particulars of his flight from Japan, could easily be dismissed for its sloppy establishment of yakuza-movie causality. However, the director pays no heed to this anticipated criticism.

I have previously identified several factors that made Kitano's films stand out in 1990s Japan—for example, "the power of the intervals between scenes where main events occur," or "the precarious effect of balance, implying a sense of looming collapse, created when the plurality of characters is superimposed on the simplicity of plot exposition." *Brother* takes these principles even further, piling on even more complex characters one after another. Just as a disk painted in wedges of primary colors gives off white light when spun quickly, this film taken as a whole puts one in a mysterious trance. Since the film is dominated to an unfortunate extent by the notion that the secret to Hollywood movies is their rapid-fire delivery of detail, the only thing that remains in the end is an intensity virtually indistinguishable from futility.

The opinion that this is not a Hollywood film, but only an upgraded Kitano film, is thus also valid. "Yakuza existence is riddled with impossibility." "All die but one." "The one who remains receives the spirit of those who died." "The time of pure play, nihilistically gaping open in the film, eludes definition." With respect to all of these points, the film appears to be a mere rearrangement of *Sonatine*. Of course, *Fireworks* was already a rearrangement of *Sonatine*, so

Sonatine, Fireworks, and *Brother* can be seen as a classic example of a minimalistic body of work composed of the smallest possible variations. Those drawn to the sense of materiality in Takeshi's taciturn screen presence will immediately be mesmerized by *Brother.* They will also be intoxicated by the shock effect of the film's cutting, which also surpasses Kitano's earlier work. (An example is the scene near the beginning where Takeshi uses a wine bottle to slash the eye of Omar Epps, who will later become the gang member closest to him.)

The problem, however, is this very sense of intoxication. The U.S. has become a coercive force worldwide under "Pax Americana," and yet it harbors in its depths poverty-stricken populations of blacks and immigrants. *Brother* seems to be delving into these depths, but in fact a real American other does not exist here. Takeshi himself is the absolute other. The film's sense of intoxication is unrelated to its depiction of the American underclass; this strange sense of intoxication comes from the on-screen violence blossoming around Takeshi. Make no mistake—the specificity of the L.A. location is bleached out of the film. Maki and the others who had been outfitting themselves with the clothes of urban black culture exile themselves from this identity and change into the black suits that are "kamikaze uniforms." In the end, the film plunges into an anonymous American desert setting. This negative "bleaching out," which has no practical benefit, is the reason for the film's sense of intoxication.

The film's nihilistic purity is discovered not only in the moments of idle play, but more broadly in the "America" that appears here—for example, when the relatively short Susumu Terajima takes off his shirt, exposing his tattoo, and desperately plays hoop with the black gang members on a court constructed in the office of Takeshi's gang. This purposeless "play of the gods," performed by gods of destruction, gives birth to a sensation that causes the margins of violence, not violence itself, to sprawl out into their surroundings. The scene is intoxicatingly beautiful.

On the other hand, the violence in this film closely resembles play, and as it abstractly increases in volume, it loses its physical deadliness. The standard of violence within the director has been transformed. It could be said that since he incorporates the use of guns in his films, the violence they cause constitutes a form of mythical weakness. The interpenetration of landscape and violence is important in this context. When the violent protagonists of Clint Eastwood's action films are denied any interiority but remorse, they are colored by a sense of the apocalypse, and the landscape is meticulously bleached out. Kitano has created something similar. America is a blank space: to make this statement, he places the "blank space called a protagonist" in the center of the film. The sound of gunfire becomes the simple frame for his work—otherwise one must endure silence. This transforms the film into a myth with an Eastwood-style sensibility.

Incidentally, the sense of "remorse" displayed by Takeshi in *Fireworks* is not found here. The atomization of Takeshi's body in *Sonatine* as he "dies" by the moment is not found in *Brother* either. In *Brother*, Takeshi is already dead. This is related to his absence of desire. Why does Takeshi purposely choose a homely mistress when he has both money and coercive power? And when she is abducted by the Chinese Mafia, why does he shoot her together with his enemies? Because of the absence of desire. The incoherence of Takeshi's gang's rise to power also relates to this point. At this juncture, one is reminded of Walter Benjamin's essay, "The Destructive Character," which elevates left-wing destructiveness to an apocalyptic level. The essay lists the characteristics of the destructive character, beginning with, "The destructive character knows only one watchword; 'make room!'" We shouldn't overlook two other sentences that give off a dull glow in Benjamin's work: "No vision inspires the destructive character. He has few desires."

This reminds me of Takeshi Kitano=Beat Takeshi's words in a recent interview in *Komanechi! 2*.[1] "I get the feeling that when it comes to building a house, too, you can only build one when you reach the point of saying 'I don't give a damn about a house.'" It seems that a sense of disappointment—caused by the disparity between the moment when he hatches a desire and the period when it is realized—is eating away at him. Over time, this feeling has transformed into an absence of desire. This is undoubtedly the reason why his film, in addition to being a myth, also has a contemporary character.

d o l l s

A HUMAN MACHINE'S PERFORMANCE OF "REMORSE"

To break free of self-restraint, and by so doing, to change the organizational method of his works—this is the artistic spirit on which Takeshi Kitano is currently staking his work. By so doing, he seeks to vigorously deny his former self. (Probably Kitano's current mood includes some regret at his most recent work, *Brother,* which was a ratcheted-up version of his previous works made with the American market in mind.) His next film, *Dolls* (2002), was born out of such a mindset. As a result, it gives off many signals of being "anti-Takeshi Kitano."

First of all, we could mention the aggressive introduction of "kinetic" camerawork, which relies on the camera's technical possibilities (its ability to travel, zoom, and so forth). The camerawork at the opening of the film, which captures a performance of Monzaemon Chikamatsu's *bunraku* puppet drama,[1] *The Courier of Hell* (Meido no hikyaku), is particularly anti-Kitano. The camera, which circles around quite close to the puppets, alternately presents total and partial views of the gestures being bestowed by the black-robed puppeteers. The technique here denies the unity of the shot itself, and yet a certain difficult-to-grasp "tenacity" appears in the camerawork. Shots of the entire stage, the narrator, and the audience are also inserted in a complex manner. Surely any viewer would be astounded by these primitive shots, which take in the entire theater audience with a fast and abrupt horizontal movement reminiscent of silent cinema. Then, just as the leading couple in the puppet play approaches their tragic double suicide and begin to look at the "human world" from a new perspective,[2] the subject of this "kinetic" camerawork shifts from the realm of puppets to the world of humans. Shots such as the abrupt and aggressively frontal reverse shots familiar from Kitano's previous films are added in. This reinforces the sense of incongruity that is intentionally created in the shooting script.

For other examples of the film's "anti-Takeshi Kitano" qualities, we could turn to the "Japanese" colors of the film, with their bright hues taken from nature. This trend was already evident in *Fireworks*, but here the colors lack any sense of restraint and float across the screen in a kind of zero-gravity state. Springtime rows of cherry trees in full bloom, the white sand and green pines of summer, the scarlet maple leaves of autumn, and the snowy landscapes of winter: these places visited by the wandering couple (composed of a deranged and "puppet-like" woman and her remorseful man) form a symbolic realm infused with Japanese sentiment—what we might refer to as the aesthetic world of "snow, moon, and flowers."[3] (This couple is tied together by red cords, and are derisively called the "tied-up bums" by the people around them.) The costumes prepared by Yoji Yamamoto for the deranged woman are made of a single fabric draped over the actress (Miho Kanno) in a fashion typical of the designer's work, but the use of primary colors stands out as atypical for Yamamoto. In the third episode of the film, where Kyoko Fukada performs in a music studio as a singer at the peak of popular success, the colors breathe under the lighting in a truly memorable way with a brightness completely lacking in depth or thickness. (Fans will recognize this as a song by Yasuharu Konishi, a popular Japanese musician.) In this scene, the camera circles its subject in an unself-conscious manner

dolls

that seems almost flippant, and, just as in the introductory puppet-theater scene, the perspective seems too close. The scene gives rise to an uncomfortable feeling, as if confronting the viewer with something fake or kitschy. This too is the product of Kitano's earnest intention to free himself from the aesthetic of self-restraint.

Puppets peer into the world of humans. And three groups of humans who have the same fate as the puppets—the fate of regret—appear on the screen. Therefore, the human worlds depicted here can be taken as "the recollections of puppets" (these recollections have a point of return at the film's conclusion). The drama begins when the humans (Hidetoshi Nishijima and Miho Kanno in the first episode, or Kyoko Fukada and Tsutomu Takeshige in the third) look back on the past from their position in the present moment. "Recollections" within this past temporality also exist. In other words, at its most adventurous, the film's temporality consists of a three-fold reminiscence: recollections of recollections of recollections. (Despite this multilayered temporality, the film never loses its underlying simplicity).

The theme of recollection appears Kitano's work from *Fireworks* onwards. In *Fireworks*, the past uncontrollably seeps into the present time, as if to corrode it away. This tendency becomes even more extreme in *Dolls*. The associative progression of reminiscence here is determined not by the necessities of narrative explanation, but by the recollections of the characters themselves—by the editing process of the characters' imaginations. (If overused, this approach could give the narrative rhetoric a half-baked quality.) We should also note that disquieting elements such as

beat takeshi vs. takeshi kitano

absence and disillusionment are introduced into the human world in order to establish it as "the recollections of puppets." Perhaps the film's sparse dialogue and extreme narrative efficiency also reflect the gaze of the puppets, who can only grasp reality in an abstract fashion. I felt this way particularly near the end of the film, when the fate of the puppets and the fate of the humans overlap. Indeed, the excessive suggestiveness of this overlap is probably unnecessary. Perhaps Kitano had in mind the example of his good friend, Taiwanese film director Hou Hsiao-Hsien. After establishing himself completely with *City of Sadness* (1989), Hou boldly reduced even the visibility of his work in order to depict the overlapping worlds of humans and puppets in *The Puppetmaster* (1993).

Let us consider the "lives of regret" that are assigned to the three pairs of characters in this film, starting with the couple played by Hidetoshi Nishijima and Miho Kanno. Nishijima is engaged to Kanno, but dumps her when he gets the chance to marry a company president's daughter, partly due to pressure from his parents. After an attempt at suicide, Kanno loses her sanity. Nishijima learns of this in the wedding hall where he is about to get married. He runs out of the hall, pulls Kanno out of the hospital, and begins to wander across Japan with her. This hackneyed theme of a man blinded by money who has a change of heart is familiar from such classic novels as Kouyou Ozaki's *Golden Demon* (Konjiki yasha). Other Takeshi Kitano films also feature the aimless wanderings of a couple—for example, *A Scene at the Sea,* where the couple consists of a surfer and his girlfriend, or *Fireworks,* where Beat Takeshi journeys across the country with Kayoko Kishimoto in the latter half of the film.

Tatsuya Mihashi and Chieko Matsubara play the second pair of characters in *Dolls*. Though lovers in their youth, Mihashi eventually becomes intent on moving up in the world and leaves Matsubara. As the young Mihashi (played by Kanji Tsuda) leaves, Matsubara shouts, "I'll wait for you on this park bench—I'll be here with your lunch every Saturday." Decades later, Mihashi, who has become a yakuza boss, happens to recall these words. Returning to the park after his long absence, he sees Matsubara sitting on the bench waiting for him, with two boxed lunches on her lap. Having betrayed all of his promises, Mihashi feels indignation at his own idle life. Even when he sits down on the bench next to Matsubara's, she still doesn't recognize him, but treats him as a stranger. We could say that this second segment takes the theme of "waiting" from a work such as Dostoevski's *White Nights,* and combines it with the Chaplinesque theme of "not recognizing the person in front of your own eyes." This story, too, has no originality.

Soon afterwards, Mihashi is killed by a hitman (Moro Morooka) disguised as a jogger, and dies the way senior gang members in Kitano films do. By this point, such a death is no longer surprising. Undoubtedly, Matsubara will continue coming to the park bench on Saturdays with her boxed lunches, waiting for her reunion with Mihashi.

Kyoko Fukada and Tsutomu Takeshige portray the third couple. Takeshige abandons all else and singlemindedly follows after the singer Fukada, taking manual jobs such as night-time road repair work. Eventually Fukada meets with a traffic accident, and irreparably injures one of her eyes, forcing her to retire. Irrationally, Takeshige seems to feel that his own love has been inadequate. He goes to visit her while she is convalescing at her mother-in-law's home. In order to prevent himself from seeing her injured and deformed face, he blinds himself by slashing his own eyes with a box-cutter. This is surely a variation on Junichiro Tanizaki's *A Portrait of Shunkin* (Shunkin sho, 1932) Fukada is touched by Takeshige's kindness, and the two quietly pass time in places such as a rose garden filled with gorgeous blossoms. However, Takeshige soon dies in a traffic accident caused by his self-inflicted blindness. Fukada waits for his return alone on the beach. (This third story, with its two traffic accidents, is mediated by Kitano's memories of his own motorcycle accident. In particular, the scene where Takeshige's blood is washed away from the pavement strikes me as an inauspicious bit of self-mutilation.)

The performances of Nishijima, Takeshige, and Mihashi grow out of Beat Takeshi's own performances. This impression is particularly strong in Nishijima and Takeshige's brusqueness, and in Mihashi's sharp-tongued Tokyo dialect. *Dolls* thus resembles *Fireworks* in that Kitano has placed versions of himself in concentric circles throughout the film. And, as in *A Scene at the Sea*, Beat Takeshi "appears" in the film though absent from it.

Each of these three episodes is lacking in imagination. The episodes are not completely independent, but touch upon each other slightly. Even when the three are superimposed upon one another, they generate no fascination. Nevertheless, we can make several significant observations about the film: the moment of remorse does not become the climax of the story in any of the three episodes. Rather, the description focusses on the continuation of regret following this moment. At the same time, Kitano shows that remorse is a transcendental quality. Therefore the three episodes are not arranged in a progressive cause-and-effect fashion. The scene on the beach where Kayoko Kishimoto, leading the blind Takeshige, passes by the first couple, played by Nishijima and Kanno, expresses the despairing philosophy that remorse is transcendental—that new regrets only overcome and renew regrets that came before.

This philosophy reminds me of the aphorisms of E. M. Cioran, who considered regret to be a given of human existence, and yet continued to curse this fact in the strongest terms. Of course each of the episodes in Kitano's work is humanistic, and this humanism is robbed of any sense of reality by the viewpoint of the puppets. Therefore, the film's title, *Dolls*, refers not only to the puppet theater, but also serves as an allegorical description of humans. Humans cannot resist fate, and so experience a chain of moments of cruelty. When these moments are sentimentalized, they become regret. Moreover, as suggested above, we can perceive in Kitano's new work an even bleaker theme of "remorse as a transcendental quality" that exists beyond any individual cause or incident of regret.

I think that Takeshi Kitano is attempting in *Dolls* to combine this deterministic or mechanistic view of humanity with an equally mechanistic structure. Doubtless he is gambling on his ability to transpose "the drama of being the plaything of fate" that he discovered at the heart of Japan's classical performing arts. There's one moment where Kitano seems to quote—intentionally or not—from the work of Kenji Mizoguchi. He captures Nishijima and Kanno's *"michiyuki"* journey[4] with a forward-moving tracking shot, and the fallen autumn leaves beneath the couple's feet change into snow. In other words, the couple is moving through time as well as space. This scene has the same quality as the famous dream-like panning shot in Mizoguchi's *The Life of Oharu* (Saikaku ichidai onna, 1952).

The biggest shock in *Dolls* comes from the cruelty of the movement by which Kanno and Nishijima fall down a snowy slope at the end of the film. The cutting around this scene is especially skillful. Saying which scene has the greatest emotional impact depends on when one thinks Miho Kanno's madness is cured. I myself think her recovery is depicted in its germinal state when Kanno wakes up from her nightmare of being raped by a group of men in tengu masks. (The summer festival that serves as the stage of this dream is shown through very schematic art direction and horizontal tracking shots. After waking up, she ties up the sleeping Nishijima's legs and cries out "your hat flew off!" Nishijima, who immediately tries to chase after his hat, falls down. I believe this scene intends to suggest Kanno's complete recovery of sanity. By continuing to wander with Nishijima, the man who had driven her to madness, even after she has recovered her sanity, she is undoubtedly testing him. When the two stop in a mountain hut, they see the "past"—their announcement to their friends that they are engaged to be married. (This is an example of the film's use of "the editing process of the characters' imaginations.") Even now, Kanno still wears the necklace she received in lieu of a wedding ring. Her changing facial expressions show the complexity of "regret" and strike to the heart. This scene clearly reveals the humiliation felt by Kanno, who has continually tested her lover.

People who have experienced regret with this theme as a premise— even those who caused the regret—become regretful. The fundamental motion of the film is this sort of melancholic cross-contamination. Kyoko Fukada and Chieko Matsubara, waiting alone for their sweethearts, are in the same position. Kitano expresses not only the transcendental nature of regret, but its all-pervasiveness: he sees it as the very sign of humanity. Perhaps the lack of originality in the film's three episodes, then, is merely a stepping stone that leads the audience to this final awareness. Of course, the narratives of Takeshi Kitano's films have always been permeated by the simplicity of "everyone only dies" and "nothing changes." However, their totality is composed of the darting motions of their details, giving them a complex luminescence. In the case of *Dolls*, the movement of these details has a mechanistic quality not seen before, and this heightens the film's allegorical feel.

dolls

translator's afterword

by william o. gardner

Actor-directors are hardly a novel phenomenon, but it is rare for the split across two different personae—and two different media—to be as radical as that of Beat Takeshi and Takeshi Kitano. Long before he established an international reputation as a film director, Takeshi Kitano had achieved a ubiquitous presence as a television personality under the name Beat Takeshi. Thus it undoubtedly came as a surprise to many Japanese television viewers when Kitano garnered the prestigious Golden Lion award at the 1997 Venice Film Festival for his film *Fireworks* and was soon being compared with Japanese film masters Mizoguchi, Ozu, and Kurosawa. While American television actors such as Ron Howard and Penny Marshall have gone on to work in film, the extremity of Kitano's transformation from TV comedian to film auteur seems more akin to Jesse Ventura's metamorphosis from pro wrestler to Minnesota governor. And while Ventura has set aside his feather boa, director Kitano continues to work not only as a film actor, but also as a TV comedian. The nature of Beat Takeshi's TV work, it should be noted, entails appearing on the most banal quiz and variety shows and performing gleefully lowbrow gags in a wide array of vaudevillian costumes and makeup. Thus the title and organizing principle of Casio Abe's book, which sets the actor and directorial personae against each other, represents an attempt to grapple with a enigmatic reality, rather than a merely literary conceit.

Nevertheless, many fans of Kitano's films outside of Japan are likely to be unfamiliar with Beat Takeshi's television work, or the idiosyncratic world of Japanese television in general. Such conversance with only one side of the Beat Takeshi vs. Takeshi Kitano formula marks a potential point of difficulty in accessing Abe's fascinating study, and this difference of audience perspective is one of the first challenges for a translator of Abe's work. Moreover, international distributors have been woefully slow in promoting the remarkable products of the 1990s Japanese independent film renaissance (especially to the American market), thereby obstructing access to part of the cinematic context of both Kitano's work and Abe's criticism. Even the historical products of Japanese cinema have only circulated outside the country in a limited fashion, centering on famous names like Ozu and Kurosawa, with such important Kitano precedents as Kinji Fukasaku's 1973 *Battle Without Honor* (Jingi naki tatakai) yakuza series remaining largely out of distribution.[1]

Such differences in background, however, give those of us outside Japan all the more reason to welcome a study that brings critical insight to both Kitano's film projects and his television persona. Abe's *Beat Takeshi vs. Takeshi Kitano* ranges freely across Japanese and Western film and television history to explore the resonances of Kitano's work in a thoroughly imaginative and original way. Abe's critical method is also original and eclectic, combining formal analysis with a concern for social and existential questions and referencing a range of sources from German critics Walter Benjamin and Wolf Lepenies to Japanese thinkers Shuzo Kuki and Shinobu Orikuchi. Such critical eclecticism may be disorienting to readers who prefer to pigeonhole film commentators into well-defined camps. But in suggesting new critical approaches, Abe's work presents a provocative alternative to Anglo-American film writing, as well as a valuable addition to the short shelf of translations of Japanese criticism into Western languages.

Seldom resting content with received categories, Abe creates his own neologisms, and has developed a critical vocabulary custom-fitted to explicate Kitano's work. Rendering this improvised, but internally consistent, vocabulary into English is another of the difficulties facing the translator of Abe's critical writing. Many of these neologisms and key critical terms are placed within quotational brackets in Abe's manuscript, and have generally been rendered inside quotation marks in this translation. While there is no space to explicate each of Abe's terms, I will briefly outline below what I see as Abe's most important critical contributions, and suggest ways in which future Kitano critics may want to engage his work.

The first of Abe's key critical contributions is the assertion that the director Takeshi Kitano treats the actor Beat Takeshi as a "body." Abe traces the progression of this body through Kitano's early films, as it transforms—in Abe's terms—from the decisive, persistent, and explosive physical presence in *Violent Cop,* to the dispersed, "tentacular" presence in *Boiling Point,* to the fatigued, death-haunted, yet strangely rapturous body of *Sonatine.* Abe highlights the extreme physical control that Beat Takeshi brings to these performances, as well as Takeshi Kitano's skill in realizing these performances in the cinematic medium. As he writes in Chapter 6, it is "as if the actor Takeshi has a voltage switch imbedded in his body, and can vary the proportion of 'strength' and 'weakness' or 'positivity' and 'negativity' [of his actions] with infinite precision." Moreover, Abe asserts that Kitano's "thought"—from his verbal responses to interviews to his expressions as a film director— is always grounded in the "rhetoric of the body." Thus, although Kitano repeatedly kills off or "suicides" his alter egos in his films, he suggests in an interview that the relative strength or adaptiveness of his body over his spirit has prevented him from actually taking his own life.

This unremitting attention to the body as a basis for Kitano's artistic vision must have seemed like an interesting if somewhat eccentric critical perspective when Abe first published *Beat Takeshi vs. Takeshi Kitano* in 1994. However, the true prescience of Abe's approach was dramatically confirmed after the actor-director's motorcycle crash the following year, which left Kitano's face partially paralyzed. Thus Abe was in a special position to follow up on his analysis of Beat Takeshi=Takeshi Kitano's physical presence as the basis for his film aesthetic, and to demonstrate how Kitano extrapolates "paralysis" into the central theme of his masterful *Fireworks*. In addition, he was able to employ the terms of his earlier critique to observe how Beat Takeshi's television screen presence shifted after his accident, moving away from the center of TV's narcissistic "interiority" to an awkward (but no less ubiquitous) position on its "margins."

Another key point of Abe's work, but one that is seldom brought to the foreground, is the observation that slapstick comedy forms a essential basis for Kitano's film grammar. In Chapter 5, for example, Abe discusses the scene in *Sonatine* where Murakawa entices the other men to fall into pits he has dug in the beach. This scene, Abe writes, has already "given up on being a gag." In other words, Kitano jettisons the overtly comical, but uses the structure of physical comedy to organize his film and to realize its theme of "discontinuity." Kitano's ability to use the gag as a structural principle reappears most prominently as true slapstick in *Getting Any?* and again as melodrama—or deadpan comedy—in the whimsical *Kikujiro*. Such thorough comprehension of physical comedy as a basis for the grammar of film connects Kitano with that other master of deadpan, Buster Keaton.

Finally, the most suggestive part of Abe's critique may not be the contrast between the actor Beat Takeshi and the director Takeshi

Kitano, but between the two media of television and film. Abe's analysis is centered, of course, on the specific contexts in which Takeshi has worked as a TV performer and film director. But his insights into television as an all-pervasive social presence, which has usurped the right to define itself as "contemporary life," and to remake contemporary life in its own image, are provocative to consider in televisual contexts outside of Beat Takeshi's Japan. Given the current trend towards "reality" television in the United States, for instance, are we able to deny Abe's description of TV as a net formed by the warp and woof of the viewers' own narcissism (Chapter 6)? And when media outlets are increasingly formed into large conglomerates that propagate this televisionesque reality even further, when companies such as CNN–AOL Time Warner continue to extend their reach across the globe, do we not have all the more reason to fear the logic of questioner=answerer (Chapter 1)? Perhaps, extending Abe's line of argument, we can conjecture that the success of Kitano's films abroad has been partly due to an unconscious recognition of the anti-televisionistic "otherness" of Beat Takeshi's performances, as realized by director Takeshi Kitano.

While Abe's arguments in *Beat Takeshi vs. Takeshi Kitano* are extremely suggestive, there are a number of issues raised by Kitano's work that he does not extensively address. Abe gives us a provocative analysis of Kitano's violent treatment of the body in the context of contemporary social "pathologies," but the question of the violence of Kitano's work, and its connection to escalating violence in Japanese and American media cultures, will doubtless remain a troubling one for many viewers. A related question is the influence of Hong Kong cinema on both the conception and the reception of Kitano's "hard-boiled" films. The misogyny that often accompanies the masculinist violence of these films is another issue deserving further scrutiny. Conversely, the homosocial and homosexual elements of Kitano's films also form an intriguing nexus for further critical exploration. A gender-based analysis of Kitano's work might elucidate the ways in which the actor-director refashions the *tateyaku* heroes and male-centered "hard school" ethos of earlier Japanese film into a new, contemporary sensibility.[2] Since Abe's strategy is to read Kitano's film work against the culture of television, however, the question of Beat Takeshi=Takeshi Kitano's position in a genealogy of Japanese film heroism remains outside the purview of his study.

One distinctive trend in Kitano's recent films is their tendency towards a rhetoric of national or ethnic identity. The shift towards a stronger delineation of "national character" is evident in the films from *Fireworks* onwards, but becomes most conspicuous—even self-consciously excessive—in *Brother*. While suicide has been a recurring theme in Kitano's films, *Brother* rewrites the act of suicide in explicitly national and ethnic terms. The implications of this nationalist reinscription will doubtless be a topic of further discussion among Kitano watchers.[3]

No matter what direction future discussions of Kitano's work may take, however, it is clear that such discussions will owe a major debt to Casio Abe's pathbreaking work. It is truly a welcome event, then, to see this work appear in the English language. We can hope that it stimulates further critical exchange between the Japanese and English-speaking film communities, and that the vigor of this discussion is exceeded only by the continuing inventiveness of Takeshi Kitano's creative work.

translator's afterword

endnotes

FOREWORD

[1] Misemono: Tradition of sideshows featuring unusual people or things that began in the Tokugawa period.

references

Miyao, Daisuke. "Blue vs. Red: Takeshi Kitano's Color Scheme." *Post Script: Essays in Film and the Humanities* 19.1 (Fall 1998): 112-27.

Sugawa, Yoshiyuki, ed. "Kitano Takeshi soshite/aruiwa [and/or] Beat Takeshi," *Eureka: Poetry and Criticism* 400. 30-3 (Feb 1998).

Yodogawa, Nagaharu, ed. *Filmmakers 2: Kitano Takeshi.* Tokyo: Kinema Jumpo-sha, 1998.

CHAPTER 01

[1] It is illegal to depict genitals or pubic hair for commercial purposes in Japan. As a result, the pubic region, and in particular the hair, is deliberately blurred in movies, videos, and magazines.

[2] The question of whether or not to notify the family when a relative has cancer has been a big controversy in Japan.

[3] Beat Takeshi co-hosted the popular 1990s TV quiz show, *Heisei Board of Education* (Heisei kyoiku iinkai) with Masataka Itsumi. In it, various celebrities try to solve questions that imitate private junior-high-school entrance exams. Itsumi would earnestly moderate the show while Takeshi made fun of him.

[4] Manzai: A Japanese stand-up comedy genre played by two partners that usually contains "cause and effect" sequences.

[5] "Takeshi Gundan": The name given to Kitano's stable of comedians. Literally translates into "Takeshi Army."

[6] Omanta: An invented word that is dangerously close to "twat" in Japanese.

[7] Beat Takeshi writes columns in several weekly publications for the so-called "salary-man." These columns are usually dictated by Takeshi and written by editors or other writers. Fumio Takada is a popular TV writer who has worked on many of Takeshi's variety shows, and is a close friend of Takeshi's. Some suspect that Fumio Takada not only wrote, but also dictated the columns, as Takeshi seemed too busy to even talk to the editors.

[8] "Ore," "oira," and "boku" are all used as male first-person pronouns. "Ore" and "oira" both sound macho and gangsterish, while "boku" sounds like something a spoiled child would say.

[9] In December 1986, Beat Takeshi and his fellow members from the Takeshi Gundan assaulted the editorial staff of *FRIDAY*, a weekly photographic tabloid that had tenaciously followed a woman who was then Takeshi's lover. In revenge, Takeshi and his followers broke into the magazine's office with bats and other weapons. Takeshi was unable to work for six months because of this assault.

[10] Kazuo Komizu: A director and actor born in 1946, Komizu (nicknamed "Gaira") joined a film production headed by Koji Wakamatsu and produced prominent x-rated films in the 1960s and '70s. He directed his first film, *Rape Me*, in 1970. Since then, he has directed and produced numerous x-rated films and videos.

[11] "Two-picture cartoon technique": A comic technique that elicits laughs by depicting two simple events that show cause and effect.

[12] Tamura Tsutomu. *Film Art Quarterly* (Eiga Geijutsu). Summer 1993.

[13] Kasahara Kazuo. *Film Art Quarterly*. Winter 1991.

[14] "The Quietest Ocean That Summer": Direct translation of the film's Japanese title, which appears on-screen at the end of the film.

[15] *The Crime of Kiyoshi Okubo* (Okubo Kiyoshi no hanzai, 1983)

[16] Kazuya Nakayama: An actor and wanna-be patriot, Nakayama crashed to his death when he dived the plane he was operating into the house of a right-wing mogul right after starring in *Serial Killer: Cold Blooded*. This exhibitionism, distinctive among criminals, is also apparent in Nakayama's acting.

[17] Kiyotaka Katsuta: From 1972 to 1984, the year he was arrested, Katsuta raped and killed nine women while drifting in the Nagoya area. He also committed many other murders. Katsuta's cruelty was much talked about at that time.

[18] Bou Nishimura: Born in 1926, Nishimura published *Demons and Ogres* (Kichiku, 1978), a novel based on a real-life murder, after working at a variety of jobs ranging from journalism to construction work. Subsequently, Nishimura continued to publish murder-mystery and porn novels, also based on real crimes. His style, which does not to try to decode criminal acts, but rather to depict them objectively, is excellent.

[19] *The Ark of Jesus* (Iesu no hakobune, 1985): Jesus Sengoku, the leader of a Bible study group from around 1980, collected and formed a large family with a group of strong female followers. Relatives of the women in the group tried to rescue them. At around that time, a newspaper reported that the Sengoku commune was like a modern-day harem, and people began to view the commune as a potential criminal case. However, when the women in the commune refused to return home, the incident gradually faded away from public consciousness. After the mid-'80s, people began to be more respectful of religious freedom.

[20] *Kim's War* (Kim no senso, 1991)

[21] "Chambara Trio": A comedy group originally formed by three of Takeshi's samurai-action trainers from a Kyoto movie studio that specializes in Japanese period dramas. ("Chambara" means samurai action.) A fourth member was subsequently added, but the group still calls itself a "trio." Based in Osaka, the trio produces very traditional comedy, and appears in Kitano's comic film *Getting Any?*.

[22] *Film Art Quarterly*. Summer 1993.

[23] Flan vital: A way of living artistically. This term is connected to the French philosopher Henri Bergson's concept of "Élan Vital" (the vital force responsible for evolution). In Japan, these two phrases were made popular by the critic Kiyoteru Hanada.

[24] Kun: A suffix added to a colleague or person of the same or lower social rank.

[25] San: A more respectful suffix than "kun"; it functions somewhat like "Mister."

[26] Johnstone, Iain. *Man With No Name: The Clint Eastwood Biography*. 1981.

[27] *Bungei Shunju*. September 1993.

[28] Jisatsu: *Ji* means "self," while *satsu* means "murders," so "jisatsu" can be described as "murdering oneself."

[29] *Film Art Quarterly*, late June 1993.

[30] Naoto Takenaka: Having distinguished himself as an impersonator on TV variety shows, Takenaka, who also loved movies, appeared in numerous films. In 1989, he made his much longed-for directorial debut (and also played the lead role) with *Nowhere Man* (Muno no hito), based on a comic book. (This work won an award at the Venice Film Festival.) At one point, he was frequently compared with Beat Takeshi as an example of a TV talent turned film director, but Takenaka's works are distinguished by a non-violent style that is humorous and quiet, and moreover, is influenced by 1960s subculture.

[31] "Skillfully crude cartoon": One of the manga trends from the late 1970s, these cartoons were mainly created by illustrators who were becoming active in the industry. Their work used wavering lines and were thought of as "crude drawings but skillful truth," which gave birth to the term "skillfully crude" (*heta-uma*). These manga staked everything on the "pop-ness" of the atmosphere, rather than their ability to create tight structure, and continued to show readers the triviality of everyday life.

CHAPTER 02

[1] Kishotenketsu: A Chinese poetry structure in which *ki* raises, *sho* inherits, *ten* transforms, and *ketsu* concludes the theme.

[2] *Film Art Quarterly*. Late July 1993.

[3] Makoto Shinozaki: Active in 1980s indie films, Shinozaki subsequently tried his hand at writing film criticism and working as a projectionist. Made his directorial debut in 1996 with *Okaeri* (the lead actor is Susumu Terajima, familiar from Takeshi Kitano's films), a film about the devotion of a husband toward his wife, who suffers from schizophrenia. Acclaimed for *Jam Session* (Kikujiro no natsu koshiki kaizokuban, 1999) which creatively depicts the behind-the-scenes filming of *Kikujiro*. Also directed *Not Forgotten* (Wasurerarenu hitobito, 2000), which refers to

old yakuza stories, and shows elderly people rallying against societal evils in a quiet tone that is distinct from most yakuza films. Shinozaki's films are characterized by a gaze that carefully examines reality without embellishment.

[4] *Cahiers du Cinéma Japon*, Volume 0.

[5] *Film Art Quarterly.* Winter 1991.

[6] *The Great Ode to Yakuza* (Yakuza zessyo): 1970 work by director Yasuzo Masumura that overwhelmed viewers with its distinct expression of emotion. It goes so far as to depict a yakuza who has an almost incestuous relationship with his younger sister. Urging her independence, he plunges into a rival yakuza organization, and comes to ruin in a state close to suicide. The main yakuza character was played by Shintaro Katsu, star of the one-armed swordsman series *Zatoichi*.

[7] *Cahiers du Cinéma Japon*, Volume 0.

[8] *Empire of Brats* (Gaki teikoku): 1981 work directed by Kazuyuki Izutsu that splendidly depicts Japanese characters and places with an Asian touch. Depicts the youth of high school boys against the background of conflict within a group of adolescent juvenile delinquents set in Osaka. One of the three lead characters is played by Bang-ho Cho.

[9] *March Comes in Like a Lion* (Sangatsu no raion): 1992 work by director Hitoshi Yazaki, who produces a film once every ten years and has continued to make delicately minimalist films. The film shows a younger sister who adores her elder brother; when he loses his memory, she pretends to be his lover, consummating her love with him. The elder brother is played by Bang-ho Cho.

CHAPTER 03

[1] *Movie & Video Yearbook 1991*

[2] Tokashiki used to be a world-champion boxer.

[3] Cutting off a finger tip is an amends according to the code of Japanese gangsters.

[4] *Movie & Video Yearbook 1991*

CHAPTER 04

[1] "3K jobs": Unpopular jobs that are hard (*kitsui*), dirty (*kitanai*), or dangerous (*kiken*).

[2] Shinozaki, Makoto. "Takeshi Kitano's 'Movie Technique'" [Location reportage of *A Scene at the Sea*.]. *Switch*. September 1991.

[3] *Scenario Magazine.* July 1993.

[4] Kunio Tsukamoto: An avant-garde *kajin* (traditional Japanese tanka poet) representative of the postwar period. Critically acclaimed for his Romanesque sensibility, mastery of metaphors, encyclopedic knowledge, skepticism toward standard tanka verse, references to haiku technique, and portrayal of beauty and cruelty, Tsukamoto was lauded as a genius by author Yukio Mishima before such praise became commonplace.

[5] This refers to the Japanese tradition of erecting one's gravestone before death so as to not unnecessarily burden others when one dies. The characters for the person's name are colored red in order to indicate that the grave is for someone who is still living: when that person actually dies, the characters are changed to black or white.

CHAPTER 05

[1] *Bungei shunju.* September 1993.

[2] Tokatonton: Word invented by Osamu Dazai in a short story written shortly before his death. Representing the sound of a carpenter's hammer (which in turn symbolizes Japan's recovery from defeat after WWII), "tokatonton" is used in the story to describes the pessimism of a man whose will to rise up from his present reality actually withers every time he hears the sound.

[3] Osamu Dazai: Popular author active from the 1930s who continues to have many dedicated fans. Fascination with his work is an adolescent rite of passage in Japan. Using an extremely rhythmical style, Dazai openly depicted psychological structures particular to the Japanese, particularly obsessions with death and shame. Thus the experience of reading his novels is very personal. Also, "he himself" is projected onto almost all the main characters of his novels. Dazai committed suicide in 1948 with his lover.

[4] Dialogue follows that published in the July 1993 issue of *Scenario*.

[5] Yoshishige Yoshida: One of a series of film directors who debuted with the film company Shochiku at the very end of the 1950s and the early '60s. Called the "Shochiku Nouvelle Vague," these directors were known for their subversion of accepted film grammar, their eroticism, and their political protests. Nagisa Oshima is representative of this group, but Yoshida's works are the most visually marvelous and impenetrable. His representative works are *Akitsu Spring* (Akitsu onsen, 1962), *Eros plus massacre* (Erosu purasu Gyakusatu, 1969), and *A Promise* (Ningen no yakusoku, 1986). He also directed *Femmes en Miroir* (2002), which premiered at the Cannes Film Festival in 2002.

[6] In Japanese folklore, ghosts are generally imagined as spirits without feet who float in the air.

[7] In Japanese, the number four (*shi*) is homophonous with the word for 'death' (*shi*).

[8] "Spirit-offering cake": Pun on the homophonous popsicle (*reika*) and spirit-cake (*reika*).

[9] "Burial kimono": This refers to the white kimono (*shini shozoku*) in which a person is buried. This garment is also worn by someone who intends to commit ritual suicide.

[10] Shinji Soumai: Garnered the most attention among Japanese film directors in the 1980s. Used program-picture-type material and expressed dynamism through long-running shots. Also gave actors' bodies a charismatic sense of reality. Representative works include *Sailor-fuku to kikanju* (1981), *Typhoon Club* (Taifu club, 1985), and *Kaza-hana* (2000). *Love Hotel* (1985) is an x-rated masterpiece that melodramatically depicts a couple's encounter and breakup. Soumai passed away in 2001 just after the domestic release of *Kaza-hana*.

[11] "The eyes of a man about to die" (Makki matsugo no me): According to traditional Japanese thought, the world takes on an appearance that is both nostalgic and real when a person is on the verge of death. The Nobel Prize-winning author Yasunari Kawabata wrote an essay by this same title.

[12] Jun Ishikawa: Master of Edo-period literature, Ishikawa went from writing about French literature to authoring novels. He was active for about sixty years, and his unique style resulted in a body of work that is cultivated and vivid, and that uses many literary devices. Ishikawa is placed in the same immediate post-World War II period literary group as Osamu Dazai due to the self-mocking attitude of his works.

13 Kinji Fukasaku: Debuted as a director with Toei, one of Japan's major film companies. One of Japan's representative directors from the 1970s who focused on contradictions within the system and on violence from a socialist perspective. Fukasaku is known for his splendid treatment of life and death, and is perhaps most highly acclaimed in Japan for the breathless rhythm and gritty documentary touch of his series of films on the reality of yakuza life (*Death of Honor* is an off-shoot of that series). However, after violent action films lost their ability to mobilize audiences, Fukasaku moved into entertaining movies based on novels. Fukusaku has a deep relationship with Takeshi Kitano-Beat Takeshi. He was originally slated to direct *Violent Cop* with Beat Takeshi as the lead actor, though this film eventually became Takeshi Kitano's directorial debut. In Fukusaku's *Battle Royale*, Beat Takeshi gives a fantastic performance as a violent teacher who guides students to self-annihilation on a solitary island. Fukasaku passed away in 2003.

CHAPTER 06

1 *Représentation.* No. 3, 1992.

2 Noh: A traditional Japanese performing art founded by Zeami during the 15th century in which masked performers dance on stage with distinctive steps while uttering poetic words. Noh is characterized by tragedy, often with the living and the dead appearing on-stage simultaneously, and the masks represent certain characteristic emotions. It continues even today with troupes of actors who maintain the teachings of Zeami. Unlike the later performing arts form *kabuki*, which appealed to the masses, noh in the pre-modern period were performances offered to the emperor and supported by the aristocratic classes.

3 "Takeshi Kitano." *CUT Magazine*. July 1993.

4 "Parting Ways with Beat Takeshi." *Bungei shunju*. September 1993

5 "Riverbed beggar": Term rooted in performances by actors and dancers at the side of Kyoto's "Shijo Gawara" district, located on the shores of the Kamo River. These performers existed outside the normal hierarchical status system of samurai or merchants. Since they earned their living using their bodies, they should have been socially shunned like prostitutes. However, if their performances were superlative, they earned the patronage of the upper social strata. In this sense, "riverbed beggars" were positioned in a liminal state in society.

6 Sekkyobushi: Narrative song popularizations of certain sermons by Buddhist monks during the medieval period. Sung by blind men accompanied by a Japanese stringed instrument (*biwa*), "sekkyobushi" it is one of the earliest representative forms of the Japanese oral tradition. During the early Edo period (1600-1867), these narrative songs were written down. This standardized them on the one hand, but also spawned odd variants. Stories (for example, a child from a wealthy family who experiences misfortune after misfortune after inheriting the bad karma of his or her parents) often start with a tragic situation and end with the characters being saved through the intervention of a Buddhist figure. The style used to tell these stories using song later influenced the *bunraku* puppet performance tradition as well.

7 *Scenario.* December 1993.

[8] Shinran (1173-1262): Kamakura-period priest and founder of the Joudo Shinshu sect of Pure Land Buddhism.

[9] Showa: Term used to calculate dates in reference to the Japanese emperor's reign. In this case, refers to the reign (1925-1989) of Emperor Hirohito. Kitano was born in 1948, or Showa 23.

CHAPTER 07

[1] *Tokarev* (Tokarefu, 1994): The fourth work by Junji Sakamoto, who made his directorial debut in 1989, the same year as Takeshi Kitano. This film depicts the revenge of a man whose son was kidnapped and murdered.

[2] This conclusion was originally published in 1994 and does not reflect the movies Kitano has in fact made subsequent to *Sonatine*.

[3] Toyotomi Hideyoshi (1537-1598): Warlord who unified Japan in the 1570s, putting an end to a century of warfare.

[4] Sen no Rikyu: 16th-century founder of the formal tea ceremony.

[5] Kanbei Kuroda: Loyal associate of Toyotomi Hideyoshi.

LONG JOURNEY OF THE MELANCHOLY KING

[1] "Two Beats": A manzai or stand-up comedy duo formed in 1974 in one of the manzai capitals of Japan, Asakusa, by Jirou Kaneko and the still-unknown Takeshi Kitano. The stage names used by the two were Beat Takeshi (Kitano) and Beat Kiyoshi (Kaneko). Kiyoshi played the straight man, while Takeshi used his wit, along with banned words, to get laughs from his audience and shock them with his sarcastic comments. Takeshi's speedy manzai technique made him increasingly popular. Eventually, Takeshi struck out on his own as a television personality. However, there has never been a formal declaration of the duo's dissolution.

[2] TV Tokyo: Local TV station headquartered in Tokyo and known for travel programs in which celebrities give tours of inns and attractions while sampling local cuisines. These low-budget, pastoral TV programs are popular among middle-aged housewives and elderly people, and are bewildering for their lack of change. This same TV station also became an expert at mining local stations for guerilla ideas. Their numerous, unprecedented variety shows have captured the public's attention. The animated TV series *Pokemon* is one of their flagship programs.

[3] "Motorcycle accident": After finishing work on August 2, 1994 Beat Takeshi got into a shocking accident while driving his scooter at breakneck speed through central Tokyo. The accident was rumored to have been a suicide attempt, and Kitano was a step away from death. While in the hospital, and during the recovery process, his life was reported on in the news every day. When he left the hospital to begin rehabilitation, he boldly revealed his partially paralyzed facial expression in an interview, causing a sensation throughout Japan. In March of the following year, he returned to television.

[4] Part of the argument in this essay refers to the work of Wolf Lepenies' *Melancholy and Society*.

[5] Team Downtown: Comedy duo that became famous in the late 1980s. Hitoshi Matsumoto, one of the pair, pioneered an autistic and grotesque style of comedy, thereby single-handedly transforming TV comedy in Japan.

[6] Ninety-Nine: Comedy duo that became famous in the mid 1990s. One of the duo, Takashi Okamura, is extremely small, and struck a chord with his "cuteness" and "dexterous amateurism." Both Team Downtown and 99 appear regularly as hosts on TV variety shows, and are widely regarded as having eclipsed Beat Takeshi's influence.

[7] Yasu-Kiyo: Yasushi Yokoyama and Kiyoshi Nishikawa, pre-eminent comedy duo of the 1970s. Yasushi's self-destructive streak, bravado, and sweetness contrasted with Kiyoshi's malicious everyman persona. This duo delivered *boke* (feigned idiocy) and *tsukomi* (pointing out the idiocy of one's partner) at a breakneck speed, setting the kind of fast-paced tempo that became a trademark for the Two Beats a decade later. However, their work also has the consistency of classical comedy. In particular, Yasushi's highly original performances drew many fans. Toward the early 1980s, the comedy duo's popularity faded, resulting in Yasushi's death. His partner, Kiyoshi, was a member of the National Diet from 1986–2004.

[8] Kokontei Shinsho (1890-1973): *Rakugo* performer known for his genius in expressing human emotions and his retelling of unique stories in a comical way. Born in the Kanda district of Tokyo, he was also well known for "drinking, gambling, and buying prostitutes." He changed his name sixteen times to escape from debt collectors.

[9] *We Are Jokers!* (Oretachi hyokinzoku): Highly popular variety program from the early 1980s that also referenced the comedy of *Saturday Night Live*. Brought together a new generation of comedy talent, such as Beat Takeshi and Akashiya Samma, who used a wide variety of gags, including the use of repetition, physical endurance, childish play, and inside jokes. Takeshi and Samma's "Takechanman" corner was especially popular. In it, the two fight while continually transforming themselves like the superheroes in children's TV programs. Relationships among the performers and their personal lives were used for gags that were obvious to the audience.

[10] *Bubble Holiday* (Shabondama holiday): Legendarily successful music/skit/variety program from the early 1960s, when TV was still in its formative years. The program brilliantly fused an urban comic sensibility with high-quality music, and suggested the tremendous potential of TV programs. New slang expressions emerged from members of the Crazy Cats, who came from a comic jazz combo. The skit writer was Yukio Aoshima, former Tokyo governor.

[11] The Drifters: Group that originated from a comic jazz combo. Like younger brothers to the above-mentioned Crazy Cats, the Drifters starred in the show *It's 8pm! Everyone Get Together* (8 dayo! Zenin shugo), which aired Saturdays at 8pm and featured live broadcasts of skits. The show was popular with adults and school kids alike, particularly from the late-1960s through the 1970s. A big part of the group's success came from its erotic gags suggesting the grownup world, which tickled kids. Beat Takeshi's *We Are Jokers!*, which had been launched as a competing program aimed at an older audience, eventually overtook the phenomenal ratings of *It's 8pm!* People considered this change as the beginning of a new era in Japanese comedy.

[12] "Ganmen Mahina Stars": Joke that combines two phrases: "ganmen mahi" and "Mahina Stars." "Ganmen Mahi" (Facial Paralysis) refers both to the bestselling book that Takeshi authored immediately after the motorcycle accident and to the injury

endnotes

that left his face partially paralyzed, a condition that would usually be the end of a career for an actor or television personality. (Takeshi eventually recovered much of his facial movements through extensive rehabilitation.) The phrase "Mahina Stars" refers to a well-known band representative of the so-called "mood kayou" genre of Japanese music that peaked in the 1960s. This big-band-type romantic music was influenced both by Hawaiian-style music and guitar-centered jazz. Though sometimes sung by female vocalists, it most often featured men singing sappy love songs in falsetto. Later, it was ridiculed by many as "corny" and "gross." The combination of "ganmen mahi" and "Mahina Stars" is both funny and evokes a certain repulsion.

13 Aum Shinrikyo: Religious practices included soaking in a 50-degree centigrade bath, which reportedly resulted in several deaths.

14 Kenji Nakagami: Novelist representative of contemporary Japanese literature who was born in 1946 and died in 1992. Nakagami began his literary work under the influence of Kenzaburo Oe. Using his hometown of Kumano as a stage, he plunged into a fictional world depicting a Faulkner-esque "saga" modeled after his own clan (a group who faced discrimination). Referring to the folklore of old timers, Buddhist sutra lectures, and other classical arts, he resuscitated the power of the "story," and at the same time realized a breathtaking eroticism. From the late-1980s onwards, he entered a period of stagnation as a writer, and died of cancer in 1992 while still holding many serials. In addition to being of the same generation as Takeshi Kitano-Beat Takeshi, he also had a similar history of having moved among many different jobs when young. The two would critique one another's work. When Takeshi was working as a bartender in a Shinjuku jazz teashop, he met Nakagami, who was a frequent customer. Incidentally, Takeshi worked in shifts with Norio Nagayama, whose serial shooting spree would later shock all of Japan. (Nagayama began writing while in prison, but was executed in the mid 1990s.)

15 Yasuo Matsukawa: Documentary filmmaker born in 1932. Though quiet, many of his films are masterpieces that poetically crystallize narrative and combine orchestral editing with experimental techniques. His films display a microscopic and highly cultivated point of view. He should be regarded as Japan's leading documentary filmmaker, due to the subtlety of his view toward subject matter, and his level of cultivation. His representative works include *Wildlife Caricature* (Choju giga, 1966), *Hands* (1974) and *The Depths of the Road* (Michi no oku, 2000).

16 Kiyoshi Yamashita (1922-1971): Painter who garnered attention after learning to paint in a facility for mentally disabled youth. While the subject matter he selected was simple, the details of his pictures and the boldness of his compositions were unprecedented. His representative works express "fireworks" through inlaying and pasting small torn pieces of paper. His childlike simplicity and innocence of expression, together with his unique style of narration, made him popular. He spent almost his entire life as a wanderer.

17 Sonnenstern: Painter of fantasia in the surrealist tradition born in Eastern Europe. Sonnenstern's style is erotic, and also minutely detailed and ornamental. According to the Japanese essayist Tatsuhiko Shibusawa, "whirlpools," "heart shapes," "snakes," and "curious symmetry" are recurring themes in Sonnenstern's work. His paintings are also characterized by an anti-historical and cosmic sensibility. Until he gained attention as an artist, he spent time in mental institutions and jail.

[18] Iki: An aesthetic that spread in the Edo period. Generally taken to mean "urban sophistication" in contrast to *yabo*, or "the un-sophisticated manner of peasants." This kind of differentiation arose among Edo (Tokyo) residents because Edo was a large city that peasants would migrate to from their hometowns.

[19] "World of suffering": In general, this means the world surrounding the women who became prostitutes. However, in Buddhism, the "World of Suffering" is the same as the world itself, as one cannot live without suffering. Shuzo Kuki understands that living in the "world of suffering" is a kind of process or journey, both because prostitutes are sold to brothels from their hometowns, and because the life they live is a continuation of that journey of suffering.

GETTING ANY?

[1] Sharaku: Woodblock print artist of the Edo period, known for the series of actors' prints he executed from 1749-1750.

[2] Shotoku Taishi (574-622): Prince and culture hero who helped to establish Buddhism in Japan.

[3] Masumi Okada (1935-present): Actor representing Nikkatsu, one of Japan's major film studios. Debuted in 1954, primarily in gangster movies. He was often cast in comical roles, and as a good-looking youth, even though he didn't look typically Japanese because of his mixed-race heritage as a son of Japanese and Danish parents. After leaving Nikkatsu in 1959, he often worked as an emcee for television or the theater. He maintained his good looks and "dandy" style even in middle age, and his popularity did not fade. His graceful aging must be something that Takeshi Kitano also seeks after.

[4] Joe Shishido: One of the headlining stars in the 1960s for Nikkatsu.

[5] Zatoichi: Series based on a 1962 film directed by Kenji Misumi, *Zatoichi Monogatari*, which was in turn an adaptation of a novel by Kan Shibozawa. "*Zato*" refers to blind male masseurs (massage was one of the few ways the blind could learn a living) who dominated the profession in the samurai age. "*Ichi*" is a person's name. Shintaro Katsu became a major movie star through his portrayal of Zatoichi, a figure that went on to be serialized on television. The popularity of the Zatoichi figure can probably be attributed to both the charm of the blind figure himself as well as his surprising and tricky use of his staff, which cleverly hid a sword. Since Zatoichi was blind, his other senses were heightened in a way that added to his hero stature. (Many Japanese men of that era would practice by pretending to wield imaginary swords with their eyes closed.) Zatoichi was seen as someone who would vanquish the evil character at the end of a film. In a way, he could be said to be the archetype of "sacred monsters" in films.

In 2003, Takeshi Kitano directed his own version of *Zatoichi*, in which he himself played the blind hero. The new film was pitched by the studios as Takeshi replicating the role formerly played by Shintaro Katsu, so the concept for this film was not original to Takeshi. To portray the character in an original way, Takeshi dyed the figure's hair blond. He also employed a great deal of computer graphics and shocking plot turns. He didn't emphasize the special "backward use of the sword" that was used in the original film, and his way of representing cuts had too much flurry. Although Takeshi probably wanted to reinvent Zatoichi in the "sacred monster" modality, he ended up turning the character into a cyborg.

6 "Three-hundred-million-yen incident": This refers to an incident that took place on December 10, 1968 in a Tokyo suburb and that shocked all of Japan. A criminal dressed in police uniform and riding a fake police motorcycle stopped an armored bank truck, claiming to have been notified of a bomb planted on the vehicle. He lit a smoke candle under the vehicle, and while the officials flinched, he drove off with the vehicle. Then he switched cars one after another and vanished. The three aluminum cases that the criminal stole contained about 300-million yen, bonus pay for employees at an electric machinery factory. The money was insured against robbery, so there was no loss to the electric machinery company. Voices of approval rose up at that time for this bold criminal act, and speculation continued as to what kind of person the criminal was, how he would live with this huge amount of money, etc. The case was closed when the statute of limitations expired on December 10, 1975 with the criminal still at large.

7 Natsuko Toda: The most famous translator of film subtitles in Japan. Also frequently translates at press conferences for Hollywood actors when they arrive in Japan. She has been involved with the subtitle translations for almost all Hollywood films, and all Japanese film fans know her name.

8 Teigin Incident: On January 26, 1948 a criminal posing as a disinfection worker from a public health center poisoned sixteen bank employees and robbed the Teikoku bank (twelve people died). An aspiring painter was arrested as a suspect, but he insisted that he was falsely charged. He was convicted in court and given the death penalty. However, in 1986 the suspect died of old age in prison at the age of 95. Kei Kumai's film *Teigin Incident: Death Row Prisoner* (Teigin jiken: Shikeishu, 1964), a socialist detective story that questions police corruption and the conscience of newspaper reporters, takes the position that the suspect was innocent.

9 Jonan Electronics: The president of this volume electronic goods seller had quickly ascended the company ranks, and was famed for carrying a Luis Vuitton trunk stuffed with cash in order to stock goods that could be sold cheaply. He appeared in Jonan Electronics TV commercials, and his bald head and his unusual vigor for an older person made him extremely popular. He appeared frequently in variety programs. (He passed away shortly after appearing in *Getting Any?*.)

10 Goemon Ishikawa, Jirokichi Nezumikozo: Famous thieves of feudal Japan.

11 *Lupin III* (Lupin sansei): Anime from the early 1970s about a hero-thief that received widespread acclaim. The main character's grandfather was Arsene Lupin. Each story overflows with ideas, as Lupin III pulls off robberies along with an expert gunman, a master swordsman, and a mysterious beautiful girl who is always trying to get the loot for herself. Stands out for its cheeky touch. The writer for the first season (a thirteen-week run) was Atsushi Yamatoya, who directed the fantasy gang film *Dutch Wife in the Desert* and other masterpieces. It overflows with fantastic ideas and expressions that are novel to anime, and also displays an outstanding horror sensibility.

12 Toei yakuza films: A series of magnificent program pictures made successful in the late 1960s by Toei, one of Japan's major film studios. Mostly set around the year 1900, they conclude with the main character, who is a yakuza client, selflessly going behind enemy lines as he tries to help local yakuza suffering under the despotism of rising yakuza. With their detailed depictions of yakuza society, the completeness of their sense of tragedy, and the heroism and dark emotions of their main characters, these films are considered a high point for Japanese films from that period. The films were

originally intended to be a twist on the pre-existing *matatabi*, or wandering samurai, type of films, but in the midst of student demonstrations, the anti-establishment thrust unique to yakuza films hit a nerve with students. From the early 1970s, Toei moved toward realistically depicting the struggle of yakuza based on actual documentation. At the same time, charismatic leading actors like Ken Takakura, Koji Tsuruta, and Junko Fuji withdrew from appearing in such yakuza films.

13 Nikkatsu "Romance Porn": In 1971, Japanese movie studio Nikkatsu found a niche for itself in violent action and erotic films. Its "romance porn" (roman poruno) films sought to capture male audiences through the sheer quantity of male/female love scenes that appeared in them. Despite the name given these films, actors were never filmed actually having sex. Instead, these films encompassed a range of genres from drama to action to comedy to suspense—as long as a certain proportion of love scenes were included, any genre was fine. These films were low budget, but freely expressive, with repeated appearances by Tatsumi Kumashiro, Noboru Tanaka, and other film directors representative of the 1970s. However, as adult videos and other media with sexually explicit content appeared, "romance porn" lost its ability to mobilize audiences, and at last disappeared in 1988. Moeko Ezawa, from the early Nikkatsu "Romance Porn" years, relied on her skill as an actress more than her beauty, and continues to be active today as a sexy middle-aged actress.

14 Hideaki Nitani, Yujiro Ishihara: Along with Hideaki Nitani, Yujiro Ishihara was a top star for Nikkatsu from the late 1950s through the mid 1960s. He gave especially brilliant performances in action films. Sanae Nakahara changed from playing princesses in period dramas made by the film studio Toei, to being a partner to action stars in the mid 1960s.

15 "Topless pizza": Practice that came about from the Japanese sex industry's attempts to avoid prosecution and harassment by the police. Similar to no-panties cafés (*no-pants kissa*), which featured young, panty-less waitresses in extremely short skirts. Owners of such establishments could run a legitimate business, while still appealing to men. The "topless" version was based on the same principle, except the waitresses were topless. The joke here is a play on the concept of pizza delivery, but in this case by panty-less or topless women. The American pizza delivery business was also seen as a funny contrast to the unique Japanese sex industry promotion of cafes.

16 Asadachi: "Morning–stand"—slang for "morning erection." The name "Asao" can thus be interpreted as meaning "morning man."

17 This citation of Benjamin's book refers to the Japanese edition, published by Shobunsha.

KIDS RETURN

1 *GS2 1/2 Godard Special*. Toju Publishers, 1985.

2 *Une femme est une femme*, the title of a 1961 Godard film.

FIREWORKS

1 See "Long Journey of the Melancholy King," notes 16 and 17.

endnotes

KIKUJIRO

[1] *3000 Leagues in Search of Mother*: A popular animation featured on TV Asahi in 1976. Based on the Italian original *Cuore* by Edmondo De Amicis, it follows the story of a young boy, Marco, who sets out to Argentina to earn money and meet his disabled mother.

[2] "Types": Tap dancers, jugglers, and mimes are all traditional performers. In old Japan, they did not belong to a specific class, and were thus considered to be closer to God. "Street-stall vendors" were a group of vagabonds who idolized Chinese gods of medicine, and who possessed the characteristics of both performers and merchants. These groups of vagabonds would later be transformed into yakuza groups. The origins and lifestyles of performers, street-stall vendors, and yakuza have been the object of ethnological (and mythological) studies in Japan. Sexual deviants can also be considered as people who belong to no particular class.

[3] Tengu: Japanese goblins purported to have originally metamorphosized from armed Buddhist priests. Tengu combine the characteristics of crows (they have beaks and fly), to which is added a strong, masculine element (they have long noses like sticks). Many of the characters in this film can thus be said to have been imprinted with a kind of cultural ethnicity.

[4] Shinobu Orikuchi (1887-1953): A tanka poet and scholar of Japanese literature and folklore who was active from early to mid-20th century. Also one of Japan's representative ethnologists. Kunio Yanagida, another representative ethnologist from around the time, researched demotic life and folklore. Orikuchi's objects of research were Japanese mythology, *Tennou* (the Japanese emperor), and the spirituality of words. Orikuchi was also an eminent tanka poet. A homosexual with mystical tendencies, Orikuchi was an advocate of the concept of the "Little God" (*chiisagami*), which refers to Japanese folktales of people the size of fingers, much like the figure of Tom Thumb in the West. Orikuchi interpreted these to be embodiments of the spirits of children who can lead adults out of danger. Orikuchi believed that all children possess this kind of spiritual power. Japanese homosexuality (called *shudo*) can be described as a type of sexual activity in which a child's spiritual power is received. There is also a general belief in Japan that children and the elderly are closer to the gods than adults.

[5] Asakusa: A corner of Tokyo's entertainment district. In the first half of the twentieth century, Asakusa housed movie theaters, panoramas, vaudeville theaters, dance halls, reviews, cabarets, amusement parks, restaurants, shrines, and temples, and was considered a place where the "entire world" could be experienced. Naturally, it also contained a concentration of "entertainment folks," which gave rise to a unique epicurean atmosphere. Before World War II, it was used as an incubation place for anarchists, and many yakuza also gathered there. Beat Takeshi, who is from the neighboring countryside area, admired Asakusa, and started his artistic career doing manzai comedy at a local strip club. However, by the time Takeshi became active in Asakusa in the 1970s, Tokyo's entertainment center had moved west to Shinjuku and Shibuya. Today, Asakusa has completely lost its former vigor, and in Japan is generally thought of as an "area reeking of the past." However, it is still strongly colored by the old atmosphere, and is a must-visit spot on the itinerary of foreigners visiting Tokyo,

BROTHER

1 *Komanechi! 2*: The title of a special issue of a Japanese literary magazine that came out in conjunction with the Japanese release of Takeshi's film *Brother* and that was edited by Takeshi himself. The original *Komanechi!* was a similar special issue released on the occasion of the Japanese release of *Hana-Bi*. The term is based on the 1976 Montreal Olympic gold medalist, Nadia Comaneci, who amazed the world with her gymnastic abilities and scored a perfect ten in her routine. A 14-year old girl at the time, she also appealed to the sexual feelings of men around the world who had Lolita complexes. Takeshi played off of this by shouting "Komanechi!" while making a "V" around his crotch to represent a woman gymnast's tights. This gag became associated with a crude sexualized gesture.

DOLLS

1 Bunraku: A performance art using puppets in which puppeteers wear black clothes and makeup while manipulating puppet strings. Popularized during the Edo period (1600-1867), it is derived from "Bunraku-za," an Edo-period puppet theatre located in the city of Osaka, and closely related to the older puppetry form of *ningyo joruri*. Bunraku shows often feature romantic stories of, for example, thwarted lovers committing suicide together. The hands, legs, eyes, and mouths of the puppets can be manipulated to great effect, and are moving for audiences even today.

2 Towards the conclusion of the puppet play by Chikamatsu (1653-1725), the protagonists hide in an empty house and secretly peer out the window at a procession of townspeople returning from a pilgrimage.

3 "Snow, moon, and flowers": These images are known as *setsugekka*, traditional Japanese poetic and artistic motifs.

4 Michiyuki: Literally "going on the road," this refers to a type of highly conventional travel scene that is included in many classical Japanese dramatic works, including the plays of Chikamatsu.

AFTERWORD

1 There are some recent signs of Kinji Fukasaku's films getting more international exposure: a Fukasaku retrospective toured New York and Los Angeles in 2001, and his work has been featured at the 2000 and 2002 Rotterdam International Film Festivals.

2 For a discussion of the *tateyaku* hero, see Tadao Sato, *Currents in Japanese Cinema* (Tokyo and New York: Kodansha, 1982). Isolde Standish briefly discusses Kitano's films in the context of Japanese film representations of masculinity in *Myth and Masculinity in Japanese Cinema: Towards a Political Reading of the Tragic Hero* (Richmond, Surrey: Curzon Press, 2000) 189-192.

3 On the question of national identity in *Fireworks*, see Aaron Gerow, "'Nihonjin' Kitano Takeshi: HANA-BI to nashonaru shinema no keisei," *Eureka* 30.3 (February 1998 special issue) 42-51, and Darrell William Davis, "Reigniting Japanese Tradition with Hana-Bi," *Cinema Journal* 40.4 (Summer 2001) 55-80.

index

index

index

PUBLISHER'S ACKNOWLEDGMENTS

This book would not have been completed without the assistance of William O. Gardner, Yutaka Sato, Akiko Ohata, Rieko Ishibashi, Ann T. Yamamoto, and Duncan Williams. The efforts and advice of Lawrence Chua, Hisami Kuroiwa, and Kyoko Hirano have also been invaluable to this process. We are grateful to Chikuma Publishing, Hiromi Sakai and the Japan Foreign-Rights Centre, and Office Kitano for the opportunity to publish this work. Special thanks to Julie Koo, Vince Schleitweiler, Kai-Ming Cha, Sandra Watanabe, Erin Shigaki, Joyce Teague, Sharon Gallagher and Avery Lozada at DAP, and everyone else who worked to make this book possible. Finally, many thanks to Casio and Ritsuko Abe for their generosity and patience.

—Sunyoung Lee, Kaya Press.

PHOTO CREDITS

Merry Christmas, Mr. Lawrence by Nagisa Oshima © 1983 Jeremy Thomas
page 22

Violent Cop by Takeshi Kitano © 1989 Shochiku-Fuji Co., Ltd.
pages 46, 48, 54, 60, 61, 65

Boiling Point by Takeshi Kitano © 1990 Bandai Co., Ltd. / Shochiku-Fuji Co., Ltd.
pages 68, 72, 73, 77, 78, 83, 84

A Scene At the Sea by Takeshi Kitano © 1991 Totsu Co., Ltd., and Office Kitano
pages 89, 96, 97, 100, 101

Sonatine by Takeshi Kitano © 1993 Shouchiku Daiichi Kougyo
pages 112, 115, 118, 126, 127, 128, 133

Fireworks (Hana-Bi) by Takeshi Kitano © 1998 Bandai Visual, Television Tokyo, Tokyo FM, and Office Kitano
pages 207, 210, 213, 218, 239, 240

Getting Any? by Takeshi Kitano © 1994 Bandai Visual and Office Kitano
pages 218, 219, 228

Kids Return by Takeshi Kitano © 1996 Bandai Visual and Office Kitano
pages 230, 231, 232, 235

Kikujiro by Takeshi Kitano © 1999 Bandai Visual, Tokyo FM, Nippon Herald, and Office Kitano
front + back cover images + pages 244, 245

Brother by Takeshi Kitano © 2000 Recorded Picture Company and Office Kitano
pages 248, 249

Dolls by Takeshi Kitano © 2002 Bandai Visual, Tokyo FM, Television Tokyo, and Office Kitano
pages 254, 255, 260